ELEMENTARY
SURVEY ANALYSIS

PRENTICE-HALL METHODS OF SOCIAL SCIENCE SERIES

EDITORS

Herbert L. Costner
Neil Smelser

JAMES A. DAVIS
Dartmouth College

ELEMENTARY
SURVEY ANALYSIS

PRENTICE-HALL, INC., Englewood Cliffs, New Jersey

13-260547-3

Library of Congress Catalog Card Number: 75-138477
Printed in the United States of America

Current printing (last digit):
10   9   8   7   6   5

PRENTICE-HALL INTERNATIONAL, INC., *London*
PRENTICE-HALL OF AUSTRALIA, PTY. LTD., *Sydney*
PRENTICE-HALL OF CANADA, LTD., *Toronto*
PRENTICE-HALL OF INDIA PRIVATE LIMITED, *New Delhi*
PRENTICE-HALL OF JAPAN, INC., *Tokyo*

SEEK SIMPLICITY AND DISTRUST IT.

—Alfred North Whitehead
The Concept of Nature

Preface

Rather than describing the greed and missionary zeal that led to the handsome volume which you hold in your hand, perhaps even with a sales slip as book marker, let me begin by thanking some extremely nice people. (The first section, Introduction, explains the purposes of the book.)

Herbert Costner, Robert O. Dryfoos, Nick Mullins, and Vanderlyn Pine did me the honor of reading various draft versions and forwarding numerous specific and helpful suggestions. Readers are easy to find, but readers who provide specific and helpful suggestions are jewels.

Four Sociology 7 classes at Dartmouth college (Fall '68, Winter '69, Fall '69, and Winter '70) hacked their way through various draft, corrected, revised, revised and corrected, etc. versions. I should feel sorry for them, but the fact is that we had fun wrestling with the thing and there is no stronger motivation for close reading than the distinct suspicion that half the numbers in the key examples are misprints.

Paul Lazarsfeld was kind enough to comment on selected sections of the book that badly needed his expertise and wisdom.

Mrs. Donna Musgrove, Mrs. Lorraine Kendall, and the linch pin of the

Dartmouth Sociology department, Miss Elsie Sniffin, promptly and efficiently typed and duplicated the various draft versions.

And some less direct debts.

The staff of Project IMPRESS, Dartmouth's experiment in using computers for student research and instruction, helped me in many ways. I am especially grateful to Edmund D. Meyers, Jr. and David Chapin. It won't mean much outside Hanover, but this book is essentially a user's manual for the IMPRESS system and its logical structure was much affected by the development of the system.

From a professional point of view, this is an attempt to mesh the seminal ideas of Paul Lazarsfeld with those of Leo Goodman and William Kruskal. It was never more truly said that "without them, this book could not have been written."

That the creation of a textbook makes for certain intra-familial readjustments is shown by the fact that it was on or about the day I tore up the third draft of Chapter 6 my wife, Martha, came to habitually refer to herself, Mary, Jimmie, Andrew, and Martha as "Mother Courage and Her Children." Cheers, Dears!

JAMES A. DAVIS

Etna, N.H.
January, 1971

Contents

3

4

5

6

Introduction

This text aims to teach you to analyze statistical materials such as sample surveys, census materials, and cross-cultural data. After studying it, you should be able to start with a set of raw figures and end up with a statistical report.

No book can teach you how to pick a brilliant hypothesis or provide the dowsing rod which points to clean, strong results, nor will an ethical violin teacher promise to make you into another Heifetz. Like your music teacher we have more limited aims: (1) to teach you simple but serviceable techniques so that you can handle simple problems on your own as soon as possible, and (2) to provide a sound foundation for advanced study.

The main emphasis is on doing research, but we claim some benefits for the purely armchair reader. A subsidiary aim of the book is to teach you to think like a sociologist. Some students find it hard to think like a sociologist, not because a sociologist's thought is so eccentric, but because at first glance it appears so similar. By and large, sociologists think about the same things everybody does: friends, family, personal opinions, groups, organizations, money, and sex. What is different is the intellectual framework: The professional sociologist tends to think in terms of a *structure of probabilistic rela-*

tionships among operationally interpreted variables. In a way, this entire book merely spells out the meaning of this phrase, beginning with *variables* and their operational interpretations, then moving to *probabilistic relationships*, and ending with *structure*. Even if you will never do any research (but you should, because that is most of the fun in sociology), the book may be of some use in explaining the style of thought of your sociology teachers and the sociologists whose books you read.

A high degree of "originality" is a bad sign in a methods text because the principles and techniques of research have been well developed by many men over many decades. Most of the materials in this book are well known to professional research workers. However, this volume differs from others in four ways: It is *antiencyclopedic*, it stresses *crude procedures*, it compromises the problem of *statistical inference*, and, as advertised, it is limited to one style of research, *survey analysis*.

Most methods books tend to be small encyclopedias in which one can find brief descriptions of a wide variety of research tools, and there is a good reason for this. Empirical research is a sequence of steps in which one (1) samples, (2) measures, (3) tabulates, (4) calculates, and (5) interprets. Within this framework, though, there are literally dozens of alternatives. For example, one of the most important calculations is that of a coefficient to describe the degree of association or correlation between two variables—a number which states how strongly the variables are related. In a standard statistics book you will find from 6 to 20 different coefficients, each of which has certain assets and certain liabilities. We, however, will use only one measure of association, Yule's Q coefficient. We do so because we feel it is better to understand and to be able to use one procedure than to have a vague acquaintance with a number of alternatives.

Similarly, data analysis always involves a number of arbitrary decisions once a procedure has been chosen. We will see, for example, that a coefficient of degree of association for two variables can range from a value of .00 to a value of plus or minus 1.00. At some point on this scale the relationship can be described as "very strong," but the choice is quite arbitrary. We will state flatly that a Q coefficient must exceed the value of plus or minus .70 before it is called "very strong." Under oath, we could give no mathematical argument that .70 is better than .69 or .50. However, with no rule at all, one tends to flounder around, unable to make any decision; or worse, one may make inconsistent decisions at different places in the research. We feel that it is better to make consistent and definite decisions than to be paralyzed with the sophisticated knowledge that such things are arbitrary. At many points in the book we will give you very specific rules even though they might appear whimsical to a sophisticate. Once you become sophisticated in research, you may choose to ignore them, but for now we believe that a somewhat authoritarian approach will get you off to a better start.

Putting these two antiencyclopedic trends together, we may say that this book presents a *system* of analysis, even though we grant that there are many other systems which are equally acceptable for research. The justification is that such oversimplification will get you started on actual research work sooner and that it all hangs together in a way that encyclopedic approaches do not.

The second trait is that the procedures chosen are crude in two senses. First, they require fairly large sample sizes to detect "significant differences" (the term will be explained later). Exactly how large is one of those arbitrary matters we will solve by fiat later. For now, all we can say is that you should not use these techniques if you have fewer than 40 or 50 cases in your sample and ideally you should have 150 or more. One might think that this crudeness is a serious drawback, but sociologists collect lots of data and you will have little or no trouble finding appropriate figures with which to work. The *Statistical Abstract* alone could keep you busy for years. Furthermore, in statistics, crudeness is the same as conservativism. The fact that our procedures require lots of data prevents you from going off half-cocked on the basis of slender evidence.

The second facet of crudeness is that we will limit our attention to crude levels of measurement, especially dichotomies. Levels of measurement will be explained in Chapter 1, but for now we can say that our approach uses all the numbers in the data but is insensitive to many of the differences and distances. This, too, is an inefficiency of sorts, but it also means that we can apply our tools to any set of data without having to assume sophisticated levels of measurement. All this will be explained in more detail later. Many research experts would challenge this approach, but we believe that it is quite appropriate for beginners and indeed we would hazard the hypothesis that our procedures will usually give the same *substantive conclusions* as more sophisticated ones; i.e., you will generally draw the same inferences about "people" with these techniques as with fancier ones.

Third, we have made some uneasy compromises on the thorny question of "statistical inference." Statistics is divided into two parts, descriptive statistics and statistical inference. Descriptive statistics are the calculations you make to summarize and reveal the results in your own sample. Statistical inference is a set of procedures for inferring, with some known risk of being wrong, whether the findings in your sample are true in the universe from which it was drawn (always assuming that the sample was drawn by what are called "probability methods"). Knowledge of statistical inference is vital for anyone seriously interested in social research, but it requires a course in itself—not because the mathematics is so formidable, but because there is so much of it (each different statistic has its own peculiar procedures for statistical inference). The result is a dilemma. If you are required to study statistics before you take a "methods course," you are likely to be bored and confused because statistics is really about the mathematics of probability, and statistics courses, particularly good ones, seldom pause to teach you the concrete details of research. If, on the other hand, you take a methods course without any background in statistics, certain parts of it just will not make much sense.

Our uneasy compromise is this: By and large, we will concentrate on descriptive statistics and not worry about whether the sample is representative (another reason why we assume large samples, for the larger the probability sample, the less likely it is that it differs from the parent universe). Here and there, though, we will present procedures for statistical inference without much explanation. We will tell you how to make the calculations and how to assess the results, but the rationale will be skimpy. This will protect you from certain pitfalls in data analysis, but this book is no substitute for a statistics course. If you have any serious interest in modern social science you should take as many statistics courses as you can, as soon as possible. We hope that this book is a good way to begin your study of research, but we know that it is a bad way to end it.

Fourth, this book is limited to one style of research, often called survey analysis, though it is not limited to the analysis of public opinion survey data. It is more accurately described as "case-classificatory, one-shot nonexperimental, multivariate research," but you can see why survey analysis is a more popular phrase. By reviewing each of these adjectives we can see how this style differs from other approaches to social science research.

The first modifier, case-classificatory, means that survey analysis treats classifications of individual cases as its raw materials. Any such classification will be called a *variable* or *measure*. The idea may appear stupefyingly banal at first glance, but it actually raises some fundamental problems about the nature of research and the field of sociology.

The elementary particles of research data are *cases*, the objects of inquiry. Usually they are people, but sometimes they are families, small groups, organizations, regions, or whole societies. What is required is that they be numerous and logically distinct. The definition of cases seldom causes problems, though sticky situations can occur. In a sample of magazine stories, should each episode count as a distinct case? In a sample of business firms, should each subsidiary of a conglomerate corporation count as a distinct case?

Given a collection of cases, what can be done with them? Obviously, we can sort them into piles on the basis of their properties, i.e., classify them. The classification can be very simple, as in classification by sex, or very complicated, as in classification by a three-item index of socioeconomic status; but at the root we are sorting our cases into piles or classes.

Having taken this fateful step, an important consequence follows, for when we work with classifications, the individual case "disappears."

Assume that we have 150 cases classified by sex and socioeconomic status.

The information with which we will work will be class frequencies—the number of men, the number of women, the number of persons with particular SES (socioeconomic status) scores, the number of men with particular SES scores, etc. The fact that a particular man, case 037, has a particular SES score, 38, will not play any further part in our research.

This case-classificatory approach is quite different from that of the biographer or historian who often seeks to give a full description of many properties of a single case. Some critics of social science feel that it is somehow immoral to study the properties of classes rather than the properties of individuals, and there are some sociologists who specialize in case studies rather than survey analysis. We feel that it is a matter of intellectual taste rather than morals, but we remind you that the sort of research we are treating aims to develop generalizations about categories of individuals rather than descriptions of particular individuals.

In addition to case studies and case-classificatory research there are at least two other important ways of organizing data, *relational analysis* and *contextual analysis.*

In relational analysis the unit is the pair of cases, not the individual case, and data consist of classifications of pairs. Such data have the generic form of a matrix in which the rows and columns are cases and the cell entries refer to the class of the relationship—in contrast to the table of frequencies which is the generic form of data for survey analysis. For example, one might list the members of a group down the rows and columns of a matrix and put a plus sign in all cells referring to good friends and a minus sign in all other cells. The result will be a sorting of all the *pairs* into the two classes, plus and minus. Studies of freiendship choice (usually called sociometric research), kinship systems, authority structures, flows of influence and information, and dominance relations are typical of this approach. Relational analysis, particularly the study of interpersonal networks, is a rapidly expanding part of sociological research, but we will not cover it in this book.

Contextual analysis organizes the data in still another way—in terms of levels of aggregation, i.e., sets and subsets. It is another rapidly developing style of analysis and no neat definition can be given at this time.[1] The central idea is the attempt to see how the distribution of cases in a higher-order subset influences some property of sub-subsets. A concrete example may help. Several studies have shown that the social class composition of high schools tends to influence the academic aspirations of students, regardless of the individual's own class background. The higher the SES level of the school, the more likely it is that a young man will plan to go to college, whether or

---

[1] For an early attempt, see James A. Davis, Joe L. Spaeth, and Carolyn Huson, "A Technique for Analyzing the Effects of Group Composition," *American Sociological Review*, 1961, *26*, 215–226.

not he is from a high SES home. You can see that the analysis divides the total cases into subsets, high schools, and sub-subsets, individuals within high schools. The finding is that the distribution of SES in the subsets influences the characteristics of the sub-subsets.

Studies of racial segregation, coeducation, ability groupings in schools, adjustment to old people's homes, efficient ways to make up work groups, etc., often fall in the category of contextual analysis since they frequently ask how a higher-order subset (a social context) affects a lower-order one.

Granted that case-classificatory research is only one of several logical approaches to sociological research, it is by far the most common one and the vast majority of research reports, books, and articles are of this type. Thus, it is the best style for beginners, even though relational analysis and contextual analysis are perhaps more "sociological" in their approach.

The second trait of survey research is that it is "one-shot." It deals with classifications at a single point in time. This is in contrast to "panel" studies in which the same classification is observed at different points in time for the same cases. For example, political sociologists often ask people their voting intention at several points during an election campaign in order to spot trends. Panel analysis tells us how a particular classification changes over time; survey analysis tells us how different classifications are related or unrelated. Survey techniques are also appropriate when one looks at different classifications at different times, e.g., grades in high school and earnings at age 35 or child care practices and later adjustment of the child. Indeed, survey techniques are quite useful in panel studies, but panel analysis also includes a number of techniques and problems which we will not cover in this book.

Survey analysis is nonexperimental, by which we mean that the data variables are not under control by the investigator. The experimental psychologist, who works with variables such as color, sounds, words, and visual patterns, can study their effects[2] by (1) dividing his cases into otherwise equal groups through *randomization* (assigning cases to groups through a chance device so that there are necessarily only chance differences between them), (2) exposing his groups to different levels (called treatments) of his variables (those with level zero are usually called the control group), and (3) measuring the groups on variables which are purportedly sensitive to the treatments (*dependent variables*). If he finds group differences, he concludes

---

[2] It is considered bad form to use the word "cause" in research texts. Hence, methods books and research reports abound in euphemisms such as "stems from," "influences," "promotes," "facilitates," "generates," etc. This genuflection to the philosophy of science is pious cant since the only sensible reason to go through the agonies involved in research is the hope that you will find what causes things. This does not mean that you can expect a high rate of success, but it does mean that whether or not it is philosophically justified, most research workers are highly interested in causes and effects.

that they stem from his treatments since randomization should have minimized any prior differences on the dependent variables.

The key ideas here are randomization and control. Control makes it possible for the groups to vary on the treatments, and randomization makes it unlikely that the subgroups vary on anything other than the treatments. Application of both randomization and control makes it possible to argue that any observed group differences were produced by the treatments and not produced by anything else.

We will return to the logic of experiments in Chapter 4, but now we merely note that most sociological variables (thank heavens!) are not amenable to experimental control and the sociologist must work with his measures "as they fall" rather than making sure that half his subjects receive high socioeconomic status and half receive low. Consequently, this book will have nothing to say about the design and analysis of experimental data.

Finally, by multivariate we mean that survey analysis deals with a number of variables (classifications) and their interrelations rather than merely reporting isolated facts. A research report which consists of reporting isolated facts is called "merely running the marginals" (marginals are explained in Chapter 2) and is considered—pardon the expression—sophomoric by the pros. We will see why in Chapters 1 and 2, but for now we merely say that multivariate analysis helps to avoid some of the limitations of nonexperimental research and it also reveals intellectually interesting structures among the variables.

IN A NUTSHELL

Since the writing in this text is somewhat condensed, we will try to help you gain some perspective on each chapter by presenting a brief outline at the end, along with a list of the more important concepts.

A. This book aims to teach you

1. How to analyze statistical materials, not necessarily with any great artistry, but
   a) *With simple, serviceable techniques so you can handle simple problems on your own as soon as possible*
   b) *Giving you a sound foundation for advanced study.*
2. To think like a sociologist, that is, in terms of a
   a) *Structure*
   b) *Of probabilistic relationships*
   c) *Among operationally interpreted variables.*

B. While almost all of it contains materials long familiar to professional research workers, it differs from other methods texts in that it

1. Is not an encyclopedia of alternative procedures, but a system of analysis including some definite answers to questions which are really arbitrary.

2. Deals with statistical methods which are "crude" in the sense that they are appropriate for large samples and unsophisticated levels of meaurement (this term is defined in Chapter 1).

3. Makes an uneasy compromise on the question of "statistical inference," teaching some specific procedures but not attempting to provide a substitute for a statistics course.

4. Treats a style of research called survey analysis, characterized as

    a) *Case-classificatory, as opposed to*
       (1) Case studies
       (2) Relational analysis
       (3) Contextual analysis.

    b) *One-shot, as opposed to panel studies in which the same classification is studied at several times to determine trends.*

    c) *Nonexperimental, because the sociologist seldom has access to the key elements of experimental design,*
       (1) Randomization
       (2) Control.

    d) *Multivariate, studying the interrelations of several variables in order to*
       (1) Compensate for some defects of nonexperimental designs
       (2) Reveal interesting structures among the measures.

Major Concepts

---

1. Case
2. Classification (variable, measure)
3. Contextual study
4. Controlled experiment
5. Panel study
6. Randomization (in an experiment)
7. Relational study

1

Variables

A variable (or classification or measure—we will use the three words as synonyms) is a sorting of the cases into two or more mutually exclusive and totally inclusive categories, such as male vs. female; age 0, age 1, age 2, ..., age 99; high status, middle status, low status, etc.

Some minor points in the definition:

1. If there is more than one variable, categories of different variables must *not* have any *logical* relationship because it is their *empirical* relationship which is the point of the research. A high correlation between educational attainment and occupational prestige becomes less impressive when one discovers that his prestige scale defines high-status occupations as those that require college training.

2. Frequently a variable is manufactured from other variables. The variable "IQ score" is made by combining answers on many test questions, each of which is technically a variable.

3. Sometimes the requirement of total inclusion must be met by defining residual categories such as "other," "not elsewhere classified," "no answer," or "not applicable." (This is discussed later in this chapter.)

Every variable has four working parts: (1) a name, (2) some sort of verbal definition, (3) a set of categories, and (4) a procedure for carrying out the sorting. Thus we have the name, "intelligence"; the verbal definition, "capacity for learning"; the categories, intelligence test scores; and the sorting procedure, a test and the details of its administration—or the name, "party preference"; the verbal definition, "usual vote in national elections"; the categories, "Democratic, Republican, other, none"; and the sorting procedure, asking interviewers to record the answers to, "In national elections, which party do you usually vote for?" We begin with the easy part, categories.

Categories: Level of Measurement and Number

Categories vary in two ways, in level of measurement[1] and in number. The notion "level of measurement" is a logical framework for classifying the inferences one is willing to make when one compares cases assigned to different categories. We usually end up assigning "numbers" to the different categories, e.g., different numbered punches in the columns of an IBM card, but, common sense to the contrary not withstanding, numbers are not simple and straightforward. The analysis of the various meanings of "numbers" will make clear what we meant in the introduction when we talked about "crude levels of measurement."

Methodologists usually distinguish four levels of measurement: (1) ratio, (2) interval, (3) ordinal, and (4) nominal. They are best understood by comparing four variables: (1) age, (2) Farenheit temperature, (3) stage of medical study, and (4) region.

Age is a *ratio* scale. If we observe that Sam is 30 years old and Saul is 15 years old, we may draw four distinct conclusions from this sorting: (1) Sam and Saul have different ages, (2) Sam is older than Saul, (3) Sam is 15 years older than Saul, and (4) Sam is twice as old as Saul. The name *ratio* comes from this fourth inference, since we could restate it as "the ratio of their ages is 2 to 1."

Now consider Farenheit temperature, an *interval* scale. If we observe that Sam's temperature is 103.0°F, while Saul's is 98.6°F, we may draw three distinct conclusions from this sorting: (1) Sam's temperature differs from Saul's, (2) Sam is hotter than Saul, and (3) Sam's temperature exceeds Saul's by 4.4°F. We may not, though, draw the fourth conclusion that Sam is 1.06 as hot as Saul because Farenheit temperature does not have a true zero but only an arbitrary one. Such scales are called interval because of the third conclusion—we can count the distance or interval between observations.

You will note that we do not provide a sociological example of an interval

---

[1] The classic paper on this is S. S. Stevens, "On the Theory of Scales of Measurement," *Science*, 1946, *103*, 677–680. See also Warren S. Torgerson, *Theory and Methods of Measurement*, Wiley, New York, 1958, pp. 13–40, for a more recent and expanded discussion.

scale. This is because there are few "natural" social science variables which have arbitrary zero points and countable intervals. There are, however, a good number of "contrived" measures such as IQ scores which are routinely *treated* as interval scales. Their properties involve technical statistical concepts which are out-of-bounds in this book.

Stage of medical study (premedical student, medical student, intern, resident) is an *ordinal* scale. If we observe that Sam is a resident and Saul is a medical student, we may draw two distinct inferences from the sorting: (1) Sam and Saul are in different stages of medical training and (2) Sam's training exceeds Saul's. We may not, however, draw the third conclusion, that Sam's training exceeds Saul's by two units, nor may we meaningfully state any ratio in terms of training. The absence of property three, distances between observations, is worth a comment. We could make the statement that they are two "categories" apart, but note how vacuous this is compared to the previous differences of 4.4°F or 15 years. Degrees and years have unique meanings, while categories do not. Similarly, we might be able to claim that they are 4 years apart (if Saul is a first-year medical student) but this amounts to substituting a new measure, years, for the stage measure.

The important logical concept in ordinal scales is *transitivity*. If A exceeds B and B exceeds C, then A must exceed C. Any classification where transitivity may be assumed, but not "arithmetical" properties, is an ordinal scale.

Region is a *nominal* scale. If Sam lives in New England and Saul lives in the South, we may draw one lone inference: (1) Sam and Saul live in different regions. We cannot arrange the regions in any order or calculate distances (except by shifting to a new scale, spatial distance) or ratios meaningfully. Such scales are called nominal because the categories and any numbers attached to the categories serve as names, like the numbers on the backs of football players.

This classification of scales has an important internal structure, as shown in Table 1.1.

TABLE 1.1 Scales and Scale Properties

	SCALE			
PROPERTY	NOMINAL	ORDINAL	INTERVAL	RATIO
1. Classification	+	+	+	+
2. Ordering	–	+	+	+
3. Distances	–	–	+	+
4. Nonarbitrary zero	–	–	–	+

Table 1.1 shows that scale properties are cumulative. Fancier scales have all the properties of less sophisticated scales plus something. Thus interval scales have the classification property of nominal scales and ordinal scales, the ordering property of ordinal scales, and the distance property.

Because of this, cumulative property scales can be arranged in an unambiguous order (i.e., scales form an ordinal scale), which is an instance of what is called a *Guttman Scale* after Louis Guttman, the sociologist who first applied the idea to social research. A test has this Guttman property if the questions vary in difficulty so that the higher scorers get all the easy questions right plus harder ones. Attitude scales often have it. Consider the hypothetical questions, "Would you vote for candiate Jones?" "Would you attend a rally for candidate Jones?" "Would you contribute money to Jones's campaign?" Presumably persons who would say yes to the third question would say yes to the first two and those saying no to the first question would also say no to the other two.

Our interest in Table 1.1 is not in its Guttman structure per se but in a dilemma related to it. On the one hand, the higher the level of measurement, the more sophisticated statistics one can use. In particular, if one can assume interval scales, a package of high-powered tools called *regression analysis* is appropriate. These statistics are not only more sophisticated in that they do not require such large samples, but they also have a number of lovely algebraic properties that enable the investigator to ask many subtle questions. (You will have to take all this on faith if you have not yet taken a statistics course.) Unfortunately, the answers to all these subtle questions are meaningful only in terms of a statistic called *the variance*, which is a number describing the spread of a distribution in terms of (here speaking quite roughly) the average distance of the observations from the mean. Now, if a scale does not have meaningful distances between observations, it does not have meaningful distances from the mean of these observations (it does not have a meaningful mean for that matter), and while one can calculate a variance, the results are inherently ambiguous.

On the other hand, the lower the level of measurement, the more likely it is that all of the variables in the study meet the measurement assumptions. After all, Table 1.1 tells us that every variable is a nominal scale—by definition. Further, as we said above, since the sociologist seldom works with brass instruments, it is rare for his measures to go beyond ordinal scaling, save by a certain amount of statistical jiggery-pokery.

As a consequence, the research worker who wishes to use advanced statistical tools (regression, analysis of variance, factor analysis) may be forced to make some queasy measurement assumptions, while the research worker who wants to make honest measurement assumptions may be forced to use statistical axes rather than scalpels.

Not all dilemmas should be resolved by a middle ground, and in this case, as the introductory chapter made clear, we will stick with those statistics which make only nominal or ordinal assumptions. Our reasons are these: (1) Our all-purpose tools can be used on any data so you do not have to worry about the sometimes complex issues involved in testing for appropriateness of sophisticated measurement assumptions. (2) As stated in the introduction, we believe that you will arrive at essentially the same substantive conclusions, i.e., verbal propositions about the variables, with these techniques as with fancier ones. (3) We can give a precise explanation of these techniques with a lot less algebra. (4) The crude statistics illuminate the central methodological ideas just as clearly as fancier ones.

Let us repeat, though, that serious students of social research should not stop with this text but go on to statistics courses, and in particular, aim for a detailed understanding of regression and *multiple* regression.

We will take one more simplifying step. You will remember that categories vary in level of measurement and number. By number we mean only how many categories there are (one, two, three, four, five, etc.). Two category variables are called dichotomies, three category variables are called trichotomies, and there are undoubtedly Greek names for all the rest.

Let's look at dichotomies, divisions of the cases into two categories such as male vs. female, favorable vs. all other, white collar vs. blue collar and farm, and Catholic vs. non-Catholic. They have the advantage that many variables are naturally dichotomous, as, for example, sex, presidential party preference, agree–disagree, and any variable can be made dichotomous by combining categories. (If driven to it, you can classify the states of the union as Nebraska vs. all others.) A less obvious property involves transitivity. Transitivity is a property of triads: If A exceeds B and B exceeds C, then A must exceed C; doubts about how to order triads are the main problem in ordinal scales. (Should it go Protestant, Catholic, Jewish or should it go Protestant, Jewish, Catholic? Or perhaps Jewish, Protestant, Catholic?) When there are only two categories, there are no triads and no problems about whether triads are transitive. (Whether the categories should be arranged Catholic vs. non-Catholic or non-Catholic vs. Catholic is a purely literary problem.)

Having raised the question of levels of measurement and number of categories, we can make it all go away by the following: *Since any variable may be dichotomized and since either nominal or ordinal techniques may be used on dichotomies, we will work with dichotomies in developing the major principles of analysis.*

Names–Definitions–Sorting Procedures

While the logic of categories and levels of measurement is neat and crisp, the discussion of names, definitions, and sorting procedures[2] is one of the sloppiest, soggiest parts of social science. It is easy to think up names—see any

---

[2] The technical phrase for a sorting procedure is *operational interpretation*, i.e., a set of concrete operations or procedures which interpret or give pragmatic meaning to the abstract concept and verbal definition.

sociology book for a list of impressive variable names. There is little problem in forming reasonable verbal definitions to go with the names. An ingenious investigator can always come up with a new way to collect data, i.e., a new sorting procedure. The problem is whether a given name, definition, and sorting procedure belong together.

What do intelligence tests really measure?

What is the best measure of group cohesion?

Do attitude scales really tap personal opinions or just what people think the investigator wants to hear?

How would you know whether America has a "power elite" or not?

Is this patient schizophrenic?

Does an income of $3000 a year mean poverty?

Each of these questions amounts to asking whether a particular linking of name–definition–sorting procedure is justified. This is called the problem of *validity*.

Validity is distinguished from *reliability*, the question of whether repetitions of a given procedure give similar sortings. Reliability, in turn, involves two forms of repetition: over time (Would you get the same result if you went back and repeated the measurement?),[3] and over slightly different models of the instrument (Do different judges agree in their ratings of small group interactions? Do form *A* and form *B* of the personality test give the same results?). The hooker is that validity and reliability are not perfectly independent. A highly reliable measure may or may not be valid. (If you measure IQ by standing subjects on bathroom scales and reading off the number on the dial, your measure will be quite reliable in either sense—the same reader will get similar results for 10 weighings of the same man within 10 minutes—different readers will call off similar readings of the same man at any given weighing, but one may doubt its validity.) But a highly unreliable measure cannot be valid. If you measure IQ by flipping a coin to get the number of correct "answers," your measure cannot be valid.

Reliability does present some technical problems. It is hard to train observers and interviewers so that their measures tend to agree, and when you repeat a measure like an attitude scale, your second reading may be contaminated by the first. However, the fundamental doctrine is clear: We want repeated measures to agree and we find out whether they do by repeating them.

Validity, in contrast, raises grave issues in both doctrine and technique. At the extreme it constitutes a philosophical thicket which makes a dandy hiding place from which antiempirical social scientists can ambush the simple-

---

[3] We assume, of course, that the variable has been defined as a relatively constant phenomenon. If you are working on a measure of "transient moods," you would be dismayed to find a strong correlation between repeated measures 6 months apart.

minded folk who want to find out what the world is like rather than speculate about it.

Since this is not a general methods text,[4] we will not delve into such concepts as *operationalism, construct validity,* and *constitutive definitions.* We merely state the following:

1. The *findings* of a research project are assertions about the statistical properties of the category data produced by the research operations (e.g., "subjects with low scores on the vocabulary test tended to have high scores on the prejudice scale").
2. The *conclusions* of a research project are assertions about variable names ("low intelligence leads to hostility toward outgroups") which become meaningful when one knows the verbal definitions of the variables.
3. The aim of research is to produce conclusions which are supported by the findings.
4. It is seldom possible to demonstrate a perfect fit between category sortings and variable names, even when there is a crisp verbal definition.

It is, of course, point 4 which makes all the trouble, its nasty nub being this: To demonstrate that our category sortings are a good reflection of the defined variable, we must show that our sortings correlate highly with a perfect measure of that variable—but if we had such a measure, we would undoubtedly be using it instead, and how did it get to be doubt-free in the first place?

Before we embrace solipsism, three somewhat more constructive assertions should be added to the list:

5. The fact that a measure is not perfect does not mean that it is useless. Only a philosopher would doubt that research operations are pretty good at sorting people by sex, socioeconomic status, political preference, occupation, etc. Even the much maligned public opinion surveys stand up extraordinarily well under those checks which can be made.
6. Data analysis itself can help the investigator to evaluate his measures (more on this in Chapter 7).
7. Weak measures are to be preferred to brilliant speculations as a source of empirical information.

If we abandon niceties of doctrine, we may view good research practice as finding the appropriate place on a spectrum. Too far to the right (or maybe left, who is to say?), sticking too close to one's data, produces triviality. After all, who wants to know only that question 14 has a moderate negative correlation with question 8? Too far to the left, soaring well beyond the findings, produces unwarranted conclusions. One should probably not infer that modern man becomes progressively alienated from the finding that college seniors are more likely to report complaints about dining hall food than college freshmen.

There is no statistical or mathematical solution to the problem, and a good part of research training amounts to a subtle exposure to the implicit standards current in the field. (One reason you should read a lot of sociology is that by learning how various measures usually behave you are in a better position to interpret them in your own data.) For now we drop the issue with this reminder: The problem of relationship between findings and conclusions —between category sortings and their names and definitions—the problem of validity—is always with us.

Practical Implications

So far we have been talking about definitions and fairly abstract principles. Now we turn to a set of rules designed to help you use these ideas in your own sociological activities.

R U L E   1.1

Learn to think in terms of variables and their relationships.

If cases and variables are the building blocks of research, it is necessary to translate your ideas (and the sociological ideas you read) into the language of variables before you can carry out or evaluate research. The experienced sociologist develops the habit of routinely translating the English he reads and hears into variables, just as a bilingual person can read in one language while thinking in another.

Ordinary English is a beautiful and flexible language, but it is lousy as a means of precise research thinking. Its categories seldom imply a complete variable, it almost never implies the necessary research sortings (*operational interpretations*), and its verbs are bad for handling reciprocal relationships between variables.

Let us begin with the categories. Ordinary English is loaded with nouns and adjectives which suggest single categories but leave the others dangling. If we read that "Americans tend to be pragmatic," we sense two variables, and we know that "Americans" is one category of one variable and "pragmatic" is a category of the other. However, we may have to do a lot of detective work to discover the remaining categories. Is it Americans vs. Chinese? North Americans vs. South Americans? Americans today vs. Americans 100 years ago? Is it all Americans or just middle-class Americans? What about American Indians? Similarly, what is the complement of pragmatic? Idealistic? Impractical? Unreflective? Or is pragmatism an interval scale such that we all vary by degrees? Usually the clues are there in other parts of the text, but it is often hard work to run them down.

To refine our rule a little:

RULE 1.1a

> To define a variable you must state its mutually exclusive and totally inclusive categories, and consequently its implicit scale level. (Obviously if the variable has a large number of categories, e.g., income in dollars, you do not have to list them all, but the point is that you could if you had to.)

Just as ordinary English is full of categories which do not imply complete variables, technical sociology is full of variable names which do not imply any categories at all. Sociologists, alas, are fond of such abstractions as "social structure," "personality integration," "social change," and "role expectations," which may be thought of as variable names in search of categories. Until one states the kinds of social structures, the levels of personality integration, the types of social change, and the particular expectations for a role, such ideas are of little use for the research worker, except as sources of inspiration.

Logical exegesis is only half the job. Before a variable is defined, it is necessary to state some concrete sorting operations even if they are quite arbitrary. It is easy enough to write, "We shall consider 'introspection' as a tendency to direct thought toward the self and assume that subjects fall into three broad classes, introspective, nonintrospective, and borderline," but even thought the statement meets Rule 1.1a, one would have no idea at all how to proceed to classify a particular individual. It may be that the operational definition is debatable, but until it is stated, there is nothing to debate.

RULE 1.1b

> To define a variable you must state (however sketchily) the research operations which are used to sort the cases into categories. In reporting your own research, describe your operations in sufficient detail for a reader to evaluate them.

Rule 1.1b takes us to the edge of the philosophical thicket. When it is carried to an extreme, we near the doctrine of "operationalism," the claim that variables have no meaning beyond the sorting instructions ("Intelligence is what intelligence tests measure"). We have rejected this position in our earlier discussion of "conclusions." What we wish to state is the reminder that although the answer may be equivocal, you are obliged to raise the question. Thus, a third subrule:

RULE 1.1c

> Always consider the alternative variable names which might be more appropriate for a given set of operations and the alternative operations which might be more appropriate for a given variable name.

If you read that an investigator combined a set of items to obtain a scale he calls *political involvement*, read the items (you should always report the exact question wordings when you are writing up data from interviews and questionnaires) and consider alternative, and usually less lofty, variable names which might fit the operations. Perhaps the scale is merely tapping information about politics, or even length of residence in town (if you just moved to town a week ago, you probably will not be registered to vote, probably will not belong to any political clubs, and probably will not have a preference for fence warden in the next election). It might even be tapping a sheepish tendency to answer "yes" to any and all questions. (This is a classic booby trap and can be avoided by always wording questionnaire items so that both "yes" and "no" answers are associated with both ends of the scale.) Similarly, you should consider other operations which might serve to sort people in terms of political involvement and ask yourself whether they might produce different results.

You will note that any serious attempt to test these suspicions will require further data—measures of length of residence in town, other measures of political involvement, and items worded so that "yes" and "no" appear at both ends of the scale. You often do not have such information available in other people's research reports, but when you design your own studies you have the opportunity to anticipate such problems if you follow the next subrule:

R U L E   1.1d

When designing research, use multiple measures for key variables whose operational definitions are problematic.

The rule allows for some degree of play. You obviously do not have to ask a respondent's sex in four different ways and you want to avoid that great plague of sociology, the overlong, boring, repetitious questionnaire. However, in designing a study you should certainly be able to list the handful of key variables even though you will gather data on others. (If you do not know which variables are important you should not be doing the research.) A reasonable rule of thumb is this: If you have to ponder about the best way to measure a key variable, it is worth measuring in two or more different ways if only by writing two slightly different questionnaire items.

You should practice translating from prose to variable language so that when reading a research report or sociological essay you can always answer these questions:

1. What are the key variables?
2. What are their categories and scale levels?
3. How are they measured operationally?

4. Are the operations
   a) Obviously appropriate?
   b) Plausible?
   c) Dubious?[5]

The first four subrules treat isolated variables, but we have already cautioned you against thinking this way in the introduction, where we italicized the phrase *structure of probabilistic relationships*, and in our patronizing comments about "running the marginals." Thus we reminded you of the last three words in Rule 1.1, "and their relationships."

If English prose is ambiguous when expressing variables, it is a disaster when it comes to expressing relationships between variables. The sentence–verb–object structure makes it difficult to describe mutual relationships. The sentence "Friends tend to have similar opinions" tends to force us to view friendship as a cause and similarity as an effect, but maybe it works the other way too; "Persons with similar opinions tend to become friends." It is very difficult to express both notions in a single clause. Also, English is quite inexact in describing the strength of these relationships. Is the tendency mild, strong, overwhelming, or what? And if you decide to write, "strong," what do you really mean? In a sense, the remaining chapters of this book are an attempt to teach you a more precise language for thinking about relationships and systems of relationships.

At this point, we can only take two steps (the second step is discussed in the following section on relationship diagrams) toward implementing the last three words in Rule 1.1.

R U L E   1.1e

Beware of one-variable findings, unless they come from ratio scales.

The rule follows from our previous discussion of levels of measurement, and the idea is painfully familiar to students who have had experience with "grading on the curve." When a teacher grades on the curve, he produces an ordinal scale with arbitrary category frequencies. If so, the grade distribution does not tell us anything much about the student's performance since the results are mostly a function of the instructor's decision about cutting points. Similarly, if we combine answers from a six-item questionnaire on economic liberalism, we might divide the cases into high–medium–low groupings, but if we then observe that 28 % are "high," this does not tell us "how liberal" the subjects really are since it could as easily have been 10 % or 45 %.

Interval scales are no better. Because the zero point on an interval scale is arbitrary (by definition), the number of cases falling above or below a given score is equally arbitrary and we can inflate it or deflate it by moving the zero

---

[5] If dubious, what is the more appropriate variable name for these operations?

point around. This is summarized by the feeble joke about the man who was terribly upset when he found out that half of the population is below average in intelligence!

It is only when we get to ratio scales that one-variable results have an intrinsic importance. If we find our cases have an average income of $6500 a year, this tells us something since zero income is not an arbitrary unit and neither are dollar distances in income.

For nominal scales, things are not so clear. Where the scale reflects "natural" classes in the population, one-variable results may be informative. The sex composition, the proportion of voters registered, and, for nonbiological purposes, racial distributions are fairly straightforward. However, classifications of occupations, regional boundaries, employment status, personality types, and the like are so arbitrary (though useful) that one-variable results should be taken with a grain of salt.

There is an irony in all of this. As social science becomes more sophisticated, it tends to move away from classifications based on obvious, "natural" nominal categories to more sophisticated measures of abstract variables (measures of anomie, social status, community structure, personality characteristics, etc.) which are ordinal or interval but not ratio scales. Thus, it is the "better" social science measures which should not be taken at face value, i.e., in terms of one-variable distributions.

We will see, however, that statistics of relationships, particularly those of the type stressed in this book, are designed to give meaningful results even when the one-variable distributions are quite arbitrary. The technical issues will be developed later, but for now we ask you to accept the claim that while the single-variable distribution on an index such as SES and an index of political attitudes may be quite "meaningless," the question of whether political attitudes are correlated with SES is quite meaningful.

Let us repeat: You should always be suspicious of single-variable results. If you read that $X\%$ of the people believe in God, oppose the incumbent administration, need the ministrations of a psychiatrist, or whatever, that fact, even though established by the most objective scientific methods, usually can be interpreted only by comparison with some other group or time (that is, in terms of a two-variable relationship) unless it is based on a plausible ratio scale.

In particular, it is well known that the distributions of answers on attitude and opinion questions will vary by 15 or 20% with apparently slight changes in question wording, even though both versions may provide valid orderings.

Be especially wary of implicit two-variable assertions based on one-variable data. Frequently a writer will imply a two-variable finding even though he has evidence on only one measure. You may read that "American youth are self-centered. Eighty-five percent of a recent sample scored high on the

Thingamabob scale of self-centeredness." No conclusion should be drawn from this finding unless scores are given for some other group. Perhaps 95% of European youth would score high (if the missing variable is the nationality of youth); maybe 100% scored high 15 years ago (if the missing variable is time).

Since assertions about relationships between variables are the heart of research, when reading you should learn to pounce on the words and phrases which claim relationships. It is often the case that pages of introductory discussion and definitions of variables yield only a sentence or two where the author "actually says something"—where he asserts a relationship between variables.

Sometimes the task is easy. Here is a sample from a famous study of voting behavior:

> Who are the interested people? Education and SES level seem to have about equal importance in creating and maintaining political interest. . . .[6]

The variables are (1) political interest, (2) education, and (3) socioeconomic status. Further reading would reveal that political interest is an ordinal scale based on the respondents' self-ratings, education is a dichotomy cut at high school graduation, and SES is a four-step ordinal rating of the respondent by the interviewer.

In terms of relationships, the authors make two claims: (1) Education is related to interest and (2) SES is related to interest. We note that, here at least, the authors say nothing about the relationship between education and SES, though after Chapter 4 we will realize that the phrase "have about equal importance" is a shorthand summary of a fairly elaborate analysis which takes into consideration the association between education and SES.

Relationship Diagrams

It is useful to summarize such exegeses by diagrams in which lines connect the variables for which relationships are claimed (see Figure 1.1).

Such diagrams will be used extensively throughout this book, and you should develop the habit of drawing them whenever you read a research report or theoretical essay, and especially when you plan a research project of your own.

Eventually we will take into consideration a number of complica-

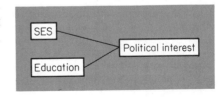

FIG. 1.1

[6] Paul F. Lazarsfeld, Bernard Berelson, and Hazel Gaudet, "The People's Choice," in William Peterson, ed., *American Social Patterns*, Anchor Books, New York, 1956, p. 136.

tions: the *sign* of the correlation (positive or negative), whether or not the relationship is assumed to be mutual (asymmetrical relationships are indicated by adding appropriate arrowheads to the lines), and the complex but fascinating implications of the fact that variables may be directly linked and also indirectly connected through paths or chains involving other variables.

For the moment, we limit ourselves to noting two kinds of assertions which you will find difficult to diagram. Frequently authors will assert that whether two variables are linked depends on whether other variables "have been controlled." For instance, an author may say, "When educational attainment is controlled, the relationship between father's occupation and son's occupation disappears." The link between the two occupations appears quite ambiguous. On the one hand, the statement that it "disappears" implies that you should have no such link in your diagram, but the innocuous "the" before the word "relationship" implies it was there before educational attainment was controlled. In Chapter 5 we will explain exactly how to handle these situations, but for now we suggest that you connect such variables with a special symbol, a "hairy line," shown in Figure 1.2. Hairy lines should be used whenever (1) the author says that a relationship disappears or changes appreciably when some variable is controlled, (2) the author says that a relationship is "because of," "due to," or "explained by" some other variable, and (3) the author says that the variables are related "indirectly" or "through" another variable or variables. (Chapter 5 will make all of this clearer, but you should get used to such diagrams before you read it.)

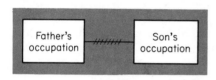

FIG. 1.2

The second problem occurs with conditional propositions where an author says that a relationship between two variables may be present or absent, depending on the category or level of a third variable. The statement "People tend to like those with whom they interact, but only if they are not in competition" involves three variables—liking, interaction, and competition. No claim is made that competition is linked to liking or interaction. Rather the statement is that liking and interaction are linked when competition is "low" and not linked when it is "high." The best way to handle this is by drawing multiple diagrams for different levels of the conditional variable (see Figure 1.3).

Warning: References to *controlled variables* and *conditional variables* may be hard to distinguish unless you read them carefully. The statement "The relationship between X and Y is due to T" *is not* the same as the statement "The relationship between X and Y depends on the *level* of T." The former calls for a hairy line and the latter for multiple diagrams.

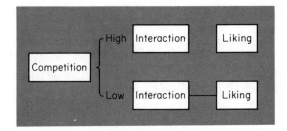

FIG. 1.3

R U L E 1.1f

Learn to analyze your own and others' arguments by diagrams in which variable names are linked by lines using
  a. Solid lines for unqualified assertions that two variables are related.
  b. Hairy lines when it is claimed that
    1. The relationship disappears or changes appreciably when some other variable is "controlled."
    2. The relationship is "because of," "due to," or "explained by" some other variable.
    3. The variables are related "indirectly" or "through" some other variable.
  c. Multiple diagrams for conditional variables.

When no assertion is made, connect the variables by a question mark, as shown in Figure 1.4.

Rule 1.1 gives advice for thinking about variables. Now we turn to more technical advice for the research worker.

FIG. 1.4

R U L E 1.2

Make sure your variables vary.

If the heart of research is to compare cases which fall in different categories, the research worker must have plenty of cases which differ in their classification. It is hard to argue with such a truism, but it is easy to forget it.

Let us begin with study design. It is extremely important that the designer of a research project plan to obtain variation in the important variables. There are a number of advanced techniques for this such as *stratified sampling*, but the vital ingredient is clear thinking.

Consider, for example, the "offbeat group" fallacy. Frequently, a novice research worker is curious about some very special group such as political extremists, corporation presidents, drug addicts, or sociology students. It seems so natural to then drawn a sample of extremists or presidents or addicts or neophyte sociologists. However, such designs remove almost all of the variation in the variable. In a group of political extremists there is little variation in extremism; among corporation presidents everyone receives high scores on "presidency"; among addicts, addiction is uniformly high; sociology students are uniformly sociological—all of which means that in order to study such a group you should have some other group for contrast, producing a variable. Political extremists may be compared with moderates, corporation presidents with government officials, drug addicts with nonusers, and sociology students with students in other fields. The precise comparison group depends on how you are defining the variable. If you compare addicts with "normals," you define it one way; if you compare them with alcoholics, you are defining a different variable. The important point is to build differences in the key variables from the beginning.[7]

A less extreme version of this design problem is naturally selected populations. We all know that college students vary in intelligence, but compared with the general population they tend to be homogeneously high in intelligence. If we use a college student sample to test some hypothesis about intelligence, we will get less variability in the key variable than if we use a population cross section. Since college students are a natural target for beginning research workers, it is important to remember that they are not an optimum study group for variables such as intelligence, social class, age, and career plans.

RULE 1.2a

In designing research, always avoid the offbeat group fallacy and try to avoid samples which are highly selected on your key variables. Always ask yourself, What groups will I compare and how many cases am I likely to get of each?

A similar issue turns up when forming dichotomies. Since you will treat all your variables as dichotomies through most of this book, we will explore the question in some detail.

Some dichotomies—but not many—are natural and the analyst has no choice. The sexes come men vs. women, and that's that. More often, dichotomies are formed by the application of cutting points to a larger set of categories, dividing the cases into high and low grade point average, more and less liberal, newcomers vs. oldtimers, etc.

We advance two rules, depending on the level of measurement:

---

[7] Be wary, however, of selecting your sample on both variables when you are interested in their relationship. If you are testing the hypothesis that corporation presidents have higher achievement drives than nuns, do not select 50 ambitious presidents, 50 nonambitious presidents, 50 ambitious nuns, and 50 nonambitious nuns. Your data would show no relationship at all between the two variables.

R U L E 1.2b

With ordinal, interval, and ratio scales, seek a 50:50 split and try to avoid dichotomies more extreme than 30:70.

1.2c If the variable is nominal, seek substantive compatibility as well as a 50:50 split.

Rule 1.2b is simple to apply. If there are many values (categories), you want to dichotomize the data at the *median*, the value above which and below which lie half the cases. Even where there are few categories, the task is simple. Assume that you have the distribution shown in Table 1.2. Inspection of the left-hand column suggests that the reasonable cuts are either I + II vs. III + IV or I + II + III vs. IV. Looking at the columns of cumulative percentages (a handy way to go about this if you have quite a few categories), the diagonal lines tell us that the first would give a 30:70 split and the second a 35:65 split. Following Rule 1.2b, one would choose the second because it is a little closer to 50:50.

TABLE 1.2 Percentage Distribution on Some Variable

CATEGORY	DISTRIBUTION, %	CUMULATIVE	
I	10	10	100
II	20	30	90
III	35	65	70
IV	35	100	35
	100		

Why does a 50:50 dichotomization maximize variation in our variable? We will explore the qustion because it helps us to set up the notion of *random pairs*, a theme which will run throughout the technical parts of the book.

But slow and steady wins the race. Before we tackle random pairs, let us first establish the notion of *random cases*.

Assume we have collected data on N cases, measuring some dichotomous variable, for example, using the Rorschach test to determine unconscious attitudes toward peanut brittle among 1538 cases, of whom 1112 are classified as "favorable" (high) and the rest, 426 cases, are classified as "nonfavorable" (low).

Further assume that for some mad reason we decide to shuffle all the cases in some helter-skelter fashion and then draw individual cases, like dealing cards from a well-shuffled deck. What is the probability of drawing a case high on peanut brittleness? Obviously it is 1112:1538 or .723. And the odds for drawing a "low"? We can get them two ways. We might figure that 426:1538 equals .277. Or, because the measure is a dichotomy, the two probabilities must have a total of 1.000, and 1.000 minus .723 is .277.

Calling the total number of cases N, the frequency of highs fh, and the frequency of lows fl, we have said that H, the probability that a random case is high, equals fh/N; L, the probability that a random case is low, equals fl/N; and $H + L = 1.000$.

Having analyzed this trivial problem, let us move on to the slightly trickier issue of random pairs. This involves the following extension of our hypothetical enterprise: We shuffle all the cases, draw a single case (case I), note its category, return it to the pot, reshuffle, draw a second case (case II), and note its category. Cases I and II constitute a random pair, and the question is this: What are the probabilities for various outcomes among random pairs? The possible outcomes are these:

1. Case I and case II are both high (we draw two highs or the same high twice).
2. Case I and case II are both low (we draw two lows or the same low twice).
3. Case I and case II differ (one is high and one is low).

And the probabilities? Since the draws are statistically independent (the outcome of one is unrelated to the outcome of the other), we calculate them by multiplying the probabilities for a random case, just as the chances of obtaining two heads in a row with flips of a fair coin is $.500 * .500$ or $.250$. (We will use the convention of indicating multiplication with an asterisk: $*$). Table 1.3 summarizes the results.

TABLE 1.3 Probabilities for Outcomes in Draws of Random Pairs from a Dichotomous Variable Where the Probability of a High is H and the Probability of a Low is L.

OUTCOME		
I	II	PROBABILITY
High	High	$H * H = H^2$
Low	Low	$L * L = L^2$
High	Low	$H * L$
Low	High	$L * H$

What we are really interested in is pairs that differ (remember this section began with the statement "The heart of research is to compare cases which fall in different categories"). Therefore, the important part of Table 1.3 is the bottom two lines, the outcomes where the pairs differ. Since we do not care which case was draw I and which case was draw II, we can combine them, and here is the key result. In random pairs, the probability of a differing pair (one in which draw I and draw II come from different categories) is

$$2 * \frac{fh}{N} * \frac{fl}{N} \quad \text{(in frequency terms)}$$

$$2 * H * L \quad \text{(in probability terms)}$$

This basic result can be used to justify Rule 1.2b, which tells us to pick cutting points near 50:50 in order to maximize the differences. Table 1.4 drives the point home by showing the value of $2 * H * L$ for selected probabilities.

TABLE 1.4 Value of $2 * H * L$ for Selected Values of H and L

H	L	$2 * H * L$
.10	.90	.180
.20	.80	.320
.30	.70	.420
.40	.60	.480
.50	.50	.500
.60	.40	.480
.70	.30	.420
.80	.20	.320
.90	.10	.180

The value of $2 * H * L$ reaches a maximum of .500 when $H = L = .500$ and it declines as we move away from that value in either direction. Clearly we can maximize the number of differing pairs in our data by setting the cutting point as close to .500 as possible, and we wish to avoid *skewed* distributions that depart strongly from 50:50. It is not always possible to get a precise 50:50 break, but we note that any cutting point in the 30:70 range gives 42% or more differing pairs, 84% or more of the maximum of 50%. This is the foundation for Rule 1.2b.

Table 1.4 also reveals some of the "inefficiencies" in our statistical approach. The decision to work with dichotomies means that we can never top 50% differing pairs. If we expanded our dichotomy to a finer ordinal scale, of course we could increase the number of differing pairs, and if we had data in which all N cases were ranked from 1 to N on the variable, the proportion of pairs that differ would reach 1.00. Our approach, though relatively inefficient, provides plenty of grist for the mill. Chapter 3 will take us deeper into this question, and there we will see that not only does a dichotomy provide plenty of differing pairs, but it also nets those pairs with the "biggest differences" in rank on the variable in question.

The case of nominal data (Rule 1.2c) is more difficult. When the scale is ordinal, interval, or ratio, the problem is simply one of where to cut the ribbon, and Table 1.4 gives us a definite answer. The trouble with nominal data is that they can be rearranged, not just "cut." This, of course, is the definition of a nominal scale. Consider the hypothetical data presented in Table 1.5.

If 50:50 splits were the only consideration, Table 1.5 would be easy to handle. We could combine humanities (20%), fine arts (5%), and engineering

TABLE 1.5 Percentage Distribution by Undergraduate Major at Hypothetical State University

FIELD	PERCENT
Engineering	25
Fine arts	5
Humanities	20
Physical sciences	15
Social sciences	15
Social work	20
	100

(25%) to get the magic 50%. Yet intuition tells us this is "wrong." Somehow, humanities does not belong with engineering, which is to say we predict that on other variables (e.g., mathematical aptitude) engineering students will be more like the physical scientists we placed in a different category than the humanists whom we put in the same category. This would tend to lower the correlation between field of study and mathematical aptitude.

We are caught in a circle, for we want to group together categories which will be similar on other variables and to separate categories which will be different on other variables—but if we knew all this, we would not be doing the research!

Clearly we are at one of those points where insight, luck, and knowledge of the research literature are more important than statistical rules. All that can be said is that one should seek to group together categories which will be similar on other variables and to segregate categories that will tend to differ on other variables.

The following rules of thumb may be of help:

1. If one of the categories is conspicuously larger in frequency than the rest, use it alone as one half of the dichotomy if it is in the 30:70 range. If not, add as few "seemingly compatible" categories to it as are necessary to meet the 30:70 criterion.

2. If you have a large number of categories with small frequencies, begin by forming "seemingly compatible" pairs; then combine pairs into sets of four, etc., until one such group reaches the 70:30 criterion.

In Table 1.5 one would probably go at it by the second route, pairing humanities and fine arts (20% + 5% = 25%), social sciences and social work (15% + 20% = 35%), and physical sciences and engineering (15% + 25% = 40%) on intuitive grounds. This gives three groups. Now all we have to do is to pair two of them. The best-split rule would be to combine humanities–fine arts–social science–social work, which would give us 60% vs. 40% in physical sciences and engineering.

In the example, the best-split rule coincides with one's intuitive feeling that students of humanities and fine arts are "more like" students of social sciences and social work than like students of physical science and engineering. It does not always work this way, and sometimes one has to make a hard choice between a cutting point which seems intuitively better and one which seems statistically better. The only advice is "Good luck!"

3. Beware of combinations where you cannot attach a category name to either half of the dichotomy.

If you are going to treat some combination of categories as a supercategory, you ought to be able to give it a name—although both halves of a dichotomy do not need names, since "other" will always do for one. Note that our first attempt for Table 1.5—humanities–fine arts–engineering vs. social sciences–social work–physical sciences—defies naming, while our final version can be called "pure and applied natural science" vs. other.

4. Scales which combine several items may be used to generate acceptable cutting points even though the constituent items are each highly skewed.

Scaling is a complex matter which cannot be covered in this book. For our purposes you may feel free to combine items in any way that seems logical. With two items, you can call "high" those who are "high on either" or those who are "high on both" depending on the cuts; with many items, you can build scales by "giving one point for each favorable answer" and dichotomizing the distribution of points near the middle. In either case you should begin by showing that your items are strongly correlated with each other (using the techniques of Chapter 2) since items that tap the same variable should show a high agreement.

There remains the frequent case which defies all these rules, the tiny category which should stand alone on substantive grounds. If one is interested in race problems, the obvious dichotomy is Negro vs. all other; yet in most U.S. samples, Negroes will run 10% or less. Again, in studies of religious behavior, it generally turns out that the most striking differences are between Jews and Christians, yet Jews constitute about 2% of the general population. In such situations you should not sacrifice substance on the altar of statistical efficiency, but proceed to make extreme dichotomies. However, you must pay a price—you will need an extra large sample to compensate for the shrinkage of differing pairs. Some concrete rules are given in Chapter 2.

The strictures above may appear frightening. However, you should remember that there is no "wrong way" to form dichotomies—or perhaps a better way to put it is this: There are only two consequences, neither fatal, of violating the rules: (1) You may get lower correlations if you group together categories which do not belong together, and (2) you may get results which are hard to interpret if you group together categories in a way which does not make sense. Neither is disastrous, but neither is desirable. Therefore, unless you have some strong reason to do otherwise, the rules should be followed.

If a particular dichotomy for a nominal scale lies uneasily on your conscience, there is no rule against repeating your analysis with an alternative version. If the results do not change much, you will feel more comfortable, and if they do, you will have learned something. However, you should be warned that (1) a reshuffling which merely slides a small minority of cases from one side of the cutting point to another will usually make only a small difference in your results, and (2) if you have several nominal variables, there are so many combinations of alternatives that the amount of work is high and you can generate an overwhelming volume of data. Thus, such a step should be reserved for one or two key variables (see Chapter 7).

Actually, forming dichotomies is a chance to exercise imagination in research. You get a chance to predict the ways in which the world is structured and you should not be bound by tradition. For instance, in Table 1.5, there is no law saying that you could not adopt a completely different strategy. You might group (humanities + social sciences + physical sciences = 50%) vs. (fine arts + social work + engineering = 50%) and call the result "pure" vs. "applied" fields. Who knows; this grouping might produce interesting results.

A final note. In addition to the substantive categories, variables often include the categories "no answer," "no information," and the like to designate cases where the classification could not be attempted because of missing information. It is important to distinguish them from "no opinion," "other," "unclassifiable," etc., which are substantive categories. Cases of the former type should be excluded from your tabulations (i.e., you should work with a reduced sample size) because you have no way of knowing where they might have been classified if the information had been obtained. Cases of the latter type should be placed in one half of the dichotomy since they constitute a sorting on the basis of the case characteristics, e.g., dichotomizing as "favorable" vs. "unfavorable and no opinion." A third special situation, "not applicable" (the question, "When did you last fight with your wife?" does not apply to single, widowed, or divorced persons), is not really a category, but a redefinition of the sample. "Not applicable" cases obviously should be excluded from the dichotomy.

Beginners have a tendency to overuse the "not applicable" category, for example, excluding those with "no opinion" when they can be legitimately treated as "not favorable" (or "not unfavorable") or tossing out the political independents, leaving only staunch Republicans and Democrats. This has the unfortunate effect of artificially inflating correlations (correlations run higher when you are working only with extreme cases) and limiting the persons to whom you can generalize your results. In general, one should be loath to classify cases as "not applicable."

IN A NUTSHELL

A. The logic of variables

1. Categories
   a) *Levels of measurement: nominal, ordinal, interval, and ratio*
   b) *The technical dilemma*
      (1) Higher-scale levels allow for more sophisticated statistics,
      (2) But since most sociological data are ordinal and interval and since cruder statistics are easier to make clear to beginners, we will limit our attention to nominal and ordinal scales.
   c) *Number of categories: the decision to limit our major attention to dichotomies.*
2. Name-definition-sorting procedure : problems of validity
   a) *Distinction between validity and reliability*
   b) *Argument for a middle position between extreme operationalism and indifference to problems of validity.*

Rules

R U L E 1.1

Learn to think in terms of variables and their relationships.

1.1a To define a variable you must state its mutually exclusive and totally inclusive categories.

1.1b To define a variable you must state (however sketchily) the research operations.

1.1c Always consider the alternative variable names which might be more appropriate for a given set of operations and the alternative operations which might be more appropriate for a given variable name.

1.1d When designing research, use multiple measures for key variables whose operational definitions are problematic.

1.1e Beware of one-variable findings, unless they come from ratio scales.

1.1f Learn to analyze your own and others' arguments by diagrams in which variable names are linked by lines.

R U L E 1.2

Make sure your variables vary.

1.2a In designing research, always avoid the offbeat group fallacy and try to avoid samples which are highly selected on your key variables.

1.2b With ordinal, interval and ratio scales, seek a 50 : 50 split and try to avoid dichotomies more extreme than 30 : 70.

1.2c If the variable is nominal, seek substantive compatibility as well as a 50:50 split.

Major Concepts

1. Conclusions	11. Operational interpretation
2. Cutting point	(sorting procedure)
3. Dichotomy	12. Ordinal scale
4. Differing pairs	13. Random pairs
5. Findings	14. Ratio scale
6. Guttman (cumulative)	15. Reliability
scales	16. Skewed dichotomy
7. Interval scale	17. Tied pairs
8. Level of measurement	18. Transitivity
9. Median	19. Trichotomy
10. Nominal Scale	20. Validity

FURTHER READING

On experimental and nonexperimental designs:

D. T. CAMPBELL AND J. C. STANLEY, "Experimental and Quasi-experimental Designs for Research on Teaching," in N. L. Gage, ed., *Handbook of Research on Teaching*, Rand McNally, New York, 1963, Chapter 5.

On the logic of measurement:

WARREN S. TORGERSON, *Theory and Methods of Scaling*, Wiley, New York, 1958, Chapters 1 and 2.

On multiple measures of problematic variables:

EUGENE J. WEBB, DONALD T. CAMPBELL, RICHARD D. SCHWARTZ, and LEE SECHREST, *Unobtrusive Measures*, Rand McNally, New York, 1966, Chapter 1.

On validity:

WILLIAM N. STEPHENS, *Hypotheses and Evidence*, Thomas Y. Crowell, New York, 1968, especially Chapters III and V.

(The main ideas of this chapter have been lifted from Stephens' lucid and sophisticated text.)

2

Two-Variable Relationships: Independence, Yule's Q, Confidence Limits for Q

An Overview

If the most important idea in research is the idea of *variables*, the next most important is the idea of *relationships between variables*. This chapter spells out the concepts and computations necessary to state whether two dichotomous variables are related at all, how strongly they are related, and what generalizations can be made from sample data to relationships in the parent population.

We begin with the raw material—a cross tabulation of two measures arranged in a *fourfold table*. Even such a simple set of data requires a lot of notation and explanation before you can begin work.

Next we attack the very concept of relationship, noting that statisticians back into it by giving a precise definition of the *absence* of relationship (called statistical independence) and then saying there is some relationship between two variables if the data do *not* meet the definition of statistical independence.

Then we shift from "some relationship" to "how much relationship," describing in detail a statistic, Yule's Q, used to describe the degree or strength of relationship. Q has some useful technical properties and also an interesting "meaning" in terms of the differing pairs defined in the previous chapter.

In the last section we treat the problem of inferring from sample to parent population (universe), that is, making rational guesses about the value of Q in the universe on the basis of the sample results and mathematical principles of sampling. This can be done only with *probability samples*, and we begin by defining various probability samples. Finally we present a procedure for calculating *confidence intervals*, a range of Q values within which we are fairly certain the parent value lies.

Fourfold Tables

When two dichotomies are cross-tabulated, the result is called a fourfold table because it has four interior cells where frequencies are entered. Such tables have nine working parts—four cell frequencies, four marginal frequencies, and a total called N. Table 2.1 is a concrete example, taken from a subsample of the 1960 U.S. census.[1]

TABLE 2.1 Sex and Earnings in 1959 Among Those Reporting Some Earnings

| | | EARNINGS | | |
		Under $4000	$4000 or more	Total
SEX	Male	2166	2754	4920
	Female	2128	413	2541
		4294	3167	7461 = N
				10478 = inapplicable (no earnings in 1959)
				17939 = Total

The example has two totals. The total number of cases in the census sample happens to be 17,939, but we decided to examine the relationship between sex and earnings only among those who had some earnings, and following the advice of Chapter 1, the inapplicable cases were excluded. The second number, N, the total for the cases in the table, is much smaller. It is imperative that (1) we make clear to our readers when we are working with a subset of the total sample and (2) our figures add up. Thus, a rule:

[1] These and other data used in this book are from a punchcard file furnished under a joint project sponsored by the U.S. Bureau of the Census and the Population Council. Neither the Census Bureau nor the Population Council assumes any responsibility for the validity of any of the figures or interpretations.

R U L E 2.1

> When reporting tables of frequencies, you must account for all of the cases in the sample by specifying frequencies such as "no answer" and "not applicable" as well as the *N* for the table.

In the abstract, the parts of a fourfold table are as shown in Table 2.2.

TABLE 2.2   Nomenclature for a Fourfold Table

		VARIABLE *Y* NOT *Y*	*Y*	
VARIABLE *X*	*X*	Frequency *A* (total cases which are *X* and *NOT Y*)	Frequency *B* (total cases which are *X* and *Y*)	Marginal frequency *X* (total cases which are *X*)
	NOT X	Frequency *C* (total cases which are *NOT X* and *NOT Y*)	Frequency *D* (total cases which are *NOT X* and *Y*)	Marginal frequency *NOT X* (total cases which are *NOT X*)
	Total	Marginal frequency *NOT Y* (total cases which are *NOT Y*)	Marginal frequency *Y* (total cases which are *Y*)	*N* (total cases in the table)

Fourfold tables are not quite so simple as they seem, and you should note the following conventions and definitions:

1. We will call the two variables *X* and *Y*, and the two categories of each *X*, *NOT X*, and *Y*, *NOT Y*.
   Warning: In this abstract notation the same letter appears as a variable name and a category name. You should be able to tell which is meant from the context. In concrete research the problem does not arise because we always pick different words for variable names, e.g., sex, education, occupation, and category names, e.g., male, high school graduate, professional.
2. The four interior cells are designated by the capital letters *A*, *B*, *C*, and *D*.
3. When you sum across a row or down a column you obtain the total frequency for a category. This is known as a "marginal" because it appears in the margins of the table.
4. If the dichotomy is collapsed from an ordinal, interval, or ratio scale, "high" is associated with *X* and *Y*, and "low" is associated with *NOT X* and *NOT Y*. In other words, values of variables increase as one moves up rows and from left to right across columns. This is important when we get to the "sign" of a correlation.
5. To check tables and to help understand certain properties of fourfold tables, note that the following must hold:
   a. Each row must sum to its marginal frequency.
   b. Each column must sum to its marginal frequency.
   c. The four cells must sum to *N*.
   d. The two marginals for a variable must sum to *N*.

While the nomenclature looks very impressive, we do not yet know whether there is any relationship between sex and earnings. Even experienced research workers have a hard time drawing conclusions from raw figures, and this is why we carry out statistical analysis—to state precisely and succinctly what is going on, if anything.

Statistical Independence

Statistical analysis backs into association (or correlation—we use the words as synonyms) rather than confronting it head on, a strategy which is quite logical but occasionally confusing to a beginner. The statistician's reasoning is something like this:

1. By definition, these data either show a relationship (however weak) or they show no relationship at all.
2. We will deduce what the table would look like if X and Y have no relationship at all.
3. Then we will compare the actual data table with the deduced "no relationship" table.
4. If the real data differ from the "no relationship" table, we will conclude that X and Y are correlated.

What do we mean by "no relationship"? The technical term is *statistical independence*. (You will remember the statistically independent draws I and II to get the random pairs in Chapter 1.) The definition is "X and Y are statistically independent if the cell probabilities equal the products of the relevant marginal probabilities."

The idea is exactly like flipping coins or drawing random pairs. If we made a fourfold table in which X is the first flip (heads $= X$, tails $= NOT\ X$) and Y is the second flip (heads $= Y$, tails $= NOT\ Y$), we would say that if the flips are independent, the probability of getting, say, a head and then a tail (which would turn up in cell A) is $.250 = (.50) * (.50) = $ (marginal probability for X) $*$ (marginal probability for $NOT\ Y$).

Independence also means that the odds for one variable are the same whatever the category of the other variable—the other variable literally does not make any difference. If sex and earnings are independent, the odds for being a high earner are the same for men and women and the odds that a case is a man is the same for high earners and low earners.

Let us translate Table 2.1 into probabilities by dividing each frequency by 7461, as shown in Table 2.3.

The probability a random earner is male is .659, and the probability that a random earner made $4000 or more in 1959 is .424 (note that both marginals are within the 70:30 norm). If sex and earnings are independent, the prob-

TABLE 2.3 Data in Table 2.1 Expressed as Probabilities

		EARNINGS		
		Under $4000	$4000 or more	*Total*
SEX	Male	.290	.369	.659
	Female	.285	.055	.340
	Total	.575	.424	.999

ability that a case is both male and a high earner would be .659 ∗ .424 = .279. This is called the "expected" value. But looking inside Table 2.3 we see that the "observed" probability is .369, not .279. We've got something:

Observed probability (cell B)	.369
Expected probability (cell B)	.279
Difference	.090

There are more high-earner males than we would expect if X and Y were independent (have only a chance relationship) and thus (by definition) there is a correlation between sex and earnings in our data.

What about the other three cells? Should we examine their observed and expected probabilities? No, because fourfold tables have this property: In each row (column) the results for observed vs. expected (whether expressed as a probability or a frequency) must be equal in value and opposite in sign. (*Warning:* This is not true for tables with more rows or columns.)

To understand the logic of association, we must explore this a little.

1. Call the cell value of "observed" minus "expected" *delta*. Generally delta is expressed as a frequency rather than a probability but the difference is irrelevant here.

2. In any cell we can substitute "expected" + delta for "observed." In cell B of the example, "observed" is .369, "expected" is .279, delta is +.090, and clearly .279 + .090 = .369.

3. In any row (column) the observed frequencies can be expressed in terms of two expecteds and two deltas. For the top row of our table:

	Under $4000	$4000 or more
Male	Expected A + delta A	Expected B + delta B

4. The two expecteds in any row (column) must sum to the marginal from the elementary algebra of probabilities.

5. So far, we have shown that
   Expected A + expected B = marginal for X
   Expected A + delta A + expected B + delta B = marginal for X.

6. The only way to square these two equations is for delta A and delta B to sum to zero.

7. Now take any arbitrary cell and calculate the value of delta.
8. Given step 6 the other delta in the row must have the same value and opposite sign, as must the other delta in the same column.
9. We have now filled in three deltas. The fourth must be equal in value and opposite in sign from the two deduced in step 8.
10. In general we can fill in all four deltas and their signs from the value and sign of any one of them.

While the mathematics is not profound, we explained delta in some detail for two reasons. First, it sets the stage for later consideration of tables with more rows and columns. Second, it leads us to the notion of the sign of a correlation. When delta differs from zero, there are only two ways in which the signs (plus or minus) can appear. These are shown in Table 2.4.

TABLE 2.4   Delta and Signs of Correlation

a. Positive correlation	NOT Y	Y		b. Negative correlation	NOT Y	Y
X	−	+		X	+	−
NOT X	+	−		NOT X	−	+

Case a in Table 2.4 is called a positive correlation because X and Y "tend to go together." If we consider "tend to be" a synonym for "occur together more than one would expect by chance," a positive correlation implies the following statements:

1. X's tend to be Y's.
2. NOT X's tend to be NOT Y's.
3. Y's tend to be X's.
4. NOT Y's tend to be NOT X's.

The nature of delta makes these four statements tautologies. If any one of them is true in a fourfold table, all the others must be true. Any or all of them provide a verbal interpretation for a positive correlation.

Warning: "Tends to be" is not the same as "most are." X's may tend to be Y's even though only a minority are Y's, provided that X's are more likely to be Y's than are NOT X's. In Table 2.1 low earners tend to be female, but *most* low earners are male, not female. This is an instance of the probabilistic nature of social research, cited in the introduction. While the sentences listed above are reminiscent of the propositions of elementary logic, they are probabilistic, not either/or, and there are a number of differences between these two forms of reasoning.

This makes for enormous difficulties when one comes to test sociological theories which are stated in traditional logic. Chapters 5 and 6 amount to a rhapsody on this theme.

The upshot of all of this is that after calculating the lone delta for Table 2.1, we may state all of the following: (1) There is a positive correlation between sex and earnings, (2) men tend to be high earners, (3) women tend to be low earners, (4) high earners tend to be men, and (5) low earners tend to be women—but we know that these are five different ways of stating the same thing, not five separate pieces of news.

To summarize:

1. Independence or complete lack of association means that cell probabilities are identical with the expected values given by multiplying marginal probabilities (or alternatively, the Y odds are the same for each category of X and vice versa).

2. A fourfold table which departs from independence is defined as showing a "correlation" or "association" between X and Y.

3. If delta (observed minus expected) is known for any one cell of a fourfold table, the other three deltas have the same value and their signs can be deduced.

4. The two possible patterns for nonzero deltas are called "positive" and "negative" correlation.

We have discussed independence in terms of probabilities, but exactly the same properties hold when we are working with frequencies since a probability is only a convenient rescaling of the frequencies. In practice, the research worker usually works with expected frequencies rather than expected probabilities. To obtain the expected frequencies for a particular cell, simply multiply the pair of relevant marginal frequencies and divide their product by N. In Table 2.1 the expected frequency in cell B is $(4920) * (3167)/7461 = 2088.4$.

Strength of a Correlation, Yule's Q

The mere fact that a table does not show independence means little in research. Tables almost never show deltas of .000, but that does not mean they always reveal breathtaking correlations. If delta is nonzero but very small, for all practical purposes the two variables can be considered independent even though the precise definition of independence is not met. Thus, we need some way to assess the degree of correlation as well as its presence or absence.

Why not use delta? After all, in any particular table, the larger delta is, the greater is the discrepancy between observed data and chance expectations.

The objections are two. First, delta is sensitive to sample size. If you double the sample size you double the value of delta. This would make it difficult to compare deltas from two different samples unless they had identical N's. The second problem is that of an upper limit. We know how small delta can get, zero. How large could it become? The frequency delta in our example, 665.6, looks big standing alone, but if we knew that the highest possible delta for our table was, say, 100 billion, we would not think 665.6 very impressive. We seek a measure which is insensitive to sample size and has meaningful upper and lower limits.

In addition, statisticians have adopted the following rules of the game when devising measures of degree of association: (1) They should equal .00 when X and Y are independent, (2) they should have a maximum of $+1.00$ for the strongest possible positive association, (3) they should have a maximum of -1.00 for the strongest possible negative association, and (4) the values should have some intrinsic meaning.

By a little algebraic fiddling around, one can obtain a coefficient which meets all these standards and is intimately related to delta (its numerator can be shown to equal delta $* N$). The coefficient is called Yule's Q. The British statistician G. Udny Yule published the first paper on it in 1912 and he named it Q to honor the pioneer statistician Quételet (1796–1874).[2]

Here is the formula:

$$Q_{XY} = \frac{(B * C) - (A * D)}{(B * C) + (A * D)} = \left[\frac{N * \text{delta}}{(B * C) + (A * D)} \right]$$

For Table 2.1,

$$Q_{XY} = \frac{(2754 * 2128) - (2166 * 413)}{(2754 * 2188) + (2166 * 413)} = \frac{(5,860,512) - (894,558)}{(5,860,512) + (894,558)}$$

$$= \frac{4,965,954}{6,755,070} = +.735$$

It is a good rule to calculate Q to three decimals, but round it to two in your report. If the third decimal is 5, round to the even; e.g., .735 becomes .74, while .725 becomes .72.

Let us take a close look at Q because, like so many aspects of fourfold tables, it is more complex than one would think. The coefficient has five statistical properties worth discussion and an interesting intrinsic meaning.

First, it has only two working parts, $(B * C)$ and $(A * D)$. They are called

[2] G. Udny Yule, "On the methods of measuring association between two attributes," *Journal of the Royal Statistical Society*, 75 (1912), 579–642.

cross products. To see why, have a good look at Table 2.2 with the Q formula in mind. This makes it easy to remember the formula, which boils down to "the difference in cross products divided by the sum of the cross products." With a little practice you can learn to estimate the rough value of Q by making a quick mental multiplication of the cross products in a raw data table.

Second, Q must equal .00 when X and Y are independent. This follows from the fact that under independence the ratio (odds) A/C will be the same as the ratio B/D (i.e., the ratio of X's to NOT X's must be the same among Y's and NOT Y's). Consequently,

$$\frac{A}{C} = \frac{B}{D}$$

We remember from high school that you can cross multiply such an equation giving $(B * C) = (A * D)$. If so, the difference $(B * C) - (A * D)$ must be zero, and since zero divided by anything is zero, Q must equal zero.

Third, for any particular table, as delta increases, the value of Q will increase. Start with the case of complete independence, where delta is zero. Then consider some positive correlation such that the value of delta is now W. From our previous discussion we see that the values of the four cells must be changed so that what was originally A, B, C, D under independence is now $(B + W), (C + W), (A - W)$, and $(D - W)$. Consequently the product $(B + W) * (C + W)$ must be larger than $(B * C)$ and the product $(A - W)$ $* (D - W)$ must be smaller than $(A * D)$, producing a positive value of Q. If delta next swells to $W + Z, (B + W + Z) * (C + W + Z)$ must be still larger and $(A - W - Z) * (D - W - Z)$ still smaller, and so on indefinitely as delta waxes. A negative correlation works the same way except that $(B * C)$ is decreased and $(A * D)$ increased when delta swells. (Note that the relative size of $(B * C)$ and $(A * D)$ determines whether the correlation will be positive or negative.)

Fourth, Q has an upper limit of ± 1.00. As one cross product swells, the other shrinks, and if the process is continued, the shrinking cross product reaches a minimum of zero and can go no further. Q will then become either $[(B * C) - \text{zero}]/[(B * C) + \text{zero}] = +1.00$ or $[\text{zero} - (A * D)]/[\text{zero} + (A * D)] = -1.00$. Since the only way to obtain a product of zero is to have one or both of the multiplied frequencies equal to zero, a fourfold table which gives a Q of ± 1.00 must have exactly one or two zero cells (if it had three, one of the item marginals must be zero, which is pretty far from 70: 30, and if all four are zero, $N = 0$, which is a very special case indeed). Table 2.5 gives three hypothetical maximum associations with identical values of $(B * C)$.

TABLE 2.5 Three Maximum Values of Q

	1				2				3	
	NOT Y	*Y*			*NOT Y*	*Y*			*NOT Y*	*Y*
X	0	100		*X*	0	100		*X*	100	100
NOT X	100	100		*NOT X*	100	0		*NOT X*	100	0

In situation 2 both A and D equal zero, while in cases 1 and 3 there is only one zero cell. In all three the product ($A * D$) will be zero and $Q = +1.00$. Sometimes students feel that "it isn't right" to allow a perfect correlation while there are still some cases in the (A,D) diagonal, but the inevitable becomes more bearable when one remembers those marginals. In situation 2, X and Y have identical 50:50 marginals (you can always check the equality of marginals from the A,D cells; when they are equal, X and Y have identical marginals). But in cases 1 and 3 the marginals differ. (In case 1, X is split 100 vs. 200, and Y is split 200 vs. 100, and in case 3 it is the exact reverse.) We may think of changes in correlation as a process of shifting pairs of cases from one diagonal to the other (raising delta by one for a positive correlation requires that we take a case from A and put it in B and one from D and put it in C—or alternatively one from D and putting it in B and one from A and putting it in C; see Figure 2.1).

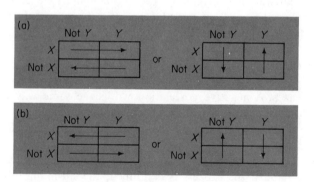

FIG. 2.1 Schematic notion of correlation as shifting pairs of cases. (a) Pair shifts which make Q more positive or less negative. (b) Pair shifts which make Q more negative or less positive.

When, however, the marginals are not identical, there will come a time when all of the cases have been removed from A (or D) while some remain in D (or A). In cases 1 or 3 in Table 2.5 there is no way we could raise delta without changing the marginals, i.e., faking the data. Thus, even though cases may appear in one of the "minus delta cells," a maximum Q means that the association has gone as far as it can go without changing the marginals.

Fifth and last, Q has the nice property that it is "insensitive to multiplication or division of row or column frequencies by a positive constant." By this is meant that you can (1) calculate Q on any table, (2) then multiply and divide A and B and/or C and D, and/or A and C, and/or B and D by any fraction(s) or number(s) you choose, and (3) the Q calculated on the new table will be identical with the old one save for tiny differences due to rounding. Why is this such a nice property?

First, it means that we do not have to have the correct marginals, provided that the cases in each category are representative of the universe. If we decide to take the advice of Chapter 1 and compare delinquents with nondelinquents, we would get only a handful of bad boys in a representative sample of adolescents, violating our 70:30 rule. Instead, we might draw representative samples of 250 nondelinquents and 250 delinquents, giving us 50:50 marginals. And we could do so with the certainty that Q's calculated on such data would be the same as those from a skewed representative sample.

Warning: This holds only for items correlated with delinquency. It would not necessarily be true if we took two other items in the data (e.g., family income and race).

A second gain is the ability to calculate Q's from other people's percentages. If, for example, you read that 34% of young people endorse some position compared with 47% of older people, you can calculate the Q for age and endorsement without access to the raw data. Simply make a table, such as Table 2.6, and proceed as usual.

TABLE 2.6 Calculating Q for Two Hypothetical Percentages

		AGE	
		Younger	Older
ENDORSE	Yes	34	47
	No	66	53
	Total	100%	100%

$$Q = \frac{(47 * 66) - (34 * 53)}{(47 * 66) + (34 * 53)} = +.265$$

The enterprise is justified by the fact that calculation of a percentage amounts to dividing the entries in each column by a constant. One would prefer to have the raw data in order to make further tests discussed below, but after reading Chapter 3 on the pitfalls of percentages, you will see why this is a handy tool.

Having reviewed five technical properties of Q, let us turn to the fourth criterion for a coefficient of correlation, "meaning." The criterion implies that when we obtain a correlation of .265 we must be able to answer the question, "Twenty-six and a half what?" For 40 years Q did not appear to have any intrinsic meaning, but was merely a useful gadget. However, in 1954 Leo Goodman and William Kruskal published an important paper[3] which not only made life meaningful for Q but also led to a considerable amount of rethinking about measures of association in general.

The groundwork was laid in Chapter 1 in the discussion of random pairs.

We already know that with one dichotomous variable there are two outcomes for random pairs, tied pairs and differing pairs, pairs from the same category of the variable and pairs drawn from both categories. With two variables, the possibilities become

1. Tied on both X and Y
2. Tied on X, differing on Y
3. Tied on Y, differing on X
4. Differing on both X and Y

By extension of the previous arguments about probabilities and the correspondence between frequencies and probabilities, it is possible to write formulas for calculating the total frequencies and probabilities for these types.

Let us now calculate these probabilities and frequencies, keeping our eyes open for familiar and meaningful formulas, for example, $(B * C)$ or $(A * D)$.

A probability is a frequency divided by the total possible different outcomes. To express our results as probabilities, we need a denominator, the total possible number of pair outcomes. That's easy enough. There are N possible outcomes for draw I (it may net any one of the N cases in the sample), and similarly there are N possible outcomes for draw II. Since the outcome of draw II has nothing whatsoever to do with the outcome of draw I, there are $N * N$ or N^2 different ways to make two draws. In Table 2.1 there are $(7461)^2$ or 55,666,521 possible outcomes!

[This total is padded a little because (1) it includes N different outcomes where the same case is drawn twice and (2) each distinct pair of cases appears twice; case i and j turn up once when $I = i$ and $II = j$ and then again when $I = j$ and $II = i$. Taking this into account, the number of distinct pairs of distinct cases is $(N^2 - N)/2$. In Table 2.1 this is a mere 27,829,530. For our purposes, though, we can stick with little old N^2.]

What is the probability that a pair is tied on both X and Y? This amounts to the probability of getting two cases from cell A or two from B or two from C or two from D. The probability of getting an A on draw I is A/N and the probability of getting an A on draw II is also A/N. Thus the probability of "shooting doubles" is the product $(A/N) * (A/N)$ or A^2/N^2. Applying the same argument to the other three cells, we always get the cell frequency squared in the numerator and N^2 in the denominator. Because all four denominators are the same, we can combine them into one expression:

[3] Leo Goodman and William Kruskal, "Measures of Associations for Cross Classifications," *Journal of the American Statistical Association*, 1954, *49*, 732–764.

Probability of a pair tied on both X and $Y = \dfrac{A^2 + B^2 + C^2 + D^2}{N^2}$

(Note that this includes the probability of drawing the same case twice in a row. If you want the probability for distinct pairs tied on both, subtract N from the numerator.)

In Table 2.1, the sum of the squared cell frequencies is 16,975,025. When divided by N^2 we obtain .305. That is, if we draw random pairs of cases from the data in Table 2.1, 30.5% of the pairs would be from the same category of both variables or the same case appearing twice.

With two variables, a pair may be tied on one item while differing on the other, for example, two men, one of whom is a high earner and the other a low earner. You may think of such cases as coming from the same column but different rows or the same row but different columns. Consider two men who differ in earnings. Being men, they must come from the top row—from cells A or B—and being different in earnings, one must be an A and the other a B. We could net an A on draw I and a B on draw II or a B on draw I and an A on draw II. Thus the probability works out to

$$\left(\frac{A}{N} * \frac{B}{N}\right) + \left(\frac{B}{N} * \frac{A}{N}\right) \quad \text{or} \quad \frac{2(A * B)}{N^2}$$

Extending this to all the possibilities, we obtain this formula

Probability of a pair tied on one variable differing on the other $= \dfrac{2[(A * B) + (C * D) + (A * C) + (B * D)]}{N^2}$

In Table 2.1,

$$\frac{2[(2166 * 2754) + (2128 * 413) + (2166 * 2128) + (2754 * 413)]}{55,666,521} = .452$$

That is, 45.2% of the random pairs would differ on one item, but not the other.

Noting that none of these cell products is $(B * C)$ or $(A * D)$, alas, we plunge on.

What is the probability for pairs differing on both items? This is a crucial concept (the previous formulas were presented just to clear away the brush) and you should study the next few paragraphs carefully.

What would such a pair look like if we reeled one in and saw it flopping on the dock? It would, of course, consist of two different people. Using Table 2.1 as an example, one would be a man and the other a woman (since the pair must differ on sex), and one will be a high earner and the other a low earner (since the pair must also differ on earnings). There are—*and this is crucial*—two ways this can happen: A high-earning man nestled next to a low-earning woman or a low-earning man consorting with a high-earning woman. In the first situation we have a case from *B* and a case from *C*. (Take a good look at Table 2.1 if you do not see this.) In the second situation, we have a case from *A* and a case from *D*.

In examining pairs with a tie, we did not pay any special attention to the different subtypes (for double ties, we did not care whether the cases came from *A*, *B*, *C*, or *D*). For pairs differing on both items, however, there is an extremely important distinction between a *B,C* pair and an *A,D* pair:

> A *B,C* pair is called *consistent* because the case that is high on one variable is high on the other, while the case that is low on one variable is low on the other.

> An *A,D* pair is called *inconsistent* because the case that is high on one variable is low on the other and vice versa.

In Table 2.1, the distinction is blurred because sex is a nominal variable. Consider, however, a table in which we substitute high education for male and low education for female. If so, a *B,C* pair would consist of one person high on education and income and another low on both variables. The differences in education and income would be consistent, high going with high and low going with low. Conversely, an *A,D* pair would consist of one person high on education while low on income and the other low on education and high on income. Such a pair is inconsistent in the sense that high lines up with low and low with high.

The formula for consistent pairs is developed from the same argument as that for pairs tied on one variable and turns out to be

$$\text{Probability of a consistent pair} = \frac{2(B * C)}{N^2}$$

$$\left[\text{For Table 2.1 it is } \frac{2(5,860,512)}{5,5666,521} = .211.\right]$$

and similarly,

$$\text{Probability of an inconsistent pair} = \frac{2(A * D)}{N^2}$$

$$\left[\text{For Table 2.1 it is } \frac{2(894,558)}{55,666,521} = .032.\right]$$

Aha! We spot our familiar cross products (*B* * *C*) and (*A* * *D*), and we begin to suspect that the Q coefficient has some meaning in terms of pairs differing on both variables. Before we get into that, we will summarize all the formulas, as shown in Table 2.7.

TABLE 2.7 Formulas for Pair Outcomes with Two Dichotomies

OUTCOME	FORMULA
1. All possible outcomes	N^2
2. All distinct pairs of distinct cases	$\dfrac{N^2 - N}{2}$
3. Probability of	
a. Tie on both variables	$\dfrac{A^2 + B^2 + C^2 + D^2}{N^2}$
b. Tie on one variable, differ on one	$\dfrac{2[(A * B) + (C * D) + (A * C) + (B * D)]}{N^2}$
c. Differ on both variables:	$\dfrac{2[(B * C) + (A * D)]}{N^2}$
Consistent paris	$\dfrac{2(B * C)}{N^2}$
Inconsistent pairs	$\dfrac{2(A * D)}{N^2}$

Just for the fun of it, let us write a formula in which the difference between the probability of consistent and inconsistent pairs appears in the numerator and the total probability for pairs differing on both variables appears in the denominator. Thus,

$$\frac{\dfrac{2(B * C)}{N^2} - \dfrac{2(A * D)}{N^2}}{\dfrac{2(B * C)}{N^2} + \dfrac{2(A * D)}{N^2}}$$

Because N^2 and 2 appear in each of the four components, we can cancel them out, and what do you know,

$$\frac{(B * C) - (A * D)}{(B * C) + (A * D)}$$

We have shown that Q can be translated as follows:

$$Q_{XY} = \frac{\text{consistent pairs} - \text{inconsistent pairs}}{\text{total pairs differing on } X \text{ and } Y}$$

or

$$Q_{XY} = \frac{\text{surplus or deficit of consistent pairs}}{\text{total pairs differing on } X \text{ and } Y}$$

The argument can be taken one step further to give a less cumbersome statement. Imagine the following drama: (1) A random pair of cases is drawn from some fourfold table, e.g., case 037 and case 1990, (2) you are told only that the cases come from *different* categories of variable Y, and (3) you are asked to guess which case is Y and which is *NOT Y*.

With no other information, you might as well flip a coin, and on the average your guesses would be correct 50% of the time.

But now, assume that a uniformed attendant slips you a little piece of paper giving you some information, the ordering of the cases on X, for example, "case 037 is a *NOT X*; case 1990 is an *X*."

Seizing at any straw, you might adopt the strategy of always predicting that the case which is X will be Y and the case which is *NOT X* will be *NOT Y*. How often would you be right if you did this for every pair in a particular fourfold table? Answer: $(B * C)$, the number of pairs where the X is a Y and the *NOT X* is a *NOT Y*! Similarly you would be wrong $(A * D)$ times.

Since it does not make any difference whether you are predicting Y from X or X from Y or taking turns at these chores, another way of thinking about Q is

$$Q_{XY} = \frac{\begin{array}{l}\text{(correct predictions of} \quad \text{(incorrect predictions}\\ \text{order on } X \text{ from order} - \text{of order on } X \text{ from order}\\ \text{on } Y \text{ or vice versa)} \quad \text{on } Y \text{ or vice versa)}\end{array}}{\text{(total different pairs for which such predictions are relevant)}}$$

And a final twist. We know that the chance level of success in making such predictions is .50, and after a little fiddling around, we can obtain the following version:

$$Q_{XY} = \frac{\text{proportion of correct predictions} - \text{chance level}}{\text{chance level}}$$

or

$$Q_{XY} = \frac{\text{surplus or deficit of correct predictions}}{\text{chance level}}$$

A hypothetical example illustrates the idea. Assume that $(B * C)$ equals 70 and $(A * D)$ equals 40. Q would equal $(70 - 40)/110 = +.272$. But we could also say that $70/110$ or .636 of our predictions would be correct, a surplus of .136 compared to chance $(.636 - .500 = .136)$. When this surplus is compared to the chance level of .500, we get $.136/.500$ or $+.272$, which is the value of Q. Thus, the most succinct statement of the meaning of Q is

A Q value of_____means that we would do_____better than chance in predicting order on one variable from order on the other by always predicting that X's are Y's and *NOT* X's are *NOT* Y's or vice versa.

The Q of $+.735$ for Table 2.1 means we would do 73.5% better than chance if we always predict that the higher earner is a male and the lower earner is a female (or alternatively always predict that the male is the higher earner and the female is the lower earner). Note that a Q of $.00$ has the comfortable meaning that we would do no better than chance, and a negative value means that we would do worse than chance (because the relation tends to go in the opposite direction). If we knew the correlation is negative, of course, we would revise our prediction strategy and end up beating chance. Thus the sign tells us which direction to predict, while the size of Q tells us how well we would do.

Because Q can fall anywhere between $+1.00$ and -1.00, it is useful to have an agreement as to what is a strong value and what is a weak one. This avoids situations where one author writes that he has found a remarkably strong Q of $+.28$, while another states that he was chagrined to turn up only a moderate Q of $+.29$. Any such rules are quite arbitrary, but following the strategy stated in the introduction, we ask you to adopt the conventions set forth in Table 2.8.

TABLE 2.8 Conventions for Describing Q Values

VALUE OF Q	APPROPRIATE PHRASE*
+.70 or higher	A very strong positive association
+.50 to +.69	A substantial positive association
+.30 to +.49	A moderate positive association
+.10 to +.29	A low positive association
+.01 to +.09	A negligible positive association
.00	No association
−.01 to −.09	A negligible negative association
−.10 to −.29	A low negative association
−.30 to −.49	A moderate negative association
−.50 to −.69	A substantial negative association
−.70 or lower	A very strong negative association

* *Correlation* and *relationship* are synonyms for *association*.

Table 2.8 fails to mention that a Q of ± 1.00 should be called a "perfect positive" or "perfect negative" relationship, but the naming of Q's that strong has not been a serious problem in the author's research experience.

With nominal variables, the "direction" of a correlation may be ambiguous without some explanation. It is a good idea to indicate the category which is scored high the first time the relationship is mentioned. We would describe Table 2.1 by saying that "there is a very strong positive correlation between sex (male) and earnings ($Q = +.74$)." The same suggestion applies to ordinal, interval, and ratio scales if the common-sense meaning is ambiguous.

Here are some examples from 1960 U.S. census sample data to give you a feel for the conventions and ways to express them.

There is a very strong negative correlation between race (Negro) and socioeconomic status (an index combining occupation, education, and income of the household head) ($Q = -.74$).

There is a substantial negative association between education (high school graduate) and age (65 and older) ($Q = -.52$).

There is a moderate positive relationship between education (high school graduate) and earnings ($4000 a year or more) ($Q = +.32$).

There is a low positive association between education (high school graduate) and urbanism (residing within a standard metropolitan statistical area) ($Q = +.18$).

The relationship between age (30 and older) and region (South) is negligible ($Q = -.08$).

A Rule of Thumb for
Sample Size

The properties of Q and the notion of expected values for cells in a fourfold table lead to a rough answer to the nagging problem, "How many cases must I have in my sample?" From one point of view, the question has no definite answer since it involves the degree of precision you demand and certain "iffy" assumptions about the universe from which your sample will be drawn. (The latter reason will make more sense when we get to confidence intervals in the next section.)

Nevertheless, many statisticians suggest that one should have *expected* frequencies of five or more in *each* cell of your fourfold tables, and this principle can lead to guidelines for minimal sample sizes. The technical reasons for the magic number five are way beyond us, but the general idea is clear now that we understand what is meant by cell expectations and Q.

You will remember that changing the value of delta by a frequency of one is equivalent to shifting one pair of cases from one diagonal to another (Figure 2.1). If some cell in the table has an expectation of size S, Q must equal .00 when S cases actually turn up there. However, if we shift no more than S pairs around, zero cases would appear in that cell and Q would be ± 1.00. A very small cell expectation means that the value of Q *could* fluctuate wildly if a handful of pairs were misclassified even though the N for the table was very large. Obviously the larger the minimal expected value, the less our results are hostage to such measurement error, and the norm of "five" is a conventional minimum standard.

It is easy to make the calculations. If you have the marginal frequencies for the set of dichotomized variables you will analyze, all you have to do is to find the two *smallest* marginals in the set, multiply them, and divide the result by N. This will give you the expected value of the smallest cell among all the fourfold tables you can make from these variables. If this result is five or greater, all other cells in your fourfold tables will have expectations of five or more.

You can get a rough idea of whether your sample size is appropriate even if you do not know the marginals (i.e., if you are about to design a new study) from Table 2.9, provided you are willing to guess them or resolve to stay in the 30:70 range.

TABLE 2.9 N Required to Have All Four Cells with Expected Frequencies of Five or More for Various Marginals

		MARGINAL DISTRIBUTION OF Y						
		50:50	60:40	70:30	80:20	90:10	95:05	99:01
	50:50	20	25	33	50	100	200	1000
	60:40	25	31	42	63	125	250	1250
Marginal	70:30	33	42	56	83	167	333	1670
distribution	80:20	50	63	83	125	250	500	2500
for X	90:10	100	125	167	250	500	1000	5000
	95:05	200	250	333	500	1000	2000	10000
	99:01	1000	1250	1670	2500	5000	10000	50000

Within the 30:70 norm for marginals, the upper left quadrant of Table 2.9, we see that a sample size of roughly 50 cases is a good rule of thumb, but if one of the items is fairly extreme (e.g., the case of Negroes discussed above), 300 cases might be required, while if more than one item has marginals of 95:05, the sample size should be at least 2000. Here is our rule:

R U L E 2.2

Make sure your smallest cell expectation in a fourfold table is equal to or greater than five.

2.2a   If all your marginals are in the 30:70 range, 50 is a reasonable minimum sample size.

2.2b   If one or more of your marginals is outside the 30:70 range, either increase your sample size to meet the standards of Table 2.9 or consult a professional statistician for special techniques which can be applied.

Confidence Limits for Q

So far we have been talking about results in our data, descriptive statistics in the language of the Introduction. Usually sociologists work with samples instead of complete counts, but their aim is to say something about the universe from which the sample is drawn. It is time to raise that dreaded topic, statistical inference. As explained in the Introduction, a thorough explanation of statistical inference is nothing more or less than a course in statistics, and we have made clear that this is not our aim. However, we can sketch the underlying ideas and give some concrete techniques, skipping the middle part—how the techniques follow from the ideas.

The first idea is that of *probability sampling*. A probability sample is one such that every case in the universe has a known chance of being drawn (i.e., a "calculatable" frequency of appearing in a sample if a very large number of samplings were taken under a specific sampling plan). We have already wrestled with the probability that a given kind of pair would be drawn in repeated samples from the cases in a fourfold table, so the idea is not really new. The basic division of samples is probability vs. all other, and the point is that in probability samples you can make some rational inferences about the universe and in all other you must depend on faith.

Probability samples divide into two kinds: *simple random samples* (SRS) and *all other probability samples*. In a simple random sample, each case in the universe has the same probability of being drawn and each combination of cases of the same size has the same probability. To be banal, we could sample the students in a class of 150 people by (1) writing their names on slips of paper, (2) putting the names in a rather large hat, (3) mixing them thoroughly, and (4) drawing out 15 slips. Under this plan every person has the same chance of being drawn (15: 150), and it can be shown that every pair of students has the same chance (though not 15: 150). Furthermore, every possible combination of 13 students has the same chance as any other combination of 13 and the principle applies to any size of combination. All combinations of the same size have the same chance.

All familiar, one may assume. However, although we will not go into it in much detail, you should realize that there are other kinds of probability samples, in which each case has a *known* probability, but the probability is not necessarily the same for each case or for particular combinations. For example, consider a *systematic* sample in which one (1) lists everyone in the universe, (2) picks a random number between 1 and N, and (3) selects every Nth person starting with the one indicated by the random number. This certainly is a probability sample, and every single case has the same chance of being drawn, 1: N. However, combinations of cases may have quite different probabilities. Cases which are N lines apart on the list have the same probability, but cases next to each other have a zero probability of appearing in the same sample. Systematic samples are probability samples, but not simple random samples.

We introduce the distinction between SRS samples and other probability samples not because one is better than the other but because the techniques for statistical inference differ.

The second idea is that of a *sampling distribution*. In principle, a mathematical statistician can always take (1) the properties of the universe, (2) a sample size, and (3) a particular sampling plan, e.g., the decision to use SRS sampling of size 100 and use them to calculate the probability that various sample results will occur—the frequency with which particular results will occur if the sampling plan is repeated time and time again. We are all familiar with the idea when applied to the problem of drawing samples from a universe consisting of two cubes with faces numbered from 1 to 6, i.e., the odds when shooting craps. You will be asked to take on faith the proposition that a statistician can also figure out the answers to such questions as:

> How frequently would one obtain a sample marginal proportion of .302 when drawing simple random samples of size 138 from a universe in which the true proportion is .540?

> How frequently would one obtain a sample value of Q equal to $+.700$ when drawing systematic probability samples of size 1504 from a universe in which the true value of Q is $+.101$?

An impressive stunt, but the statistician must know the universe value before he can deduce the distribution of results in repeated samplings. This sounds like bad news because our problem is that we do not know the results in the universe, just those for our single sample. Statistical inference amounts to turning these ideas, probability sampling and sampling distributions, upside down so that we can make some inferences from sample to universe.

We will illustrate the underlying logic of statistical inference by walking through the steps in finding "confidence limits" for Q. We will talk about specific numbers, e.g., a universe Q of $+.38$, but they are purely hypothetical. We did not work out the exact calculations and this book does not tell you how to do so. The point is to show the logic of statistical inference, not the procedures. Later in the chapter we will give you some formulas so that you can calculate confidence intervals for Q's in your data. The argument proceeds in six steps.

Step 1

From the principle of sampling distributions, it follows that for any particular universe value of Q and a particular SRS sample size, we can work out the frequency (probability) with which various sample results for Q would turn up in a long run of samplings.[4] Thus, when the universe value is $+.38$

---

[4] In practice, mathematical statisticians usually assume that the statistic is continuous and generate curves rather than results for each specific value. However, we do no injustice to the argument by assuming 201 discrete two-decimal values of Q and a probability for each one.

and one draws repeated SRS samples of size 1832, we can figure out how often one would obtain sample Q's of $+.74$, $-.38$, $.00$, and so on. This done, it is easy to obtain cumulative probabilities, e.g., the probability of sampling a Q of $+.74$ *or higher* or the probability of sampling a Q of $-.38$ *or lower*.

Step 2

Let us, quite arbitrarily, decide that a sample result that turns up less than 5 times in 100 is "rare" and a sample result that turns up 5 times or more per 100 samplings is "frequent."

Step 3

We next divide all the results found in step 1 into frequent results and rare results and then divide the rare results into the .025 lowest Q's and the .025 highest Q's $(.025 + .025 + .950 = 1.000)$. All this can be represented by a diagram (Figure 2.2).

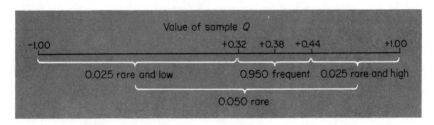

FIG. 2.2   Hypothetical sampling distribution of Q's for a universe where $Q = +.38$ and SRS samples are of size 1832.

Remembering that the example is hypothetical, we may interpret Figure 2.2 like this: If we drew many, many SRS samples of size 1832 from a universe in which the value of Q is $+.38$, (1) 95% of the sample Q's would be between $+.32$ and $+.44$, (2) 2.5% would be higher than $+.44$, and (3) 2.5% would be lower than $+.32$. In other words, sample results higher than $+.44$ or lower than $+.32$ would be rare (not impossible, but rare).

Step 4

What we can do for one universe value of Q, we can do for each, and having done so, we can combine the line diagrams like Figure 2.2 into a graph like Figure 2.3 The line from Figure 2.2 has been drawn across the graph to show how the graph is really just a smoothed collection of such lines.

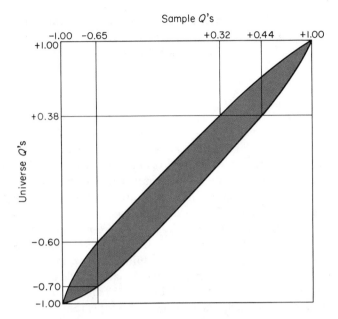

FIG. 2.3   Schematic diagram of confidence limits for Q in SRS samples of size 1832 (results are all fictitious).

While the points in Figure 2.2 refer to samples, the points in the two-dimensional graph like Figure 2.3 refer to combinations—the combination of a particular universe value and a particular sample result. What does the graph tell us about such combinations?

Notice that the graph consists of a shaded band running from lower left to upper right and two unshaded areas above and below. The shaded band is made up of the "frequent" zones from the various lines and the unshaded areas are made up from the "rare" ends of the various lines. The shaded area consists of all the frequent sample results and the light areas are the infrequent overestimates and underestimates.

Notice further that if we set out to estimate a large number of universe Q's by drawing SRS samples of size 1832, 95% of the sample results would fall in the shaded area—whatever the universe Q's might be. If the universe Q's were all positive, our results would be concentrated in the upper end of the shaded area; if the universe Q's were all negative, our results would be concentrated in the lower end of the shaded area; and if the universe Q's were strung out from positive to negative, our sample results would turn up throughout the shaded area: *but* from all the above arguments, 95% of our samples over the long run would fall somewhere in the shaded area.

In short, the shaded area of the graph represents frequent combinations in repeated SRS samplings of size 1832, the unshaded area above represents rare overestimates, and the unshaded area below represents rare underestimates.

Step 5

Now, confidence intervals. Assume that in a particular SRS sample of 1832 cases we observe a Q of $-.65$ for the correlation between X and Y. What may we infer about the universe, using Figure 2.3 as our crystal ball? We locate $-.65$ on the horizontal (sample Q) scale and drop a vertical line all the way down. Then we run perpendicular lines out where the vertical line cuts the top and bottom of the shaded area, noting that these new lines cross the vertical (universe Q) axis at $-.60$ and $-.70$.

The result is a vertical version of Figure 2.2. We have divided sample Q's of $-.65$ (in repeated SRS samplings of size 1832) into three types: frequent combinations of universe and sample result, rare overestimates, and rare underestimates. We may infer that (1) combinations of universe values between $-.60$ and $-.70$ and sample values of $-.65$ are common, (2) combinations of universe values higher than $-.60$ and sample results of $-.65$ are rare (not impossible, but rare), and (3) combinations of universe values lower than $-.70$ and sample results of $-.65$ are rare (not impossible, but rare).

Gorged with all this information, we fold our hands over our tummies and confront the crucial question, "What is the universe value of Q?" We seem to have two choices: (1) The universe value of Q is between $-.60$ and $-.70$ and a frequent combination of universe and sample has taken place, or (2) the universe value is above $-.60$ or below $-.70$ and a rare combination of sample and universe has taken place. Granted that rare combinations occur, it must also be granted that they occur rarely (about 5% of the time), and therefore we plump for the first alternative. Our inference, to make a long story short, is that the universe Q is somewhere between $-.60$ and $-.70$, these two numbers being the upper $(-.60)$ and lower $(-.70)$ confidence *limits* on our estimate and the span from $-.60$ to $-.70$ being our confidence *interval.*

Step 6

Steps 1 through 5 justify the notion of statistical inference (why we are willing to guess anything about an unknown universe) and the concepts of upper limit, lower limit, and confidence interval. There remains the concept of "confidence" itself. Conventionally, we say that we make the estimate of the interval at the ".95 confidence level." What does this mean? It certainly does not mean that our estimate is 95% right. On the contrary, our estimate is either right (the true value lies within our limits) or it is wrong (the true value is above or below our limts), though we will never know. Rather, our confidence lies in the entire procedure. If we use it again and again and again, 95% of the time we will include the true value within our confidence interval and, alas, 5% of the time we will not. When we say that our confidence level is .95 we mean that we are using a crystal ball that is known to work 95 times out of 100, although on any given trial it either works or fails.

In practice, when determining confidence intervals for Q we do not use charts, since it would be necessary to have a different chart for each possible sample size. Instead we make calculations using (1) the sample value of Q, (2) the cell frequencies A, B, C, D, and (3) a formula which will not be explained. The formula assumes a confidence probability of .95. Others could be used, but .95 is conventional in scientific research. Here are the formulas:

$$\text{Upper limit} = Q_{XY} + (1.96) \sqrt{\frac{(1.00 - Q_{XY}^2)^2 \left(\frac{1}{A} + \frac{1}{B} + \frac{1}{C} + \frac{1}{D}\right)}{4}}$$

$$\text{Lower limit} = Q_{XY} - (1.96) \sqrt{\frac{(1.00 - Q_{XY}^2)^2 \left(\frac{1}{A} + \frac{1}{B} + \frac{1}{C} + \frac{1}{D}\right)}{4}}$$

The formula looks complicated, but confidence is hard to come by in this wicked world. In words,

1. Square the sample value of Q (note that the result will always be smaller than the original and positive since you are squaring a decimal).
2. Subtract this from 1.0000.
3. Square the result of step 2.
4. Take the reciprocal of each cell value (i.e., divide 1 by the cell frequency).
5. Add the four reciprocals.
6. Multiply step 5 by step 3.
7. Divide the result of step 6 by the value 4.
8. Take the square root of the result of step 7.
9. Multiply the result of step 8 by 1.96.
10. To get the upper limit, add the value of step 9 to the sample Q; to get the lower limit, subtract the value of step 9 from the sample Q.

For Table 2.1, we obtain an upper limit of $+.763$ and a lower limit of $+.708$ around our sample value of $+.735$. We infer that in the total U.S. population Q is between $+.76$ and $+.71$ and do so at the "95% confidence level."

We cannot hope to explain the formula and its justification,[5] but we do call your attention to three of its parts. First, the value of 1.96, which is explained in any statistics book, sets the confidence level at .95, a larger value being used for higher probabilities such as .99. You can see that the less risk you are willing to take, the broader your estimate must be. Second, note that if you multiply A, B, C, D by some value larger than one (i.e., increase the sample size), you would lower the value of the result under the square root notation and make the confidence interval smaller. Thus, all other things equal, the larger the sample size, the more precise the estimate. Third, note that if Q is quite strong, whether positive or negative, $1.00 - Q^2$ will be quite small and this will bring down the width of the interval. All other things equal, strong universe values of Q show smaller sampling fluctuations than weak ones.

A final word on confidence limits for Q, and a new concept, "significance." If we observe confidence limits with the same sign (e.g., $+.72$ and $+.48$ or $-.72$ and $-.48$), we not only have a range for the estimate, but we are confident that the sample did not come from a universe where the value of Q is .00. We are confident that Q is nonzero. On the other hand, if our limits have opposite signs (e.g., $+.19$, $-.24$) or one of them is .00, the value of .00 is within the confidence interval. If so, we have little confidence that there is *any* correlation between X and Y. In the former case we say the relationship is "statistically significant" or "significant." In the latter, we interpret the relationship as if it were $Q_{XY} = .00$ even though the sample results may be other than .00.

One should always state the risk level. For the formula given here the appropriate way is "Q is statistically significant $(P \leq .025)$" or "Q is not statistically significant $(P \geq .025)$." Note that .025 is half of .05. Our risk of estimating Q too high is half that of estimating it too high or too low.

R U L E **2.3**

To assess the strength of relationship in a fourfold table, calculate Q and its confidence limits.

2.3a   Calculate Q to three decimals, but report it to two, rounding to the nearest even number if the third decimal is 5.

2.3b   If the two confidence limits have the same sign you may say Q is "statistically significant at the .025 level."

2.3c   If the confidence limits have opposite signs or one of them is .00, you should say that it is "not statistically significant $(P \geq .025)$" and interpret it as if the sample value were .00.

[5] For the statistically trained reader, see Leo Goodman, "On the Multivariate Analysis of Three Dichotomous Variables," *American Journal of Sociology*, 1965, *71*, 290–301; or M. G. Kendall and A. Stuart, *The Advanced Theory of Statistics*, Vol. 2, Charles Griffin & Co., London, 1961, p. 540.

Some Fallacies and Thorny Problems

The evaluation of relationships in fourfold tables involves three concepts: (1) independence, association, and sign; (2) degree of correlation as described by Q; and (3) statistical inference, significance and confidence intervals for the relationship. They are logically distinct but interrelated, and their interrelations present some problems. Here we list some common booby traps and difficult decisions.

1. When writing a report use the word "significant" only to refer to the outcome of a procedure for statistical inference and make the point clear by stating the confidence intervals and risk level when you use the word. Thus, "The relationship is significant (with .95 confidence limits of $+.47$ and $+.62$)." If you also use "significant" as a synonym for important, interesting, profound, or puzzling, the result will be confusion.

2. Do not confuse magnitude and significance! This is probably the single most common mistake made by beginning researchers. We have seen that confidence limits are a function of both the value of Q in the sample and the sample size. As a result, significant results can come from (a) a very large Q and a relatively small sample, (b) a very large sample and a relatively small Q, and (c) a very large Q and a very large sample. You should never assume that a significant Q must be large or a large Q significant unless you have examined the data. In particular, when working with samples of several thousand, almost all Q's will be significant, even when their magnitude is negligible.

3. Probability samples other than SRS present a thorny problem. Many of the data with which social scientists work come from probability samples which are not SRS. We mentioned systematic samples and there are also "multistage," "cluster," "stratified," and others. They are just as "scientific" as SRS, and indeed more sophisticated scientifically, but they create a problem. The inference techniques we describe (and all of those you will meet in most statistics books) assume SRS, but sophisticated probability samples give broader confidence limits for the same sample size. Thus if you calculate SRS limits of $+.38$ to $+.49$ on a sophisticated sample, the "correct" limits might be something like $+.31$ to $+.56$.

The problem is that the inference calculations for sophisticated samples are so complex that they require electronic computer programs rather than the relatively simple formulas we give you.

We advise you to use SRS formulas anyway for the following reasons:

1. If your relationship is not significant, you may assume that more sophisticated calculations would agree. (If you do not see why, reread the first paragraph in this section.) Since a large part of research consists of screening out relationships which have no promise at all, SRS is quite dependable when it says "no."

2. When you do get a significant relationship, your confidence limits may be assumed to be somewhat too narrow and some of your significant relationships may not deserve the accolade. However, you are using a consistent decision maker which, fallible as it is, is more objective than the eyeball method of determining significance. SRS techniques may have their faults, but they are the best available to you.

3. Everybody does it anyway. We advance this point, not from mob psychology, but because it means that your statistical decisions will agree with those of most professional sociologists. You may wonder why the professionals use non-SRS samples if their confidence bands are wider. The question is one of overall efficiency. For reasons too complex to explain, you can usually afford to collect so many more cases with sophisticated sample plans that this offsets the fact that each case is less informative. You end up getting more information for your money with sophisticated samples.

4. There remains the problem of applying statistical inference to data which are not probability samples at all but complete counts or arbitrary collections of cases. The "quota samples" used by market research firms fall here. This issue involves extremely difficult problems reaching to the philosophical roots of probability and inference and is hotly debated in social science. Our advice is to go ahead and calculate confidence limits anyway. If the relationship turns out to be significant, fine. If not, you have received a warning: Do not attempt to claim that your results apply to anything beyond this particular set of numbers.

IN A NUTSHELL

A. Fourfold tables

1. Four cell frequencies
2. Four marginal frequencies
3. N

B. Statistical properties

1. Independence and association
   a) *Definition of expected cell values in terms of marginal frequencies*
   b) *Delta, the difference between expected and observed*
   c) *The possible patterns for delta and sign of an association*
2. Degree of association, Yule's Q
   a) *Formula: cross product difference divided by cross product sum*
   b) *Technical properties*
      (1) .00 under independence
      (2) Extremes of +1.00 and −1.00 with one or two zero cells
      (3) Insensitivity to multiplications

c) *Meaning in terms of random pairs: relative improvement in prediction*
d) *Conventions for describing various magnitudes*

3. Rules of thumb for minimal sample size based on expected values in the table

4. Confidence intervals for *Q*

   a) *The key in statistical inference*
      (1) Sampling
         (*a*) Nonprobability
         (*b*) Probability
            i) SRS
            ii) Other
      (2) Principle that sampling distributions can be calculated for probability samples of particular sizes for particular universe values
      (3) The notion of confidence intervals—estimation of a range in which the universe value lies using a guessing device which will be correct 95% of the time as demonstrated by the properties of the sampling distribution
   b) *Calculation of confidence limits*
      (1) The formula
      (2) Properties of the sampling of *Q*
         (*a*) The larger the sample, the narrower the confidence band
         (*b*) The more extreme the universe values of *Q*, the narrower the confidence band
      (3) Statistical significance : the inference that a universe value of .00 is excluded from the confidence interval

5. Fallacies and thorny problems

   a) *Use of the word "significant" only in its technical sense*
   b) *Advice that one should use SRS techniques even when*
      (1) The data are from sophisticated probability samples
      (2) The data are not from probability samples

Rules

R U L E 2.1

When reporting tables of frequencies, you must account for all of the cases in the sample by specifying frequencies such as "no answer" and "not applicable" as well as the *N* for the table.

R U L E 2.2

Make sure your smallest cell expectation in a fourfold table is equal to or greater than five.

   2.2a If all your marginals are in the 30 : 70 range, 50 is a reasonable minimum sample size.

   2.2b If one or more of your marginals is outside the 30 : 70 range, either increase your sample size to meet the standards of Table 2.9 or consult a professional statistician for special techniques which can be applied.

R U L E 2.3

To assess the strength of a relationship in a fourfold table, calculate Q and its confidence limits.

2.3a   Calculate Q to three decimals, but report it to two, rounding to the nearest even number if the third decimal is 5.

2.3b   If the two confidence limits have the same sign, you may say that Q is "statistically significant at the .025 level."

2.3c   If the confidence limits have opposite signs or one of them is .00 you should say that the relationship is "not statistically significant $(P \geq .025)$" and interpret it as if the sample value were .00.

Major Concepts

1. Confidence limits
2. Consistent pairs
3. Cross products
4. Delta
5. Expected cell frequencies
6. Inconsistent pairs
7. Independence
8. Marginals
9. Observed frequencies
10. Probability sampling
11. Sampling distribution
12. Sign (of a correlation)
13. Significance
14. Simple random sample (SRS)
15. Universe

FURTHER READING

On the logic of statistical inference:

IRWIN D. J. BROSS, *Design for Decision*, Macmillan, New York, 1953. A sophisticated but nontechnical explanation of probability and the logic of statistical inference.

On sampling, especially sophisticated samples:

JAMES MORRIS SLONIM, *Sampling*, Simon and Schuster, New York, 1960 (paperback). A highly popularized but essentially sound introduction.

PHILIP J. McCARTHY, "Sample Design," in Marie Jahoda et al., eds., *Research Methods in Social Relations, Part Two: Selected Techniques*, The Dryden Press, New York, 1951, pp. 644–680. More technical than Slonim, but accessible to the beginner who is willing to work at it.

On probability:

JOHN G. KEMENY, J. LAURIE SNELL, AND GERALD L. THOMPSON, *Introduction to Finite Mathematics*, Prentice-Hall, Englewood Cliffs, N. J., 2nd ed., 1966, Chapter IV, pp. 127–216. The standard text, lucid and reasonably detailed.

3

Two-Variable Relationships: The Percentage Difference, Gamma, Contingency Tables

An Overview

Having described Q in loving detail, we are not about to abandon it just because some other pretty little coefficient comes along. On the contrary, Chapters 4, 5, and 6 will expand our use of Q by applying it to three, four, and five or more variables. Nevertheless, we will pause in this chapter to sketch some alternative approaches to the analysis of two-variable tables. The reader who has a firm purchase on the materials up to this point will find that exposure to "the percentage difference," "gamma," and "contingency tables" will deepen his understanding of statistical relationships. However, if you are still a little shaky on Chapter 2, it might be a good idea to skip to Chapters 4, 5, and 6 and then return to this chapter after you have a firm grasp of our "Q-uixotic" system.

The main idea here is that Q is not the only coefficient you can use to describe the degree of association in a fourfold table, and fourfold tables are not the only way you can use the concept of consistent and inconsistent pairs.

The percentage difference, called D, is a common measure of degree of association in fourfold tables. Since it boils down to comparing the "percent

Y among the X's and the percent Y among the *NOT X*'s," it is a familiar idea. When we say that "65% of the men agreed with the item, in contrast to 45% of the women," the difference, $D = 65 - 45 = 20$, is a measure of association between sex and agreement with the item. Matters become a little more complicated when we dig in further, for we find some nonobvious properties: (1) The formula for D is closely related to the formula for Q in a way that illuminates what we meant when we said that Q is "insensitive to multiplication of marginals." (2) One always has the option to calculate the percentage Y among the X categories or the percentage X among the Y categories, which raises the interesting problem of asymmetry in coefficients. (3) D is closely related to the "regression" statistics used for interval scale data and thus is sort of a bridge between ordinal and interval approaches.

When a table has more than two rows or more than two columns, you cannot calculate Q (or at least you cannot do so with the information we have given you). However, if both variables are ordinal or one is a dichotomy and the other ordinal, you can calculate a coefficient called gamma. It turns out that gamma is exactly the same as Q in its logic and interpretation, because, like Q, gamma amounts to the surplus or deficit of consistent pairs. Even though our advice is to collapse the data into fourfold tables, we will explain gamma and how to calculate it so that you will see the advantages and disadvantages of sticking to fourfold tables.

There remains the case of large tables where one or both variables are nominal (e.g., region ∗ religious preference). There is no satisfactory way to state the degree of association in such tables because they have many associations rather than a single effect like delta. However, you can examine such tables by applying the notion of observed and expected cell values. This will often give you a good idea of *what* is going on even if you cannot state *how much* is going on.

The Percentage Difference

Most sociological research reports present results in the form of percentage tables and many authors use the difference between two percentages to describe the magnitude of a correlation. Table 3.1 gives the sex and earnings correlation from Chapter 2 in percentage form.

Fifty-six percent of the men earned $4000 or more compared with 16% of the women, giving a percentage *difference* of 40.

Many research sophisticates consider percentages a lowbrow form of statistics, and we will treat them as a supplement to Q rather than a major tool for analysis. Nevertheless, although a naïve domestic, you might be amused by their presumption.

First, percentages are the only statistic which is always meaningful to a nonprofessional reader. If you are reporting your research to an audience

TABLE 3.1   Sex and Earnings in 1959

SEX	PERCENT EARNING $4000 OR MORE AMONG EARNERS
Male	56%(4920)
Female	16%(2541)
	N = 7,461
Inapplicable (no earnings in 1959)	10,478
	17,939

other than your instructor or Ph.D.'s in social science, you can be sure that your readers do not know much about Q, delta, and significance tests. But almost anyone can read Table 3.1 and get the point without pausing for a course in statistics. So much research is reported to bosses, clients, newspaper readers, fellow students, and similar untrained worthies that the advantage is quite persuasive. Or to turn it around, you should understand the ins and outs of percentages because others will use them on you.

Second, the raw figures can be recalculated from percentage tables but not from Q. There is no way to deduce the raw-data table from the value of Q, but when the bases for the percentages are reported (as they always must be), a reader who wishes to rework the data or challenge your conclusions can reconstruct the original figures save for very small errors due to rounding. In a percentaged fourfold table you simply change the percentages to proportions in your mind, multiply them by their bases to give the numbers showing the characteristic, and subtract these results from the bases to give the numbers not showing the characteristic, giving the four cell values.

These two assets are so important we begin with a rule:

R U L E   3.1

Always present your key data in percentage form as well as the results of your more complex statistical analysis.

3.1a   Always present the case bases, putting them below and to the right of the percentages and in parentheses. (This makes it possible for the reader to compare the two percentages without other numbers getting in his way.)

3.1b   Report your percentages rounded to whole numbers. (Decimals added to the percentage give an air of scientific precision, but only in samples of tens of thousands of cases is a difference of less than 1% statistically significant.)

3.1c   Place a percent sign (%) next to each percentage to make clear which figures are percentages and which are frequencies.

3.1d   In the case of elaborate multivariate tabulations (to be discussed in later chapters), you may put the raw figures in an appendix if a percentage table would be extremely cumbersome.

The third reason to consider percentages is that their statistical properties are less obvious than one might think. You can deepen your understanding of correlation by a thorough review of the technical side of percentage differences.

First, we note that the percentage difference, called D, unlike Q, is an *asymmetric* relationship. While Q_{XY} must have the same value as Q_{YX}, the percentage difference D_{XY} does not necessarily equal the percentage difference D_{YX}. There are always two ways to percentage a fourfold table, giving either D_{YX} from the percentage Y among the X's and *NOT* X's or D_{XY} from the percentage X among the Y's and *NOT* Y's.

The calculation is so easy that a formula is not required, but if we look at the formulas we can see what is going on:

$$D_{YX} = \frac{(B*C)-(A*D)}{(B*C)+(A*D)+(A*C)+(B*D)} = \frac{(B*C)-(A*D)}{(\text{sum } X)*(\text{sum } NOT\ X)}$$

$$D_{XY} = \frac{(B*C)-(A*D)}{(B*C)+(A*D)+(A*B)+(C*D)} = \frac{(B*C)-(A*D)}{(\text{sum } Y)*(\text{sum } NOT\ Y)}$$

For our example, Table 2.1.

$$D_{\text{earnings/sex}} = \frac{(5,860,512)-(894,558)}{(5,860,512)+(894,558)+(4,609,248)+(1,137,402)}$$
$$= +.397$$

$$D_{\text{sex/earnings}} = \frac{(5,860,512)-(894,558)}{(5,860,512)+(894,558)+(5,965,164)+(878,864)}$$
$$= +.365$$

The value of $+.397$ is what we would get from simply comparing the two percentages in Table 3.1 ($56 - 16 = 40$) and the other D is what we would get from running our percentage table the other way (Table 3.2).

TABLE 3.2   Sex and Earnings in 1959

1959 EARNINGS	PERCENT MALE
$4000 or more	87%(3167)
Less than $4000	50%(4294)
	$N = 7,461$
Inapplicable (no earnings in 1959)	10,478
	17,939

The formulas look familiar. In each, the numerator $(B*C)-(A*D)$ is our old friend, the cross-product difference, the numerator of Q. Immediately, we can draw some conclusions:

1. When X and Y are independent, Q, delta, D_{XY}, D_{YX} will all have the value of zero.

2. Q, D_{YX}, and D_{XY} will always have the same sign.

The denominators are less familiar. The first two terms at the left are our long-lost buddies, the denominator of Q. However, they have been joined by two new terms which appear in Table 2.7, the catalogue of pair types. The set $(A * C)$ and $(B * D)$ in the first formula turns out to be pairs "tied on Y, differing on X" while the set $(A * B)$ and $(C * D)$ in the second formula turns out to be pairs "tied on X, differing on Y."

Seeking a common meaning for all four terms in the denominators, we may say that in D_{YX} they are "all pairs differing on X" and in D_{XY} they are "all pairs differing on Y." (This explains the right-hand versions of the formulas since the total pairs differing on X can also be obtained by multiplying the totals for X and NOT X and similarly for Y and NOT Y.)

Because any positive term which appears in the denominator of a coefficient but not in the numerator will lower its absolute value, we can now state the logical difference between Q and D. We use the convention that the *dependent* variable—the variable or effect being predicted—is the one that appears as percentages, while the *independent* variable—the cause or predictor—is the one that appears as case bases. Note that this use of the word "independent" has no connection with "statistical independence" in Chapter 2.

The percentage difference is Q with a handicap for all pairs which differ on the independent variable but are tied on the dependent variable.

Is this handicap just? A rationalization can be found in terms of the prediction scenario we wrote for Q in Chapter 2. You will remember the tense scene where pairs differing on both items are drawn at random and you are asked to predict order on one variable from order on the other.

Our new ordeal might be this: Pairs differing on X but not necessarily on Y are randomly selected, and you again predict that the X fellow is Y and the NOT X fellow is NOT Y. How well will you do?

For pairs which differ on Y as well as X you will have the same success as before. Now, however, you will also be making predictions about pairs which turn out to be tied on Y. (Remember that the new ground rule is that pairs differ on the independent variable, but no promises are made about the dependent variable.) How successful will you be for these tied pairs? You will be half right and half wrong on each pair every time since you will be predicting one Y and one NOT Y for pairs which are Y, Y or NOT Y, NOT Y. Regardless of how long you continue you will have neither a deficit nor surplus or correct predictions since you will break even on every single trial.

Viewed this way, there is an implicit "zero" in the numerator for D, the inevitable "surplus equals deficit" for pairs tied on the dependent variable. Granted that imaginary zero, the numerator means exactly the same thing it means for Q—the surplus or deficit of correct predictions and the denominator is still total predictions. We may summarize the three measures this way. The improvement in prediction vis-à-vis chance is

   a. Q, when you are predicting either variable, among pairs differing on both variables
   b. D_{XY}, when you are predicting X from Y, among pairs differing on Y
   c. D_{YX}, when you are predicting Y from X, among pairs differing on X

This gives us a logical connection between seemingly different statistics, one of the reasons that the concept of random pairs advanced by Goodman and Kruskal has been so important in research methodology. And we note two more technical properties of D.

   3. The absolute value of Q will always be higher than either percentage difference unless there are two zero cells, in which case Q and both percentage differences will be 1.00 (here we assume a decimal in front of the percentage difference).

This is because there will always be one or more ties on X and Y unless there are two zero cells (ties always involve cases from both diagonals) and ties lower the value of the D coefficient.

   4. You will always get a bigger percentage difference when the independent variable is cut farther from 50:50.

Property 4 is not entirely obvious, and it occasionally leads to fallacious conclusions among beginning research workers. It follows from the principle that the denominator of D amounts to the total pairs differing on the independent variable. (This was shown by the two versions of the equations for D.) If X and Y have the same number of differing pairs, D_{XY} must equal D_{YX}, and when they are unequal, D will be greater when we use as the denominator the variable with fewer differing pairs (that is, dividing the cross-product difference by a smaller number). We know from Chapter 1 that the number of pairs which differ on a given variable has nothing to do with the inside of the fourfold table but is given by the marginal distribution. We also know that the more skewed the marginal, the fewer the differing pairs. Putting this all together, we see that when we choose the more skewed item as the independent variable, we will have fewer differing pairs, a smaller denominator, and a large value of D. In slogan form: "With more skewed bases, the difference rises."

   In the sex and earnings data, X and Y have similar marginals (66 vs. 34 and 42 vs. 58) and the two percentage differences are similar. Where there is a gross difference in the marginals, the two D's can be quite different. Table 3.3 shows race and earnings from the same census sample data.

TABLE 3.3 Race and Earnings in 1959

a. Raw Data

		EARNINGS		
		Under $4000	$4000 or more	*Total*
RACE	Negro	606	118	724
	Other	3688	3049	6737
	Total	4294	3167	7461 = *N*

$$10,428 = \text{Inapplicable}$$
$$\text{(no earnings)}$$
$$\overline{17,939} = \text{Total}$$

b

RACE	PERCENT HIGH EARNINGS
Negro	16%(724)
Other	45%(6737)

c

EARNINGS	PERCENT NEGRO
$4000 or more	4%(3167)
Less than $4000	14%(4294)

Q is $-.62$ with 95% confidence limits of $(-.56$ to $-.68)$. What about the values of D?

The marginals for earnings are as before (58 vs. 42),[1] but those for race are highly skewed (10 vs. 90), though it is safe to analyze the table since the expected number[2] of high earner Negroes is $(724) * (3167)/7461$ or 307.3.

As property 4 implies, Table 3.3c with the less skewed marginals for the independent variable has the smaller percentage difference $(14 - 4 = 10)$; Table 3.3b with the highly skewed marginals has the larger difference $(45 - 16 = 29)$.

Clearly percentage differences standing alone may be quite deceptive. If someone tells you that he found a 10% difference, while someone else proudly boasts of finding a 29% difference, you cannot compare the results unless you know the marginals for the two tables.

[1] For reasons too complicated to explain here, the census sample data never have "no answers." When there are "no answers" on items U and V, the marginal for item W may vary a little when the table U by W is compared with the table V by W. The difference is seldom appreciable. If there should be an appreciable difference, the situation merits some inquiry. Either an error has been made or "no answers" on one of the items are correlated with W. It is good practice to check the marginals of each of your tables against a master set of figures in your *Code Book*.

[2] You will remember that we obtain expected probabilities by multiplying the relevant marginal frequencies and dividing by N^2 while we obtain expected frequencies by multiplying the relevant marginal frequencies and dividing by N.

This ambiguity might be reduced if there were an unambiguous rule for choosing the direction to percentage. In sociology, there is a tradition that when two items have an asymmetrical causal relationship, one should use the cause (independent variable) as a base and calculate the percentage showing the effect (dependent variable).[3] Dodging for the moment any tight definition of cause—that useful but slippery concept—it seems plausible that race affects one's income more than income affects one's race (though a wealthy light-skinned Negro might have some interesting anecdotes to tell us on this one), and following the tradition, we would prefer Table 3.3b to Table 3.3c and, as a consequence, a 29% difference to a 10% difference.

The rule is a good one, and you should follow it, but not take it too seriously.

When asymmetry is assumed, the structure of English forces us to follow the percentaging convention because it has asymmetrical causal assumptions built into it in the form of subjects, verbs, and direct objects. It just "sounds better" to write that "Negroes tend to be low earners" rather than "Low earners tend to be Negroes," and consequently it is more natural to present Table 3.3b rather than 3.3c.

The rule certainly has literary merit, but its scientific standing is dubious. Granted that some empirical relationships are asymmetrical and granted that D is an asymmetrical coefficient, we still lack a compelling reason to assume that the two asymmetries have any connection. The difference between the two D's comes from the marginal frequencies, not the characteristics of the relationship. Indeed when the relationship between X and Y is truly asymmetrical, if X affects Y while Y does not affect X, a symmetry-sensitive coefficient should show D_{YX} to be strong while D_{XY} is zero—a mathematical impossibility. The argument that many empirical relationships are asymmetrical does not lead us to any grounds for choosing between D_{XY} and D_{YX} except that of literary smoothness.

In sum, follow the rule that the categories of the independent variable provide bases for the percentages, but do not read any high-powered causal inferences from it. Thus,

R U L E 3.2

Use as bases for your percentages the categories you will use as subjects in the sentences you will write, and use as percentages the categories you will use as verbs and objects.

Having shown that the percentage difference is a more sophisticated measure than one might think, why do we still urge you to use it as a supplement for Q to improve communication rather than as a major tool? We

[3] Hans Zeisel, *Say It with Figures*, Harper & Row, New York, 1957, 4th rev. ed., Chapter II, pp. 24–41.

have no argument with its "meaning" for it does seem reasonable to penalize the relationships for ties because if X tends to make a difference in Y, the pairs which differ on X ought to differ on Y. Rather, our objections are technical.

First, the percentage difference lacks a natural upper limit. A maximum difference of 100 can occur only in tables where two zero cells are possible, and this obtains only in the rare cases where (1) the marginals of X and Y are identical and (2) if the marginals are other than 50:50, the direction of association is such that the "fatter" category of X tends to go with the fatter category of Y. In general, we have no way of knowing whether the percentage differences in Table 3.3 (29 and 10) are near their maxima or not without making some calculations, but we know that the Q of $-.62$ is 62% of the maximum Q which could occur in a table with these marginals.

Second, the value of the percentage difference can be affected by manipulating the marginals. If we were less than ethical practitioners, we could pump up our percentage differences by setting extreme cutting points, and even though we are quite ethical practitioners, we realize that cutting points for sociological measures are often arbitrary. Luckily Q is indifferent to such hanky-panky.

Third, the asymmetry of the percentage decision introduces an arbitrary and unnecessary decision into the analysis. We are all for arbitrary decisions, but not unnecessary ones. Since there are no clean scientific grounds for choosing between the two differences (which is a different problem from choosing between the two tables on the basis of literary style and causal assumptions), we might as well avoid having to make the decision at all.

A Note for Those Who Have
Taken (or Will Take) Statistics

The analysis of relationships among interval and ratio-scaled variables usually involves a collection of techniques known as *regression analysis*. Our discussion of the percentage difference can be extended to build a bridge between these two statistical families, though these paragraphs will not mean much unless you know some statistics.

If the categories for variables X and Y in a fourfold table have (or are arbitrarily given) interval scale values (e.g., score X as 1 and *NOT X* as 0; or X as 108 and *NOT X* as -37), a product moment correlation (called r, or sometimes a Pearson correlation after Karl Pearson, the pioneer British statistician) can be calculated as can the "slopes" of the two regression lines. This special case of the product moment correlation is called PHI. When you do this, it turns out that:

1. The two regression slopes will be the two D coefficients.

2. PHI equals the square root of the product of the percentage differences, their geometric mean (this is always the case in regression analysis).

The implications are:

1. If you apply product moment correlation techniques to fourfold tables your correlations will be smaller in absolute value than Q and somewhere between the two values of D (except at the ± 1.00 special two-zero-cell case described above and, of course, when X and Y are independent).

2. When $D_{XY} = D_{YX}$, they will equal PHI.

3. The use of PHI as a measure of association is probably preferable to D since it eliminates the ambiguity of asymmetry, but PHI, like D, is sensitive to arbitrary, skewed marginals.

4. If the marginals for all your items are close to 50 : 50 you will get roughly the same pattern of results whether you use Q or regression techniques on fourfold tables, although the absolute sizes of the correlations will run higher for Q. If the marginals vary a lot, no such guarantee can be made.

5. In sum, survey statistics and classic regression statistics are a lot more similar than partisans of one or the other sometimes claim.

R by C Tables: Gamma

Cross tabulation tables are classified by the number of rows and the number of columns. Thus a 4 * 8 table is one with four rows and eight columns. When we are talking about tables in general, without specifying the numbers of rows and columns, we speak of "R by C" tables. In Chapter 2 and the previous section of this chapter we limited our attention to 2 * 2 tables. Now we want to consider, although not in much detail, larger tables.

Again level of measurement is the key concept. You will remember that an ordinal scale is one where the arrangement of categories is "transitive" and also that among dichotomies we can dodge the issue of transitivity because it is a property of triads. Thus, we can divide larger tables into two groups: (1) those where both items are ordinal or one is ordinal and the other a dichotomy and (2) all other. The difference is that in group 1 we may use the notion of order to analyze the table, while in group 2 we cannot.

Table 3.4 gives the raw data for the cross tabulation of two ordinal measures, family income and educational attainment of the head of the household. The data come from the U. S. Census[4] and refer to family income in 1966 and years of school completed by the head of the family (or individual living alone) as of March 1967. Frequencies are reported to the nearest one thousand.

Ordinarily we would dichotomize both variables close to 50 : 50 as indicated by the lines in Table 3.4 and calculate Q from Table 3.5.

Q equals $+.54$, a substantial positive correlation which means that con-

---

[4] *Current Population Reports, Consumer Income*, Series P-60, No. 53, December 28, 1967, Table 7, p. 27.

TABLE 3.4 Family Income and Educational Attainment of Household Head

	EDUCATIONAL ATTAINMENT						
INCOME	Less than 8 yr HS	8 yr HS	1–3 yr HS	4 yr HS	1–3 yr coll.	4 or more yr coll.	TOTAL
$10,000 or more	575	1356	2111	4761	2079	3606	14,488
$7000–$9999	956	1698	2328	4319	1396	1247	11,944
$4000–$6999	1771	2369	2544	3744	986	738	12,152
Under $4000	3147	2369	2004	1916	485	402	10,323
	6449	7792	8987	14,740	4946	5993	48,907

TABLE 3.5 Fourfold Table for Data in Table 3.4

		EDUCATIONAL ATTAINMENT	
		Less than 4 yr HS	4 yr HS or more
FAMILY INCOME	$7000 or more	9,024	17,408
	Under $7000	14,204	8,271
			48,907

sistent pairs—those where the family head with higher education has the higher income—are much more common than inconsistent pairs.

Let us now consider treating the same data as a larger R by C table. Returning to Table 3.4, we note that both items are ordinal. (You might think that income is a ratio scale, but if you ponder the four categories used in the table you will finally agree that *here* it is an ordinal scale.) Consequently we can find some consistent and inconsistent pairs which were hidden in Table 3.5. Consider, for example, the 2079 cases with 1–3 years of college and incomes of $10,000 or more and the 4319 cases with 4 years of high school and incomes of $7000 to $9999. They produce $2079 * 4319 = 8,979,201$ pairs that were considered to be tied in Table 3.5 but are actually consistent—the member higher on education is higher on income. Or again, look at the 575 cases with incomes of $10,000 or more and less than 8 years of education along with the 2369 cases with incomes of under $4000 and 8 years of education. They give us $575 * 2369 = 1,362,175$ inconsistent pairs where the member with the higher income has the lower education and vice versa. (If you have not already done so, go back to Table 3.4 and locate these cell frequencies.)

When a fourfold table has been collapsed from a larger R by C table with two ordinal variables, it is always possible to go back to the raw data and find inconsistent and consistent pairs that would be treated as ties in the calculation of Q.

Having found *all* these hidden pairs, thre is nothing to prevent us from calculating all their cross products and adding them to the appropriate places in the numerator and denominator of our Q formula. The result is the coefficient gamma, invented by Goodman and Kruskal, the statisticians cited in Chapter 2.

Forgetting for the moment how to do this, you will see that gamma and Q have the same meaning, "the surplus (or deficit) of consistent pairs divided by the total pairs differing on X and Y." The only difference is that gamma uses the differences that contribute to Q *plus* all the finer differences that turn up when the table is enlarged from 2 by 2 and many of the ties are "broken." Turning it around, Q is merely the special case of gamma when the data are in the form of a 2 by 2 table.

How do you calculate gamma? Alas, no simple formula like $(B * C) - (A * D)/(B * C) + (A * D)$ can be given because there is a different formula for each value of R and C and in large tables the formula is cumbersome. However, it is possible to give a set of fairly simple (though sometimes tedious) instructions for work with a desk calculator.

1. Arrange the table so that the top row and right-hand column are assigned to the positive ends of the two scales.
2. To calculate CP, the total cross product for consistent pairs:
   a) Begin with the upper-right-hand cell frequency (3606 in Table 3.4) and multiply it by every frequency below and to the left of it (there are 15 of them in Table 3.4), cumulating the sums of these products.
   b) Next take the frequency to the left of the one in step a (2079 in Table 3.4) and multiply it by every frequency below and to the left of it (there are 12 of them in Table 3.4), cumulating the sums of these products.
   c) Continue across the top row of frequencies in this fashion until you get to the left-hand row (575 in Table 3.4). It has no cases below and to the left, so ignore it.
   d) Move to the right-hand frequency in the second row and proceed similarly across the second row until you get to the left-hand frequency, which is ignored.
   e) Continue down the rows until you are about to begin the last row. Frequencies in the bottom row have no other frequencies below and to the left so the entire bottom row may be ignored.
   f) The grand sum of all these cumulative multiplications, that is, the cumulative total of all possible multiplications where one frequency is above and to the right while the other is below and to the left, is CP.
3. To calculate IP, the total cross product for inconsistent pairs:
   a) Begin with the frequency in the upper-left-hand corner (575 in Table 3.4) and multiply it against all frequencies below and to the right, cumulating the products.
   b) Move from left to right across the top row, multiplying each frequency by all frequencies below and to the right, cumulating the products as before. Ignore the right-hand frequency, which has no cases below and to the right.
   c) Continue the process, moving across the subsequent rows and ignoring the right-hand column until you have completed the next to bottom row.

d) The grand sum of all these cumulative multiplications, that is, the cumulative total of all possible multiplications where one frequency is above and to the left while the other is below and to the right, is IP.

4. The formula for gamma is

$$\frac{CP - IP}{CP + IP}$$

Should one use Q or gamma? The question is actually unfair, for they are the same coefficient. The difference is in how you organize the data not in the coefficients. If you make fine distinctions you will use gamma; if you use only dichotomous distinctions the result will be Q. It is possible for you to carry out all of the complicated operations described in Chapters 4 through 7 with gamma rather than Q, and the research logic will be the same. Thus, the question should be rephrased: Should one refine his data beyond dichotomies? The considerations seem to be these:

1. Gamma requires a lot more work, particularly in multivariate analysis treating several variables at one time. Indeed, multivariate analysis using gamma is almost impossibly tedious without an electronic computer and, even with one, the programming is complex.

2. Gamma uses more of the information in the data, allowing more of the possible pairs to contribute to the conclusions.

3. Gamma will be more sensitive to how the relationship operates at the extremes. If, for example (counter to the facts in Table 3.4), college graduation does not raise income beyond the income associated with 1 to 3 years of college, this would "pull down" the value of gamma but would not affect Q.

4. Gamma may be used only if all your variables are ordinal,[5] while Q may be used on any variable regardless of level of measurement.

5. Gamma will generally run a little lower in magnitude on the same data. This is because it includes more of the small differences in the variables and they generally are less consistent (less positive if Q is positive, less negative if Q is negative). You are more likely to get a consistent income difference when you compare college graduates with those completing less than eighth grade than when comparing those completing 2 years of college with those completing 1 year of college. Table 3.6 illustrates this for the data in Table 3.4. It gives the values of gamma calculated for various groupings of the two variables.

The table shows that as we refine the categories for either variable, the value of gamma declines. Comparing the extremes, we get a Q value of $+.536$ and when the data are treated as a 4 * 6 table, a gamma of $+.412$.

Such sensitivity to grouping does not follow of mathematical necessity, and with a little fiendish ingenuity you can construct tables where gamma

---

[5] You can, of course, calculate gamma when one or both items are interval or ratio scales because both have the ordinal property plus their various distance properties.

TABLE 3.6 Values of Gamma for Various Groupings of Income and Education in Table 3.4

	EDUCATION			
INCOME	C = 2 (4 HS or more; less than 4 HS)	C = 3 (1 or more coll.; 4 HS; less than 4 HS)	C = 4 (1 or more coll.; 4 HS; 1–3 HS; 8 or less)	C = 6 (as in Table 3.4)
R = 4 (as in Table 3.4)	+.474	+.441	+.421	+.412
R = 2 ($7000 or more; less than $7000)	+.536	+.499	+.478	+.468

is stronger than Q or even has a different sign. However, when the XY relationship is uniform—that is where one would get the same sign for the cross product difference for fourfold tables constructed for all possible pairs of categories from X and from Y (a condition that statisticians call "isotropism")—it is a safe rule of thumb that Q and gamma will be fairly close in value but Q will be a little stronger. Even with mild departures from isotropism in a category or two, the rule is sound.

While there is no reason to prefer a coefficient just because it is bigger, the rule of thumb does lead us to an argument for Q, i.e., an argument for fourfold tables. When a coefficient is sensitive to the refinement or coarseness of the groupings, all one's variables should have the same number of categories and similar marginal frequencies. Otherwise two coefficients may differ in magnitude merely because of the category structure, not because of differences in the strength of the relationship. Since we can dichotomize any variable and can more often than not get its marginals near 50 : 50, the use of Q helps standardize the tables for all the relationships.

We believe these considerations argue that we should be in no hurry to trade in Q for the flashier gamma. Q is much easier to calculate, it tends to give similar results (if only because the pairs in Q are a considerable proportion of the pairs in gamma), and it standardizes the categories and marginals.

Perhaps the best advice is to rely on Q but to use gamma to check the isotropism of key relationships in the analysis (when the levels of measurement are appropriate). If you turn up a striking difference between the two, you would do well to examine the table cell by cell using the techniques explained in the following section.

R by C Tables: Cell Analysis

A 3 * 3 or larger table where one or both variables is nominal cannot be analyzed meaningfully with gamma. There is nothing to prevent you from making the calculation, but we dare you to interpret it. Consider, for example, a table for region (northeast, south, midwest, west) by income and a pair where the higher earner is from the midwest and the lower earner from the northeast. Is this a consistent pair or an inconsistent one? Unless we assume some order among the regions the question cannot be answered and gamma would be literally meaningless.

Such large tables with nominal variables are often called "contingency tables" because their analysis amounts to asking whether the row probabilities vary with (are contingent on) the columns and vice versa.

Here is an example. Table 3.7 gives the frequencies for a cross tabulation of region and urbanism. Again the data are from the sample drawn from the 1960 U.S. census. Regions are divided into northeast, midwest, south, and west. The categories for urbanism of residence are three, (1) central city of a metropolitan area (central city), (2) outside the central city but in a metropolitan area (suburb), and (3) outside a metroplitan area (nonmetropolitan).

TABLE 3.7   Raw Frequencies for Region and Urbanism

| | | REGION | | | | |
		Northeast	Midwest	South	West	Total
	Central city	1628	1651	1534	959	5772
URBANISM	Suburb	1984	1447	1134	1046	5611
	Nonmetropolitan	867	2063	2820	806	6556
	Total	4479	5161	5488	2811	17939

There is no satisfactory way to state the degree of association in such a table, but one can use the now familiar concept of observed and expected cell frequencies to see what is going on in particular cells. Just as in the case of a fourfold table, we may calculate the cell frequencies that would turn up if the two variables were independent. To do so, we merely multiply the relevant row marginal times the relevant column marginal and divide by N, exactly as in Chapter 2. For example, if urbanism and region are independent, we would expect the frequency for suburban southerners to be $5488 * 5611 /17939 = 30,793,168/17939 = 1716.55$. Since we observe 1134 cases rather than the expected 1716, we may say that there are fewer suburbanites in the south than one would anticipate from a chance association between region and urbanism. The procedure so far is exactly the same as that explained in Chapter 2.

What we can do in one cell, we can do in any, and Table 3.8 shows the result in the form of the difference between observed and expected values for each of the cells.

We may draw a number of conclusions from Table 3.8. For example, suburbanites tend to be concentrated in the northeast and west in contrast to the midwest and south; northeasterners have a less-than-chance proportion living outside the metropolitan areas, etc.

TABLE 3.8   Value of Observed Minus Expected Cell Frequencies for Table 3.7

| | | REGION | | | | |
		Northeast	Midwest	South	West	Total
	Central city	+187	− 10	−232	+54	−1
URBANISM	Suburbs	+583	−167	−583	+167	0
	Nonmetropolitan	−770	+177	+814	−221	0
	Total	0	0	−1	0	−1

What is extremely difficult is to find an overall summary of the degree of departure from chance. Rather than the single statistic, delta, which can be used to develop Q, Table 3.8 has 12 different deltas whose only restriction is that they must sum to zero in each row and column (the −1 entries in Table 3.8 are because of discrepancies due to rounding). Despite a number of attempts, no one has come up with a bug-free coefficient to describe the overall degree of departure from chance expectations essentially because $R * C$ tables can depart from chance in many different ways (different patterns of plus and minus for cells), and each way has a different maximum possible deviation from chance expectations.

Confronted with such a table, the analyst can only inspect the pattern of signs in his table and attempt to draw a coherent verbal statement. Table 3.8 yields a reasonably simple one: "Northeasterners and westerners are disproportionately concentrated in metropolitan areas (both in central cities and suburbs) while midwesterners and southerners are disproportionately concentrated in nonmetropolitan places." Not every $R * C$ table, however, will allow so crisp a summary.

$R * C$ tables have a further technical problem, statistical inference. Before rushing into print with findings, one would like to know whether the departures from chance exceed those to be expected by random sampling both for the table as a whole and for particular cells. Statistical tools for this exist, but they take us beyond the scope of this book, and when confronted with the problem, you should consult with a trained statistician.

Cell analysis, as suggested previously, can be of help in interpreting discrepancies between Q and gamma. We said that when the relationship between X and Y is uniform across all the categories (isotropic) Q and gamma should be in fair agreement, with Q being of slightly larger magnitude. You can make a rough check for such consistency by calculating the observed minus expected values for each cell in the table. Table 3.9, for example, shows the signs of these differences for the data in Table 3.4.

You will note a distinct pattern. The plus signs are concentrated in a band running from the lower left corner to the upper right corner. This is what one would expect when the relationship is isotropic (of course, the band would run from upper left to lower right if the correlation were negative). The general rule is that there should not be any minus signs *between* plus signs in

TABLE 3.9 Sign of Observed Minus Expected Cell Values in Table 3.4

	Less than 8 yr	8 yr	1–3 yr HS	4 yr HS	1–3 yr. coll.	4 or more yr coll.
$10,000 or more	−	−	−	+	+	+
$7,000–$9,999	−	−	+	+	+	−
$4,000–$6,999	+	+	+	+	−	−
Under $4,000	+	+	+	−	−	−

any row or column. One or two exceptions do not mean doom, but if the pattern is quite different (say, with the minus signs concentrated in the center of the table and the plus signs at the edges), gamma is an inappropriate statistic. In such a case something is going on—the items are certainly not independent—but it is not the sort of isotropic consistency between differences in two orders that is described by gamma.

IN A NUTSHELL

A. Advantages of percentages

1. Ease of communication to nonprofessionals
2. Ability to reconstruct the raw data from percentage tables

B. Statistical properties of the percentage difference, D_{XY} and D_{YX}

1. Two formulas
2. Meaning in terms of improvement in prediction when one selects random pairs differing on the independent variable but not necessarily on the dependent variable
3. Specifics
   a) Both Q and D will equal zero when X and Y are independent.
   b) Q, D_{XY}, and D_{YX} will have the same sign.
   c) The absolute value of Q will be larger than D.
   d) Sensitivity to marginals in contrast to Q ("with more skewed bases, the difference rises").

C. The decision about direction to percentage

1. Causal and literary rules for choice
2. Distinction between choice of a direction to percentage and choosing between the two D's as a measure of association, the latter being generally arbitrary.

D. Disadvantages of the percentage difference

1. Lack of a meaningful upper limit
2. Sensitivity to artificial differences in marginals

E. *R* by *C* tables

1. When both items are ordinal or one is ordinal and the other a dichotomy, one may measure the degree of association with the coefficient gamma.

    a) *Gamma is closely related to Q, and indeed consists of the pair frequencies used in Q plus others that are treated as ties when the data are collapsed into a fourfold table.*

    b) *Gamma will generally be close to Q but a little smaller in magnitude if the relationship is uniform (isotropic) across the categories.*

2. When the ordinal assumptions for gamma do not apply

    a) *One can gain some insight into what is going on by calculating the difference between observed and expected frequencies for each cell in the table,*

    b) *but no satisfactory coefficient exists to describe the degree of correlation in such tables.*

    c) *Cell analysis may be used to examine departures from isotropism in tables where Q and gamma show sharp divergence.*

Rules

RULE 3.1

Always present your key data in percentage form as well as the results of your more complex statistical analysis.

> *3.1a* Always present your case bases, putting them below and to the right of the percentages and in parentheses.

> *3.1b* Report your percentages rounded to whole numbers.

> *3.1c* Place a percent sign (%) next to each percentage.

> *3.1d* In the case of elaborate multivariate tabulations, you may put the raw figures in an appendix if a percentage table would be extremely cumbersome.

RULE 3.2

Use as bases for your percentages the categories you will use as subjects in the sentences you will write; use as percentages the categories you will use as verbs and objects.

Major Concepts

---

1. *D* coefficient
2. Gamma coefficient
3. Isotropism
4. *R* by *C* table

4

Three Variables

An Overview

Having observed the correlation (or lack of correlation) between two variables, we usually introduce a third variable into our tabulations. The results give greater depth to our analyses because they reveal how our relationship is affected by or is impervious to other variables.

By tradition, we call the original variables X and Y and the new variable T, which stands for *test* variable, a variable introduced to test the properties of Q_{XY}.

In essence, what we do is to recalculate the Q coefficient among subgroups of cases that are similar in their category of T. For example, if we introduce sex as a test variable, we calculate Q_{XY} among men and Q_{XY} among women and then combine them to give a statistic known as a partial correlation coefficient. We say that "T has been controlled."

When the partial coefficient is compared with the original (zero-order) coefficient for XY, it may be higher, lower, or just the same. Any value for a partial can coexist with any value for a zero order.

Certain combinations of zero-order and partial coefficients are of special importance in research and they have been given names: "explanation," "no effect," and "suppression."

When the zero order is nonnegligible but the partial is .00 or negligible, we say that "T explains Y." That is, the reason we observed the XY correlation was because we had not controlled for T, and when we do, the relationship is no longer there. This is actually an operational definition of a common-sense idea. When we say that permissive child rearing explains the deplorable behavior of today's college students compared to the exemplary deportment of their predecessors, we mean that among people from families similar in permissiveness there would no longer be any correlation between date of birth and deplorability of adolescent behavior.

Sometimes, T does not affect the XY relationship at all and the partial correlation is the same as the zero order. Such an outcome is important when you are testing the hypothesis that X and Y are "really correlated" and you want to show that the correlation is not produced by some outside variable. On paper, a controlled experiment is the best way to demonstrate your claim, but sociologists seldom can use this powerful tool for their variables. The best we can do is to control for as many different test variables as possible, though there are always many which escape the net (if only because we do not know about them). Thus, multivariate analysis, while analogous to experimental design, does not have the power of a true experiment.

It can happen that the partial correlation is even stronger than the zero order. If so, we call T a "suppressor variable" because it has been acting to suppress the "true" strength of the relationship which only becomes apparent when T has been controlled.

A fourth outcome, "specification," is a little different. The partial correlation combines the results of two conditional correlations, say Q_{XY} among the men and Q_{XY} among the women (where T is sex). Occasionally, these two conditional Q's are quite different in size and sometimes even have opposite signs. When this happens, we say that "T specifies XY" in that you have to specify which category of T you are talking about before you can say how strong or weak the XY correlation is.

From a technical point of view, multivariate analysis is justified by an equation which shows that a zero-order Q can be expressed as the weighted average of Q_{XY} among pairs of persons "tied" on T and secondly Q_{XY} among pairs of persons differing on T. The former is the "partial" and the latter is called the "differential." The weights are the proportions tied on T and differing on T among consistent and inconsistent XY pairs. It is extremely important that the research worker have a good grasp of this equation, and in particular how the three component Q's (zero-order, partial, and differential) are interlocked so that if one goes up, another must go down.

From a practical point of view, data seldom come out as cleanly as our discussions of explanation, no effect, suppression, and specification might suggest. At the end of the chapter certain rules of thumb are presented to help you make consistent decisions in your own research.

There is a further technical problem. With some variables, a division into two "control" categories of T reduces variation in T but does not eliminate it. Thus, when we control income by dividing incomes at the $6000 a year point, there are still a lot of income differences in the group we call "high" and within the group we call "low." Thus, our multivariate analysis amounts to calculating Q's within subgroups which have *relatively* greater and lesser differences in T. You can sometimes check a partial correlation by recalculating sub-Q's in finer categories of T to see whether further refinement of the test variable has any further effect on the value of Q.

Working Parts

When you cross-tabulate three dichotomies (X, Y, T) you get $(2 * 2 * 2) = 8$ cell frequencies that can be presented in an eightfold table, which turns out to be two fourfold tables, and that is the key to the whole thing. The standard layout for such tables is presented in Table 4.1.

TABLE 4.1   Layout and Notation for an Eightfold Table

VARIABLE T	VARIABLE X	VARIABLE Y NOT Y	Y	SUM
T	X	AT	BT	$T\underline{X}$
	$NOT\ X$	CT	DT	$T\overline{X}$
	Sum	$T\overline{Y}$	TY	
$NOT\ T$	X	$A\overline{T}$	$B\overline{T}$	$\overline{T}\underline{X}$
	$NOT\ X$	$C\overline{T}$	$D\overline{T}$	$\overline{T}X$
	Sum	$\overline{T}\overline{Y}$	$\overline{T}Y$	

Although there are three possible pair relations among the variables (XY, TX, TY), the table is laid out to emphasize the XY relationship. You could, of course, arrange it to emphasize one of the others by scrambling the variables around. This gives us our first clue to the hieroglyphics in the cells: the familiar (from Chapter 2) letters A, B, C, and D indicate the values of X and Y, A standing for cases that are X and $NOT\ Y$, B for cases that are X and Y, etc.

Careful inspection of the table shows that A, B, C, and D each turn up twice. In other words, Table 4.1 consists of two fourfold XY correlation tables stacked on top of each other. Such subtables are called "conditional tables" and you can see that there would be no obstacle to the calculation of two different Q's, $Q_{XY:T}$ and $Q_{XY:NOT\ T}$, the notation after the colon indicating the relevant category of T.

The letters after A, B, C, and D stand for category scores, using the traditional notation of a line above the letter standing for "not" ($\bar{T}$ means *NOT T*).

Note further that each conditional table has a set of four marginal frequencies, and they have a pattern. The row marginals (TX, $T\bar{X}$, $\bar{T}X$, $\overline{TX}$) are the cell frequencies for the correlation between T and X. The column marginals ($T\bar{Y}$, TY, $\overline{TY}$, $\bar{T}Y$) are the cell frequencies for the correlation between T and Y.

This is the first important point about eight-fold tables: They may be seen as two conditional tables for the correlation of X and Y with marginals provided by the cells of the TX and TY correlations.

Having named the parts, let's see how they work. If we wanted to, we could calculate the correlation between X and Y, ignoring T. This is called a "zero-order coefficient," the order of a coefficient being the number of test variables. Q_{XY} is a zero-order coefficient because zero additional variables have been controlled or made to differ. $Q_{XY:T}$ is a first-order coefficient because one variable, T, has been controlled. Practically speaking, we may say that the order of a coefficient is the number of variables that appears after the colon in the subscript for Q.

How do the two conditional Q's and the zero-order Q fit together? It goes like this. Returning to our theme of random pairs, we can say without much fear of contradiction that there are two kinds of pairs involving T, tied pairs and differing pairs. If we calculate Q_{XY} ignoring T, i.e., the zero-order coefficient, we can say that Q_{XY} is the relationship between X and Y among pairs some of which are tied on T and some of which differ on T. Let us now see whether we can build Q_{XY} from the bottom up from the XY relationship among pairs tied on T (the two conditional tables) and the pairs differing on T, whose location in Table 4.1 is not immediately obvious.

First, let us find a formula for Q_{XY} using only those pairs tied on T.

Remembering that the coefficient for X and Y is made out of consistent and inconsistent pairs, we seek the consistent pairs tied on T and the inconsistent pairs tied on T. This search boils down to a hunt for $(B * C)$ and $(A * D)$ cells that have the same category of T. Thus the total for consistent pairs turns out to be $[(BT * CT) + (B\bar{T} * C\bar{T})]$ and the total for inconsistent pairs $[(AT * DT) + (A\bar{T} * D\bar{T})]$. We now use these to write a coefficient:

$$Q_{XY:\text{TIED }T} = \frac{[(BT * CT) + (B\bar{T} * C\bar{T})] - [(AT * DT) + (A\bar{T} * D\bar{T})]}{[(BT * CT) + (B\bar{T} * C\bar{T})] + [(AT * DT) + (A\bar{T} * D\bar{T})]}$$

Or in plain English we sum the positive cross products in the two conditional tables to get the total consistent pairs and sum the negative cross products in the two conditional tables to get the total inconsistent pairs and then calculate Q in the usual fashion.

We may call this coefficient alternatively

1. The partial Q between X and Y, controlling for T.
2. The Q between X and Y among pairs tied on T.
3. The improvement in prediction for X and Y when we predict only among pairs tied on T.

There remain those pairs which differ on T. They are less obvious when one glances at Table 4.1, but if you will work at it a little, you will see that the pairs which are consistent on XY and differ on T are given by the cells that are B and C but have a different value on $T: [(BT * C\bar{T}) + (B\bar{T} * CT)]$. Similarly the inconsistent pairs differing on T are $[(AT * D\bar{T}) + (A\bar{T} * DT)]$. From this we write a second coefficient:

$$Q_{XY:\text{DIFF }T} = \frac{[(BT * C\bar{T}) + (B\bar{T} * CT)] - [(AT * D\bar{T}) + (A\bar{T} * DT)]}{[(BT * C\bar{T}) + (B\bar{T} * CT)] + [(AT * D\bar{T}) + (A\bar{T} * DT)]}$$

We may call this second coefficient alternatively

1. The differential Q between X and Y when T differs.
2. The Q between X and Y among pairs differing on T.
3. The improvement in prediction for X and Y when we predict only among pairs differing on T.

The trap is almost ready to close. We know that there are only two kinds of T pairs, tied and differing; we know Q_{XY}, the zero-order relationship, is based on both tied and differing T pairs; and we know that all the pairs which differ on X and Y appear in one of the two formulas for the partial and the differential. We are sorely tempted to claim that Q_{XY} is some sort of average of the partial and differential coefficients, and it is. It is not, however, the simple average one would get by summing the partial and differential Q's and dividing by two. Rather, it turns out to be a weighted average of the two, where the weights consist of the proportions of pairs tied and differing on T. We define two weights:

$$W1 = \text{weight 1} = \frac{(BT * CT) + (B\bar{T} * C\bar{T}) + (AT * DT) + (A\bar{T} * D\bar{T})}{[(BT + B\bar{T}) * (CT + C\bar{T})] + [(AT + A\bar{T}) * (DT + D\bar{T})]}$$

= proportion of pairs tied on T among pairs differing on X and Y

$$W2 = \text{weight 2} = \frac{(BT * C\bar{T}) + (B\bar{T} * CT) + (AT * D\bar{T}) + (A\bar{T} * DT)}{[(BT + B\bar{T}) * (CT + C\bar{T})] + [(AT + A\bar{T}) * (DT + D\bar{T})]}$$

= proportion of pairs differing on T among pairs differing on X and Y

The formulas look ferocious but are really quite tame. The numerators are simply the denominators of the partial and differential, or the frequencies of tied and differing T pairs. The denominator (the same for both weights) is the total number of pairs differing on both X and Y. This, of course, is merely the denominator of Q_{XY}, but it appears in a gaudy form here because it is added up from eight cell frequencies in tables like Table 4.1 rather than the fourfold tables we are used to.

We will skip the algebra, but it is easy to show that

$$Q_{XY} = (Q_{XY:\text{TIED }T} * W1) + (Q_{XY:\text{DIFF }T} * W2)$$

This is the main mathematical result in multivariate analysis of three dichotomies.[1] It can be stated in two different ways:

1. Q_{XY} is a weighted average of the partial Q and the differential Q, where the weights are the proportions of pairs tied on T and differing on T.

Or, since the weights must sum to 1.00 and can be construed as probabilities,

2. Improvement in prediction for X and Y among pairs differing on both = $\begin{pmatrix} \text{improvement for} \\ \text{pairs tied on } T \end{pmatrix} * \begin{pmatrix} \text{probability} \\ \text{of a tie on } T \end{pmatrix}$

$+ \begin{pmatrix} \text{improvement for} \\ \text{pairs differing on} \\ T \end{pmatrix} * \begin{pmatrix} \text{probability} \\ \text{of pair dif-} \\ \text{fering on } T \end{pmatrix}$

Most of the rest of this book will be an exploration of implications of this equation. To set the stage, we call your attention to the following mathematical necessities:

Considering the zero order, partial, and differential,

Principle 1. If any two are equal in sign and size, the third must have the same sign and size.

Principle 2. If the partial is less than the zero order, the differential must be larger than either.

Principle 3. If the partial is greater than the zero order, the differential must be smaller than either.

Principle 4. Whatever the value of the zero order, the partial can have any value between $+1.00$ and -1.00, provided that the weights and the value of the differential are appropriate.

Having outlined the algebraic system for multivariate analysis, we turn to its research implications.

---

[1] G. Udny Yule and M. G. Kendall, *An Introduction to the Theory of Statistics*, 14th ed., Hafner, New York, 1950, pp. 34–37.

Outcome Regions and
Explanation

Principle 4 in the previous section—that any value for the partial can coexist with any value of the zero order—gives us a way to review the possible outcomes of a three-variable analysis. We may think of a two-dimensional space in which the vertical axis is the value of Q_{XY} ranging from $+1.00$ to -1.00 and the horizontal axis is the value of the partial $Q_{XY:\text{TIED } T}$ also ranging from $+1.00$ to -1.00. For the moment we may ignore the value of the differential since the equation shows us that its value is determined, given the zero order, partial, and weights. As far as the equation "cares," three-variable-research results may lie anywhere in the space. If we limit Q to two decimals, there are 201^2 or 40,401 possible outcomes.

Luckily we will not have to discuss each of them, thanks to a classic paper by the sociologists Patricia L. Kendall and Paul F. Lazarsfeld.[2] Kendall and Lazarsfeld show that the space can be divided into meaningful regions and instead of discussing 40,401 possibilities, we may limit our attention to a mere five, as shown in Figure 4.1.

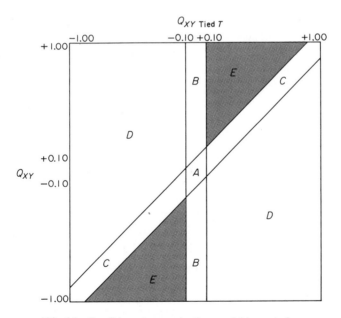

FIG. 4.1   Possible outcomes in three-variable analysis.

[2] Patricia L. Kendall and Paul F. Lazarsfeld, "Problems of Survey Analysis," in Robert K. Merton and Paul F. Lazarsfeld, eds., *Continuities in Social Research*, Free Press, New York, 1950, pp. 135–167.

The first region, designated by the letter A in Figure 4.1, includes those situations where the zero order, the partial and necessarily the differential are .00 or negligible. In other words, there is no relationship between X and Y whether or not T is controlled. This all too common outcome of research is too discouraging to deserve a name, and we quickly move on to a more interesting possibility.

The area labeled B above and below A in Figure 4.1 defines those outcomes where the zero-order relationship is nonnegligible but the partial is negligible or .00.

Kendall and Lazarsfeld call such outcomes "explanations" and following them we advance this rule:

R U L E 4.1

If we observe a nonnegligible zero-order association between X and Y, we say that T explains the relationship if $Q_{XY:\text{TIED }T}$ is negligible or zero.

In other words, Kendall and Lazarsfeld have suggested an operational definition of the English word "explanation" or "because."

An example may persuade you that the definition is apt. In a survey of the reading habits in a probability sample of 1850 women in Baltimore, the sociologist Jan Hajda observed a low negative correlation between age (under 45 vs. 45 and older) and book reading (the number of books the respondent claimed to have read in the previous year). See Table 4.2.

TABLE 4.2   Age and Book Reading in a Probability Sample of Baltimore Women*

AGE	PERCENT HIGH ON BOOK READING
45 and older	37%(867)
Under 45	49%(983)
	$N = 1850$

* Number of no answers not available from the unpublished data. $Q = -.24$, 95% confidence limits = $-.15$ to $-.33$.

Why are age and reading correlated? Well, what do you mean by why?

Since we have defined research in terms of the properties of variables, the answer has to be in terms of variables and will have the general form, "because of_____, a variable other than age and reading." But strictly speaking, it is not the variable which does the job; it is differences in the variable. (When we say that "age" and "reading" are related, this is just a convenient shorthand way of saying that "differences in age" are related to "differences in reading.") We might as well call the new variable T and restate the answer as "X and Y are correlated because of differences in T."

If we wish to provide evidence for that claim, we are obliged to show that (1) when T differs, X and Y are related; (2) when T does not differ, X and Y

are not related. And our equation is designed for that very purpose. The statement that "$Q_{XY:\text{TIED }T} = .00$" is an operational translation of the phrase "when T does not differ, X and Y are not related," and from principle 2 above, we know that when (2) is true, (1) must be true, given a nonnegligible zero-order correlation.

In the case of age and reading, Hajda reasoned that educational attainment might be the test variable which explains the relationship between age and reading. His raw data are given in Table 4.3.

TABLE 4.3   Raw Data for Age, Education, and Book Reading

		READING	
EDUCATION	AGE	LOW	HIGH
High school	45 and older	215	263
	Under 45	373	453
Less than	45 and older	335	54
high school	Under 45	133	24

$N = 1850$

From the formulas for the various weights and coefficients we may calculate a solution to the equation

$$Q_{\text{age, reading}} = (Q_{\text{age, reading:TIED, ed.}} * W1) + (Q_{\text{age, reading:DIFF ed.}} * W2)$$

$$-.241 = (-.001 \quad * \quad .498) + (-.480 \quad * \quad .502)$$

The low negative correlation has been decomposed into two parts, a negligible partial among the .498 pairs tied on education and a moderate negative association among the .502 pairs differing on education.

From this Hajda concludes that education explains the relationship between age and reading.

What we have here, of course, is an agreement about how to link English words and research operations—not a mystical insight into the deeper essence of reality. However, it is hard to argue with the link as long as one thinks in terms of variables and their relations. As an exercise, call to mind some explanation or plausible explanation involving variables. For example, "Why do high-status people vote for conservative parties?" "Because they have an interest in defending the status quo." We predict that you can always translate your verbal statements into zero orders and "vanishing" partials and the result will be a fair copy of your implicit reasoning. For example, "There is a positive correlation between SES and voting for conservative parties. When, however, interest in defending the status quo is controlled—when one takes cases which are similar in interest in defending the status quo—the correlation vanishes. Thus differences in interest explain the relationship."

In algebraic terms, explanations are clear and simple, but unless you have been well steeped in this sort of research, the whole business may seem a little magical. Again, percentage tables may be used to make clearer to you and to your readers what is going on, as well as to meet the requirement that raw figures appear in the research report.

To illuminate both the partial and the differential, we need two tables, given as Tables 4.4 and 4.5.

TABLE 4.4 Conventional Arrangement for a Percentage Table to Present a Partial (Percent Y)

VARIABLE T	VARIABLE X NOT X	X	DIFFERENCE
T	%( )	%( )	$D_{XY:T}$
NOT T	%( )	%( )	$D_{YX:NOT\,T}$
Total	%	%	D_{YX}
			N

The percentage difference being just as asymmetrical as it was a chapter ago, we have to choose one of the variables as dependent, and by convention it is assigned the letter Y, X being the independent variable. Notice further that the case bases are placed below and to the right of the percentages in parentheses, again so they do not get in the way of percentage comparisons. Table 4.5 is the partial for Hajda's data.

TABLE 4.5 Age, Reading, and Education (Percentage of high book readers)

EDUCATION	AGE UNDER 45	45 AND OLDER	DIFFERENCE
High school	55%(826)	55%(478)	0
Less than high school	15%(157)	14%(389)	− 1
Total	49%	37%	−12

The table makes clear that there is a percentage difference in the zero-order data but not within the two conditional tables.

It is harder to make clear through percentage tables why a differential is so high. (In fact, it is hard to make clear, period.) From our knowledge of Q, we can say that a high value for the differential means that if we select pairs which differ on T they will tend to have a positive or negative XY correlation. If the correlation is positive, this amounts to saying that one category of T has a surplus of $++$ pairs for XY, the other a surplus of $--$ pairs for XY. When we compare T's and $NOT\,T$'s, we have a surplus of $++$ and $--\,XY$ pairs, that is, a positive correlation. For a negative value of the differential, one category of T tends to have a surplus of $+-$ pairs for XY and the other a surplus of $-+$ pairs. Table 4.6 is a percentage table that will usually make the pattern clear.

TABLE 4.6 Conventional Arrangements for Percentage Tables to Present a Differential

	Y	$-$		$+$		
		a. If the differential is positive				
X		$-$	Other	$+$	Total	N
T		CT	$(AT + DT)$	BT	100%	( )
NOT T		$C\bar{T}$	$(A\bar{T} + D\bar{T})$	$B\bar{T}$	100%	( )

	Y	$+$		$-$		
		b. If the differential is negative				
X		$-$	Other	$+$	Total	N
T		DT	$(BT + CT)$	AT	100%	( )
NOT T		$D\bar{T}$	$(B\bar{T} + C\bar{T})$	$A\bar{T}$	100%	( )

The Hajda data (Table 4.7), where the differential has a value of $-.48$, will serve as an illustration.

TABLE 4.7 Education, Reading, and Age

EDUCATION	YOUNGER HIGH READING	OTHER	OLDER LOWER READING	TOTAL	N
High school graduate	35%	49%	16%	100%	(1304)
Less than high school	4%	34%	61%	99%	(546)

High school graduates are more often younger high readers (35% vs. 4%) and non-high school graduates are more often older low readers (61% vs. 16%). This makes it intuitively clear that where there are educational differences there will be an excess of combinations which produce a negative correlation between age and reading.

Since the percentage table for differentials cannot be broken down to give the raw data (because of the "other" category), it should not be used if you are only going to present one percentage table. But when it is necessary to clarify an otherwise confusing set of findings, percentaged differential tables make a good supplement to the more conventional partial percentage tables.

No Effect

Region C in Figure 4.1 lies along the diagonal running from lower left to upper right. It includes those cases where the partial and zero order (and necessarily the differential) are essentially the same. In region C there is a relationship between X and Y whether T is controlled, varies, or is ignored. At first glance, this outcome seems as uninteresting as the limbo of region A. Nevertheless, it is one of the most important patterns in data analysis because there are many situations where it is as crucial to show that T does not explain XY. In particular, region C is a favorable outcome when one is testing an hypothesis without the insurance of an experimental design.

Harking back to the Introduction, we remember that the persuasiveness of an experiment rests on manipulation and randomization. In their absence we may think of the XY table as an analogy to a simple experiment, with X and NOT X standing in for the experimental and control groups. A zero-order correlation between X and Y resembles a difference between experimental and control groups on the dependent variable, Y.

A randomized experiment stops right there, because the experimenter does not have to worry about test variables.[3] Why? The answer is a little complicated, but again we will wallow in the details. The effort is justified by the importance of understanding the differences and similarities between experiments and surveys and also by a very handy rule of thumb that emerges, the *sign rule*.

Let us make the following dark assumptions: (1) The experimental conditions X have no effect on the dependent variable Y, that is, the two conditional XY correlations are zero; and (2) there is some outside variable T strongly associated with Y. The question is this: Could T produce a zero-order correlation between X and Y, a phoney favorable outcome for the experiment.

Using fictitious percentage table data, the situation might be as shown in Table 4.8, with our veteran letters A, B, C, and D representing the case bases for the percentages.

TABLE 4.8   Hypothetical Data

| | (PERCENT Y) | | |
	NOT X	X	Total
T	72%(A)	72%(B)	72% (A + B)
NOT T	45%(C)	45%(D)	45% (C + D)
Total	?	?	

Remembering that we can always calculate Q from the percentages, we ask what the percent Y will be among the total X's and what it will be among

---

[3] Those familiar with experimental design will note that the statement is somewhat of an exaggeration. An investigator may frequently go to some lengths to control certain test variables in order to make his design more efficient, i.e., to get away with using fewer cases. This, however, is a matter of technique, not basic logic.

the total *NOT X*'s. Answer: We do not know. It will depend on the frequencies for *A*, *B*, *C*, and *D*. In other words the percentages are weighted averages in which the weights are *A*, *B*, *C*, and *D*. The percentage *Y* among the *X*'s will be $(72 * B/B + D) + (45 * D/B + D)$, and among the *NOT X*'s it will be $(72 * A/A + C) + (45 * C/A + C)$.

The reason we chose these four letters is that if we removed them from the table and looked at them standing alone we would see that they are nothing more or less than the frequencies in the fourfold table for the correlation between *X* and *T*. There are three possibilities: no correlation, a positive correlation, or a negative correlation.

First, let us assume that *X* and *T* are independent. From Chapters 2 and 3 we know that the percentage *T* must be the same among the *X*'s and *NOT X*'s—which is to say that $B/B + D = A/A + C$. Aha! This means that the weights will be identical among *X*'s and *NOT X*'s, and as a consequence there will be identical results for the percentage *Y* among *X*'s and the percentage *Y* among the *NOT X*'s.

What we have shown is this: When *T* is independent of *X*, it cannot explain a zero-order correlation between *X* and *Y*. That is, if $Q_{TX} = .00$, it cannot be the case that Q_{XY} is nonnegligible while $Q_{XY:T} = Q_{XY:NOT\ T} = .00$.

And this principle, of course, explains the smug refusal of the experimentalist to worry about the test variables. When he randomizes (see the Introduction), he tends to make the correlations between *X* and any possible *T* close to zero and as a consequence he knows that there is no *T* anywhere that can explain his *XY* correlation. And the beauty of it is that he even rules out variables which he cannot measure and those which have not yet been discovered, since randomization randomizes everything!

The survey analyst has no such assurance and therefore is obliged to test each of the outside variables that constitute potential threats to his assertion that *X* and *Y* are correlated. This adds to his work and because he cannot measure all the variables in the universe, survey analysis can never have the validity of a controlled experiment.

We can take it one more step by considering the signs of the correlations. Tables 4.9 and 4.10 provide hypothetical data identical except that in Table 4.9 *TX* is positive while in Table 4.10 *TX* is negative.

While Tables 4.9 and 4.10 are identical except for the sign of Q_{TX}, their

TABLE 4.9 Hypothetical Data with a Positive Correlation Between *X* and *T* (Percent *Y*)

	NOT X	X
T	72%(20)	72%(80)
NOT T	45%(80)	45%(20)
Total	50%(100)	67%(100)

TABLE 4.10 Hypothetical Data with a Negative Correlation Between X and T (Percent Y)

	NOT X	X
T	72%(80)	72%(20)
NOT T	45%(20)	45%(80)
Total	67%(100)	50%(100)

results are opposite. In Table 4.9 there is a positive correlation between X and Y which is explained when T is controlled. In Table 4.10 there is a negative correlation between X and Y which is explained when T is controlled. You can further see that the signs of the zero order for Q_{XY} would be reversed in each case if we were to reverse the signs of the TY conditional relations in Tables 4.9 and 4.10. By flailing around with all possible combinations of signs, a special case of the famous *sign rule* emerges.

RULE 4.2a Sign Rule for Explanation

A test variable T that explains Q_{XY} must have a zero-order correlation with both X and Y. If Q_{XY} is positive, Q_{TX} and Q_{TY} must have the same sign (both positive or both negative). If Q_{XY} is negative, Q_{TX} and Q_{TY} must have opposite signs (one negative and one positive).

The principle is of some help to the survey analyst since it tells him that he need not "fear" test variables unless they are correlated with both X and Y. Occasionally investigators forget this principle and proudly announce their findings to hold in test after test after test—without showing that the test variables were related to both X and Y. In such a way, one can run up a seemingly impressive score without really grappling with important issues. The investigator is obliged, not merely to run a lot of test variables, but to run those whose pattern of zero orders suggests them to be threats to his claim that Q_{XY} is nonnegligible.

We have been talking about situations where the investigator is testing the hypothesis that X and Y are correlated and he is concerned that his finding might be phoney. What about the opposite situation where the investigator's aim is to explain Q_{XY}? Obviously he should seek potential explanatory variables that meet the sign rule. If he is explaining a positive correlation he will look for test variables with same sign correlations with X and Y; if he is explaining a negative correlation, he will look for test variables with opposite signs for Q_{TX} and Q_{TY}.

However, we are talking about a "necessary" not a "sufficient" condition. *The mere fact that a variable meets the sign rule does not imply that the partial will be lower.* Note in Table 4.9 that X is a likely candidate for explaining Q_{TY} (it has a positive correlation with T and Y), but that the partial is exactly the same as the zero order. The best we can do is the following rule of thumb:

RULE 4.2b   *Sign Rule of Thumb for Explanation*

When seeking a test variable to explain Q_{XY} the zero-order correlations should not only fit the sign rule, but, generally speaking, Q_{TX} and Q_{TY} should be stronger than Q_{XY}.

Hadja's success in explaining the relationship between age and reading becomes more understandable when we note that his zero-order relationship is $-.24$ for age and reading while the zero orders involving T are $-.62$ (education and age) and $+.76$ (education and reading).

Suppressor Variables

Region D in Figure 4.1 locates those outcomes where the partial is even stronger than the zero order or is opposite in sign. That is, when T is controlled, the relationship between X and Y does not vanish; it either swells or changes its sign. In either event, one views T as masking the "true" relationship, which only appears when T is controlled. Thus, when the outcome is in the D region, we call T a "suppressor variable."

Sex is often a suppressor variable in sociological research. More data from the 1960 census are given in Table 4.11. They are from the published census tables, not the sample used in the previous examples, and are rounded to the nearest hundred thousand. All the zero-order relationships are highly significant, as they almost always are in extremely large samples.

TABLE 4.11   Sex, Occupation, and Earnings in 1959 Among Employed Persons (frequencies rounded to the nearest one hundred thousand)

SEX	OCCUPATION	EARNINGS	
		UNDER $4000	$4000 OR MORE
Male	White collar	58	93
	Blue collar and farm	175	97
Female	White collar	95	13
	Blue collar and farm	81	2
			Total = 614

The zero-order $Q_{\text{occupation, earnings}} = +.28$, a low positive association. (Confidence limits are not reported since the frequencies in the data are artificially shrunken.) However, when sex is controlled, the equation has the following value:

$$\text{Occupation, earnings} = (\text{partial} * W1) + (\text{differential} * W2)$$

$$+.28 = (+.50 \quad * \quad .55) \quad + (+.02 \quad * \quad .45)$$

Among earners of the same sex (55% of the pairs differing on occupation and income) there is a substantial positive association, $+.50$. Thus, sex is operating as a suppressor variable, and unless it is controlled, we get an "unrealistically low" estimate of the correlation between occupation and earnings.

Suppressor variables were implicit in our discussion of the sign rule and the rule can be extended as follows:

S I G N   R U L E   4.2c   *Sign Rule for a Suppressor Variable*

When T raises a positive XY correlation, it must have opposite-sign zero-order correlations with X and Y.

When T strengthens a negative XY correlation, it must have same-sign (both positive or both negative) zero-order correlations with X and Y.

When T reverses the sign of a correlation, the sign rule conditions for explanations must hold.

Again the rule states a necessary but not sufficient condition. When one is searching for suppressor variables, the best advice is this.

S I G N   R U L E   4.2d   *Sign Rule of Thumb for a Suppressor Variable*

If you "want to make" the XY correlation more positive (or reverse a negative correlation), seek a test variable where TX and TY have opposite signs and both are of greater magnitude than XY.

If you "want to make" the XY correlation more negative (or reverse a positive correlation), seek a test variable where TX and TY have the same sign (both positive or both negative) and both are of greater magnitude than XY.

In the case of sex, earnings, and occupation, we have a positive zero order for sex and occupation and the T correlations are opposite in sign. Sex and earnings have a positive correlation ($Q = +.81$) while sex and occupation have a negative one ($Q = -.40$). Thus Rule 4.2c applies. If this appears mysterious, remember that a secretary has a white collar occupation with relatively low earnings.

Suppressor variables are relatively rare in day-to-day sociological research but are well worth remembering. In particular, when one is testing the hypothesis that X and Y are correlated and finds that the zero-order results do not support the hypothesis, it is always possible that some T has been operating as a suppressor variable, and when it is controlled, the hypothesis will come flying home. Again, however, one must seek test variables with particular patterns of TX and TY signs, and again, the T correlations have to be quite high before controlling T has any practical impact on the partial.

Region E: The Twilight Zone

There remains one area, region E, indicated by the shaded portions of Figure 4.1. Here lie those cases where the zero-order correlation is nonnegligible, the partial is nonnegligible, and the partial is less than the zero order. These are the situations which hover between explanation and lack of explanation.

Though this is a very common outcome in social research, it has no neat label. The situation has an "Is the glass half full or is it half empty?" air to it. On the one hand, one may argue that T goes some distance toward explaining XY since it is undeniable that we can lessen the value of Q_{XY} by controlling for T. It is equally undeniable that T cannot account for the XY relationship since, even after T has been controlled, there is a nonnegligible relationship between X and Y.

The situation is further complicated when T is collapsed from a larger set of ordinal, interval, or ratio categories. Consider, for example, dichotomizing years of schooling at high school vs. non-high school. When we calculate some XY relationship within these two categories, it is easy to say that we have "controlled education," but obviously we have not. Within each of our groups there are lots of differences in education roaming around quite uncontrolled. What we have done is to control the biggest differences in education (e.g., Ph.D.'s vs. no school at all, M.A.'s vs. first grade only, etc.) along with some of the smaller differences near the cutting point (e.g., eleventh grade vs. 1 year of college). It is thus possible that differences in education *within* our control categories are sufficient to account for the remaining XY relationship in the partial.

This leads to another perspective on the equation, which may be seen as values of Q_{XY} for groups which vary in the amount of T difference. In the differential we have those pairs with the biggest difference in T, in the partial we have those pairs with the least difference in T, and in the zero order we have pairs with an in-between level of T differences. A result in the twilight zone may be thought of as something like this, assuming, for example, that

$$Q_{XY} = +.40, \; Q_{XY:\text{TIED }T} = +.22 \text{ and } Q_{XY:\text{DIFF }T} = +.64$$

We see from Figure 4.2 that the less the level of T difference, the lower is Q_{XY}. Our temptation is to extrapolate (indicated by the dotted line) and claim that if we controlled T more finely, the value of Q_{XY} would equal zero. However, the scale for "level of T" is quite arbitrary (i.e., ordinal) and we can make the outcome of any extrapolation look better or worse, depending on where we choose to locate "high," "medium," and "low" in the horizontal scale.

Frequently, we can actually refine T further and see what happens. All we need to do is this:

1. Divide T into as many levels as we can.
2. Lay out the fourfold table for X and Y within each of these levels.
3. Calculate the cross products in each of the new tables.

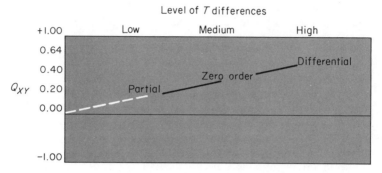

FIG. 4.2   Schematic notion of multivariate analysis as a correlation between level of T differences and value of Q_{XY}.

4. Sum all the $(B * C)$ cross products to give a super $(B * C)$.

5. Sum all the $(A * D)$ cross products to give a super $(A * D)$.

6. Calculate a new partial Q from the super $(B * C)$ and $(A * D)$.

If the new, more fully refined partial is negligible, we may say that T can explain XY when controlled sufficiently; if the new partial is equal or greater than the old partial, we may infer that T cannot explain XY even when further refined; but if the new partial is still in region E, we are back where we started from. This leads to a rule.

RULE 4.3

If a test variable reduces the zero-order correlation but the partial is still nonnegligible, test to see whether a partial Q calculated among finer groupings of T will lead to a negligible partial.

Whether a given finding merits such attention is left to the judgment of the investigator.

We end the dicussion of outcome regions by stating the most general form of the sign rule:

RULE 4.2   *The Sign Rule*

To predict the sign of "D minus P" (the value of the differential minus the value of the partial), multiply the signs of TX and TY.

Thus, if TX is positive and TY is negative, we predict that the differential will be less positive (more negative) then the partial because $(+ * - = -)$; if either TX or TY are zero or negligible, we predict that the partial and differential are the same $(+ * 0 = 0)$; if both TX and TY are positive, we predict that the differential will be more positive (less negative) than the partial $(+ * + = +)$.

Specification

Specification is an additional outcome of three-variable analysis, but one which does not appear in Figure 4.1. It is a new facet, which has been kept under covers until this point.

It all stems from a point which turned up when we were talking about the sign rule. $Q_{XY:\text{TIED } T}$ combines the results from two different conditional tables which do not necessarily have identical values of Q when calculated separately. In other words, the partial coefficient is a weighted average of the two conditional coefficients, just as the zero order is a weighted average of the partial and the differential.

The multivariate equation can be rewritten to show this:

$$Q_{XY} = (Q_{XY:T} * W1a) + (Q_{XY:NOT\,T} * W1b) + (Q_{XY:\text{DIFF}\,T} * W2)$$

where $W1a$ is the proportion of pairs differing on X and Y that are both $T =$

$$\frac{(BT * CT) + (AT * DT)}{(BT + B\bar{T}) * (CT + C\bar{T}) + (AT + A\bar{T}) * (DT + D\bar{T})}$$

and where $W1b$ is the proportion of pairs differing on X and Y that are both $NOT\ T =$

$$\frac{(B\bar{T} * C\bar{T}) + (A\bar{T} * D\bar{T})}{(BT + B\bar{T}) * (CT + C\bar{T}) + (AT + A\bar{T}) * (DT + D\bar{T})}$$

The weights $W1a$ and $W1b$ add up to the old $W1$, and "the partial" is seen as a weighted average of the two conditionals where the weights are pair proportions as usual.

There is no mathematical reason these two conditional Q's should be identical or even similar, no reason $Q_{XY:T}$ cannot be $+1.00$ and $Q_{XY:NOT\,T}$ -1.00, though substantial differences are not common.

A substantial difference in the conditional relationships is called a *specification* since T serves to specify the conditions under which Q_{XY} will be higher or lower. Occasionally, when one of the conditional Q's is .00 and the other is nonnegligible, we may say that T (or strictly speaking, the level of T) specifies whether or not there will be any XY relationship.

Specifications are tricky to handle, and you should note the following:

First, specifications may or may not fit in with analysis in terms of outcome regions. If both conditionals are higher than the zero order, but quite different, one may say that T is a suppressor variable and a specifier; if one conditional is higher than the zero order and the other lower while the partial is close to the zero order, we may say that T serves to specify but not otherwise affect the relationship. However, other situations may occur where, for example, one conditional is substantially positive and the other is substantially negative. Such outcomes just do not fit neatly into the explanation–no-explanation–suppressor package, and in your interpretation you may have to abandon the framework of outcome regions.

Students frequently confuse "specification" and "suppression." Make sure you understand the difference, remembering that specification involves a difference between conditional relationships while suppression is a general accentuation or reversal of a correlation.

Second, beware of specifications where T is highly skewed. If, for instance, the marginal for T is 90:10, the average level of T differences is much higher in the larger category than the smaller. If then one observes a difference in Q_{XY}, it may stem from uneven control rather than a true specification process. Within the 70:30 cut rule this is not a serious problem, but other investigators may not have read this book. There is no correction you can make for this possibility, but when you encounter a specification where T is highly skewed, take the results with a grain of salt.

Third, when you work with conditional tables, your sample sizes are reduced considerably. Make sure that each of your conditional tables meets the cell expectation standards of Chapter 2 before you take them seriously.

Fourth, there is no useful sign rule for specifications, no pattern of zero-order relationships which suggests that a specification will occur. However, there is always a possibility where Q_{XY} equals zero, since this might stem from a situation where one conditional is a high positive, the other is a high negative, and the differential is zero. Such "pure" specifications, however, are rare.

Fifth and most important, always consider sampling variation as the source of a specification. If we draw any two subsets of cases from our data (for example, cases whose middle names have odd and even numbers of letters) and calculate Q_{XY} in each, the inevitable variation of samples around the true universe value almost guarantees that we will not get identical coefficients. Just as statisticians can calculate the likelihood for various Q's when the true Q is zero, they can calculate the frequency for drawing different Q's when sampling from populations where the Q's are identical.

Again there is a procedure for statistical inference,[4] and again we will not explain it in detail. Rather we give you a formula:

Chi square $=$

$$\frac{(Q_T - Q_{NOT\,T})^2}{\left[\dfrac{(1.00 - Q^2_{XY:T})^2\left(\dfrac{1}{AT} + \dfrac{1}{BT} + \dfrac{1}{CT} + \dfrac{1}{DT}\right)}{4}\right] + \left[\dfrac{(1.00 - Q^2_{XY:NOT\,T})^2\left(\dfrac{1}{A\bar{T}} + \dfrac{1}{B\bar{T}} + \dfrac{1}{C\bar{T}} + \dfrac{1}{D\bar{T}}\right)}{4}\right]}$$

[4] Leo Goodman, "On the Multivariate Analysis of Three Dichotomous Variables," *American Journal of Sociology*, 1965, *71*, p. 291.

You will note that the formulas in the denominator are the same as those used in calculating the confidence limits for zero-order Q's, and without going into detail you can appreciate that the larger the confidence interval for each conditional Q, the less likely we are to have much faith in any difference we observe in our sample.

The result of solving the formula is a statistic called "chi square," and for present purposes, all we need to say is this:

If chi square is greater than 5.00, we may have the same confidence in our specification that we set for our zero-order correlation, i.e., chi square will exceed 5.00 less than .025 times in SRS samplings of this size from universes where both Q's are identical.

If chi square is less than 5.00 we may say that the difference is "not significant" and sampling error cannot be ruled out as the source of the difference.

We warn you that it takes a rather whopping difference in the conditional Q's and hefty sample sizes to meet these criteria. This makes common sense because with two coefficients, both are subject to sampling error and each is based on a smaller sample size. Thus when examining a difference between Q's we have a double source of error and less protection against it from sample size. The consequence is that we require a very large difference because it is based on more dubious evidence.

R U L E 4.4

Before you claim to have found a specification, make sure that (1) the conditional Q's differ by 10 units, (2) the difference is statistically significant, and (3) both conditional tables meet the standards for expected cell frequencies. Even then be wary of the finding if T is highly skewed.

It is not our aim to dissuade you from seeking specifications, which can be most interesting and suggestive. However, we do warn you that they are a more delicate and complex statistical property and you should avoid the temptation to shout "Eureka" every time you see some minor difference in the two conditional Q's.

When X, Y, and T are assigned to the three variables ahead of time, it is fairly easy to interpret a significant specification. The general formula is "Among the T's the XY correlation is____, but among the NOT T's the XY correlation is____." When, however, one is fishing around with sets of variables, verbal translations are often very difficult. Generally speaking, you will find that whenever T specifies XY, X will specify TY and Y will specify TX. This is because a specification is really a three-way "interaction" among the variables. The best way to proceed is with percentage tables, like Table

4.4. Here is an example, with data reanalyzed from a 1954 national survey.[5] The variables are

$Y =$ presidential preference in the 1952 election ($+$ = Eisenhower, $-$ = Stevenson)

$X =$ political party identification ($+$ = Republican, $-$ = Democrat)

$T =$ region ($+$ = South, $-$ = all other)

The raw data are shown in Table 4.12.

TABLE 4.12 Raw Data from Stouffer Survey

	PREFERENCE	
PARTY AND REGION	STEVENSON	EISENHOWER
Republican		
South	26	231
Other	26	1061
Democratic		
South	505	327
Other	930	297
	N = 3403	
	Other and NA = 1530	
	4933	

The relevant calculations are given in Table 4.13.

TABLE 4.13 Coefficients for Data in Table 4.12

	PARTY AND PREFERENCE	PARTY AND REGION	REGION AND PREFERENCE
Zero order	+.97	−.48	−.15
Conditional			
Third item +	+.86	−.67	+.34
Third item −	+.98	−.30	−.64
Chi square	18.626	53.230	107.789

All three chi square values exceed 5.00 so we have a triple specification. To begin we pick one item as Y, the dependent variable in the table. Intuition suggests that preference for president is the best. Then we lay out a percentage table, as shown in Table 4.14.

[5] The data are from Samuel A. Stouffer, *Communism, Conformity and Civil Liberties*, Doubleday, New York, 1955, reanalyzed from copies of the raw data on file in the data bank of the Dartmouth College Department of Sociology. Robert Dryfoos brought the example to the author's attention.

TABLE 4.14   Data in Table 4.12 in Percentage Form

	DEMOCRATS	REPUBLICANS	Q
South	39%(832)	90%(257)	+.86
Other	24%(1227)	98%(1087)	+.98
Q	+.34	−.64	

Table 4.14 can be read across the rows or down the columns. Interpreting across rows we can say "Party affects preference less in the South than in other regions." Reading down the columns we may say, "Among Democrats, Southerners were more likely to vote for Eisenhower, while among Republicans Southerners were less likely to vote for Eisenhower." You are free to choose the interpretation that seems more plausible.

Another way to view such a table is in terms of one cell percentage that seems "out of line." From a statistical point of view, there is no way to know which of the four cells is aberrant (we could make the specification disappear by changing any one of the cell percentages), but from our commonsense knowledge of politics, the 39% for Southern Democrats is a likely candidate. If it were lower, the Q of $+.86$ might rise to $+.98$ and the Q of $+.34$ might decline to $−.64$. Thus an alternative way to interpret our triple specification (and remember that most specifications will be triples) is that Southern Democrats had a special attraction to Eisenhower.

In this example, as is often the case, there is no clear-cut choice among the three alternatives, but percentage tables are the best way to gain a purchase on these complex patterns, even though you may have to percentage the data three ways (assigning each variable to Y in turn) before you find a sensible framework.

To summarize:

R U L E 4.5

To interpret a three-way specification, arrange the data in a percentage table and seek a plausible statement in terms of (1) column differences in a row correlation, (2) row differences in a column correlation, or (3) a particular cell with an especially high or low percentage.

Some Rules of Thumb

Real data have the disconcerting tendency of avoiding the neat extremes so elegantly defined by Kendall and Lazarsfeld, and the practicing research worker usually finds that his data are quite "iffy." Again, we propose some rules so that your decisions, if arbitrary, at least will be consistent. To the extent that there is any principle at work, it is simply a repetition of our previous arbitrary rule that differences of less than 10 points on the scale of Q should be considered negligible.

R U L E 4.6   *Rule of Thumb, D minus P*

If the difference between the partial and the differential is less than 10 points on the Q scale, treat the data as falling in regions A or C, depending on the value of the zero order.

If there is a difference of 10 points or more:

a)   You may say that T explains XY if the partial is negligible and the zero order is nonnegligible.

b)   Otherwise assign the results to region D or E depending on the values of the coefficients. If the results lie in region E, consult Rule 4.3.

IN A NUTSHELL

A. The multivariate formula:

1. With three variables, any one of the zero orders can be decomposed into two Q's, one among pairs tied on T (a partial) and one among pairs differing on T (a differential).
2. The zero-order coefficient is a weighted average of these two Q's where the weights are pair proportions.
3. The partial coefficient, in turn, is a weighted average of two conditional Q's.

B. Possible outcomes of interest to the research worker:

1. Explanation
2. No effect
3. T as a suppressor variable
4. The "twilight zone"
5. Specification

Rules

R U L E 4.1

If we observe a nonnegligible zero-order association between X and Y, we say that T explains the relationship if $Q_{XY\,:\,\text{TIED}\ T}$ is negligible or zero.

R U L E 4.2   *The Sign Rule*

To predict the sign of "D minus P" (the value of the differential minus the value of the partial), multiply the signs of TX and TY.

4.2a   *Sign Rule for Explanation*   A test variable T that explains Q_{XY} must have a zero-order correlation with both X and Y.

If Q_{XY} is positive, Q_{TX} and Q_{TY} must have the same sign (both positive or both negative).

If Q_{XY} is negative, Q_{TX} and Q_{TY} must have opposite signs (one negative and one positive).

4.2b *Sign Rule of Thumb for Explanation*   When seeking a test variable to explain Q_{XY}, the zero-order correlations should not only fit the sign rule, but, generally speaking, Q_{TX} and Q_{TY} should be stronger than Q_{XY}.

4.2c *Sign Rule for a Suppressor Variable*   When T raises a positive XY correlation, it must have opposite-sign zero-order correlations with X and Y.

When T strengthens a negative XY correlation, it must have same-sign (both positive or both negative) zero-order correlations with X and Y.

When T reverses the sign of a correlation, the sign rule conditions for explanations must hold.

4.2d *Sign Rule of Thumb for a Suppressor Variable*   If you "want to make" the XY correlation more positive (or reverse a negative correlation) seek a test variable where TX and TY have opposite signs and both are of greater magnitude than XY.

If you "want to make" the XY correlation more negative (or reverse a positive correlation), seek a test variable where TX and TY have the same sign (both positive or both negative) and both are of greater magnitude than XY.

RULE 4.3

If a test variable reduces the zero-order correlation but the partial is still nonnegligible, test to see whether a partial Q calculated among finer groupings of T will lead to a negligible partial.

Whether a given finding merits such attention is left to the judgment of the investigator.

RULE 4.4

Before you claim to have found a specification, make sure that (1) the conditional Q's differ by 10 units, (2) the difference is statistically significant, and (3) both conditional tables meet the standards for expected cell frequencies. Even then be wary of the finding if T is highly skewed.

RULE 4.5

To interpret a three-way specification, arrange the data in a percentage table and seek a plausible statement in terms of (1) column differences in a row correlation, (2) row differences in a column correlation, or (3) a particular cell with an especially high or low percentage.

RULE 4.6   *Rule of Thumb, D minus P*

If the difference between the partial and the differential is less than 10 points on the Q scale, treat the data as falling in regions A or C, depending on the value of the zero order.

If there is a difference of 10 points or more:

   a)   You may say that T explains XY if the partial is negligible and the zero order is nonnegligible.

   b)   Otherwise, assign the results to region D or E depending on the values of the coefficients. If the results lie in region E, consult Rule 4.4.

Major Concepts

1. Conditional tables
2. Differential coefficient
3. Explanation
4. Partial coefficient
5. Refining a test variable

6. Sign rule
7. Specification
8. Suppressor variable
9. Test variable
10. Zero-order coefficient

5

Three Variables:
Causal Systems

An Overview

With three variables it is usually more rewarding to examine all three at once rather than looking at one relationship as affected by a third variable. Although it is impossible to classify all the possible outcomes as we could in Chapter 4, the notion of "causal models" helps to pull things together.

Causal models are assertions (hypotheses) about the presence, sign, and direction of influence for relations among *all* pairs of variables in a set. They may be represented by diagrams like the ones here.

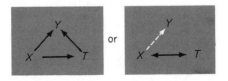

With a particular causal model one can make specific predictions about the statistical results when partials and differentials are calculated for all three relationships. These stem from three rules about (1) partials, (2) the difference between the differential and partial (called $D - P$), and (3) a special rule for certain models where one of the variables is a consequence of the other two.

There are a large number of possible models for three variables since any one of the three sides can have a positive, negative, or zero causal relationship and nonzero relationships can be mutual or asymmetrical. Nevertheless, it is possible to classify the possibilities into meaningful groups, organized according to the number of nonzero causal assertions—0, 1, 2, 3.

Reviewing the various causal models helps the investigator know what he should look for in his data and helps to build a bridge between sociological theory and sociological research.

In Chapter 4 we extracted three coefficients, Q_{XY}, $Q_{XY:\text{TIED } T}$, and $Q_{XY:\text{DIFF } T}$, from the eightfold table. To some readers that may seem a surfeit, but it is merely a beginning because an eightfold table is a cornucopia of coefficients. There are at least six more which have been ignored, the zero orders, partials, and differentials for TX and TY.

From a mathematical point of view, the axes in Figure 4.1 are two dimensions in a six-dimensional space which contains all possible *combinations* of outcomes for XY, XT, and TY. Alas, no successor to Kendall and Lazarsfeld has come along to define meaningful regions within the six-dimensional space, and the problem is further complicated by logical interlockings among the possibilities. While for two variables, any value of the partial can occur with any value of the zero order, the results for XY are not independent of the results for XT and TY. The mathematical principles have not been worked out (to the author's knowledge), but it is reasonable to assume that certain combinations of outcomes just cannot occur. The algebraic tools for handling this problem have been provided in the previous chapters, and any reader who wishes to attack it is invited to become coauthor of the revised edition of this treatise.

But life must go on and in this chapter we will discuss *selected* outcome combinations for three variables, those which give operational meaning to common causal models in sociology.

By a causal model we mean assumptions about the existence, sign, and direction of causal relations among variables. By causal relation, we mean this: Two variables have a causal relationship when a reordering of cases on one would be followed by a reordering on the other. For example, the hypothesis that social class causes political ideologies means that if we were to shuffle people around so that their relative class positions were reversed, their relative standing on various political dimensions would tend to reverse. In the absence of a randomized experiment it is impossible to "prove" such causal propositions, but we often can determine whether the data are consistent with our causal model. If not, the model lacks credibility. If the data are consistent, the model gains credibility. *Consistent results are not proof though,* for the argument "*A* implies *B*, *B* is true, therefore *A* is true" is not valid in logic. However, all of science is built on such arguments, and sociology is no exception.

For three variables, the models may be represented by triangles with lines connecting the pairs of variables. The lines may have single or double arrowheads, depending on one's assumption about causal direction. Conventionally, positive relationships are indicated by solid lines, negative relationships by dashed lines, and negligible relationships by no line at all. If, for example, we assume that there is a positive relationship between a father's income and his son's education and that the former influences the latter, but not vice versa, we would draw it as shown in Figure 5.1.

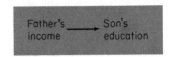

FIG. 5.1

If we wish to be mildly pretentious, we can say that Figure 5.1 defines a two-variable causal model. We can put the model to a very simple test: if the variables are connected by a line, they should have a nonnegligible zero-order correlation; if not, the zero order should be negligible. Thus, if we find a positive correlation between father's income and son's education we could proudly report that the evidence tends to support the causal model in Figure 5.1.

Two-variable models are really trivial statistically, but they provide a base line for the more complicated properties of larger models involving three or more variables.

Obviously we can draw a considerable number of three-variable models by varying the signs and directions of the causal assertions. The trick is to find out whether the data support our predictions. To test the models we need operational rules to link them to the properties of data. In the case of three variables, it boils down to three rules.

The first rule involves partials and differentials, and in particular, whether they are equal, the partial is greater, or the differential is greater. For convenience we will call the value of the difference obtained when the partial is subtracted from the differential $D - P$ (See Rule 4.6). The rule is

R U L E 5.1

For all pairs of variables, the sign of $D - P$ is the product obtained by multiplying the signs of the causal relations involving the third variable.

The rule, which is closely related to the *sign rule* (Rule 4.2) in Chapter 4, will be explained and illustated as we consider various specific models. For now, let us merely illustrate (Figure 5.2) the process. Beginning with XY we observe that T has a positive relationship with X and a negative relationship with Y. Hence the product, $+ * -$, is negative. We predict that D minus P will be negative; i.e., the differential for XY, controlling T, will be less than the partial. For the second pair, XT, we obtain the same result. For TY, the third pair, both relations involving X are positive, and their product, $+ * +$, is positive. We predict that $D - P$ will be positive; i.e., the differential for TY controlling X will exceed the partial.

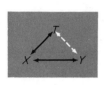

FIG. 5.2

The second rule is this:

R U L E 5.2

The partial for each pair of variables should have the sign of the causal assertion in the model, except when there is a pair of one-way arrows running into the test variable.

The third rule covers the exception to Rule 5.2:

R U L E 5.3

When there are two one-way arrows running into the test variable, delete the test variable when predicting the relationship between the other two.

We will explain both rules in the context of specific examples. For now, we merely note that in Figure 5.2 none of the variables has a one-way relationship, so Rule 5.2 applies, not Rule 5.3. We would predict the partials for TX and XY to be positive and the partial for TY to be negative.

With a little practice you can use these rules to predict the statistical properties for any three-variable model, and in Chapter 6 we will see that they may be extended to cover models with four or more variables. However, it is useful to classify the possibilities, and the best way seems to be in terms of the number of sides which have a positive or negative (nonzero) line. Obviously the possibilities are zero, one, two, and three.

Type 0, Complete Independence

A model with zero causal assertions would look like Figure 5.3. It is not the most interesting sociological analysis that ever came down the pike, but it will get us off to a start.

FIG. 5.3

Since there are no causal assertions, there cannot be any variables that receive two one-way arrows; hence, Rule 5.3 may be ignored.

Because all three legs are zero and zero times zero is zero, the prediction is that $D = P$ for all three relationships, and the prediction for the partials (Rule 5.2) is that they are all zero. In other words, we are predicting that none of the three pairs of variables has a nonnegligible relationship, whether the third variable is controlled, varied, or ignored.

We may summarize this inauspicious start as follows:

Type 0: A model with no causal assertions gains credibility when all of the partials are negligible, and $D - P$ is within 10 units on the Q scale for all three multivariate analyses.

Type I: A Single Relationship

Type I models, with only one causal assertion, are somewhat more interesting than type 0, but not much.

Let us begin with a silly model involving three variables: (1) reading conservative vs. liberal magazines, (2) holding conservative vs. liberal opinions, and (3) attitudes toward dill pickles. Ignoring the fact that the variables are badly defined by the standards of Chapter 1, let us consider the causal relations among them. Our model (yours might be different) goes like this:

Magazine reading and political opinions have a mutual causal relation. Attitudes toward dill pickles have no causal relation with magazine reading.

Attitudes toward dill pickles have no causal relation with political opinions.

We are asserting that if one could change orderings on magazine reading, political opinions would tend to come into line; if one could switch people's political opinions, their magazine reading differences would switch; if one changed magazine reading or opinions, ranks on favorableness toward dill pickles would remain the same; and if one could rearrange people on the dill pickle scale, no rearrangments would take place in politics or magazine reading.

The diagram for our causal model is shown in Figure 5.4. If we were to measure the three variables in some appropriate sample, how should the results come out? Again, Rule 5.3 cannot apply because there is no variable that receives two one-way arrows.

FIG. 5.4

Since two of the legs are zero, all of the products implied by Rule 5.1 will be zero. For prose and politics it is $0 * 0 = 0$; for pickles and prose it is $+ * 0 = 0$, and for pickles and politics it is $+ * 0 = 0$. For the partials we predict that one of them, prose and politics, will be positive and the other two will be zero. Remembering that when $D = P$ the zero order must have the same sign and value as the partial, we can say that prose and politics should have a positive zero-order correlation that will be unaffected when pickles is introduced as a test variable, while the other two relations will have negligible zero orders that are unaffected when the third variable is introduced as a control.

To summarize:

> Type: I: A model with a single causal assertion gains credibility when one of the partials is nonnegligible and $D - P$ is within 10 units on the Q scale for all three multivariate analyses.

Type II: Two Causal Assertions

With two-assertion models things begin to become interesting, since unlike types 0 and I, type II forms a true causal system in which all three of the variables are related directly or indirectly. Here the question of Rule 5.2 vs. Rule 5.3 emerges for the first time. Let us, however, begin with a hypothetical situation where Rule 5.3 does not apply.

We can change Figure 5.4 into a type II model by sending pickles back to the bench and substituting party preference.[1] We make the following assumptions:

> There is a mutual causal relationship between party preference (Republican) and politics (Conservative).
>
> There is no (direct) causal relationship between magazine reading and party preference.

Our new diagram looks like the one shown in Figure 5.5, or, if you prefer, like the one in Figure 5.6. Let's predict! For prose and politics, the dogleg involving party has a product of zero $(+ * 0 = 0)$; hence $D - P = 0$. But the model predicts a positive partial. From the equation it follows that the zero order will be positive and the same as the partial and differential in magnitude.

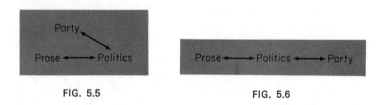

FIG. 5.5   FIG. 5.6

[1] We are quite aware that *liberal* and *conservative* are almost meaningless and that party preferences are complex and changing. The example is chosen to illustrate a technique, not as a contribution to the theory of political behavior.

For party and politics, the situation is exactly the same, and the prediction is a positive partial correlation, equal to the zero order, which is unaffected when prose is introduced as a control.

The case of party and prose is different. Here the dogleg has a positive sign ($+ * + = +$), even though the partial is expected to be zero. We expect a partial of zero and a differential which is positive. As a consequence, there will be a positive zero-order correlation between party and prose since the equation tells us that the zero order will be the weighted average of a positive Q and a negligible one.

You can see that if we were examining party and prose using the concepts of Chapter 4 we would say that politics explains the correlation between party and prose. In general, it is two-relationship models like Figure 5.5 which produce explanations and the example makes clear why the sign rule is only a rule of thumb. We would get a positive product for all these pairs when we multiply the signs of *zero orders* following the sign rule, but in only one of them, prose and party, would the partial differ from the zero order. In other words, the sign rule should be considered a necessary, not a sufficient, condition. You can also see why we advised you to seek test variables which have stronger relations with X and Y than the XY zero order. In causal models like Figure 5.5, the zero order which vanishes will usually be quite weak since it is "diluted" by the vanishing partial, the entire relationship being produced by the differential Q.

In the example we assumed positive correlations for the causal relations, but they may be positive or negative. If both are negative, their product will be positive and so will the zero order for the variables linked indirectly. The situation is equivalent to merely reversing the labels for "high" and "low" in the test variable. That is, if we shifted the meaning of high and low for politics, both causal assertions would be negative—but obviously the result would be identical. If, however, the test variable has opposite signs for its two assertions, there will be a negative zero order for the two indirectly linked variables.

Here is an example, with real data from a survey of an introductory sociology class at Dartmouth College in the spring of 1968. The survey dealt with kinship and the students were asked to rate their relationships with their aunts and uncles on three scales:

X: Proximity ($+$ = lives in same community or within 100 miles of hometown; $-$ = lives 100 miles or more from home town)

Y: Sentiment ($+$ = I feel personally close to this person; $-$ = I do not feel personally close to this person)

T: Interaction ($+$ = visits, gift exchange, correspondence, etc., two or more times a year; $-$ = less than two times a year)

Following the theories of George Homans, we may advance this causal model in Figure 5.7[2] The model asserts a mutual positive correlation between interaction and sentiment (people will get in touch with relatives they like and come to like those relatives with whom they keep in touch) but no direct causal link between proximity and sentiment (sheer distance from relatives is unrelated to sentiment unless proximity stimulates interaction). It further asserts that there is a one-way relationship between proximity and interaction (one tends to have contact with relatives who live near, but one does not tend to relocate near those relatives with whom one is in contact).

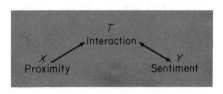

FIG. 5.7

We have about run out of cases where we can avoid Rule 5.3, but this one is safe so let us consider our predictions from Rules 5.1 and 5.2.

If the model is correct, we predict (1) the partial for XT will be positive and $D - P$ will be negligible, (2) the partial for TY will be positive and $D - P$ will be negligible, and (3) the partial for XY will be negligible and $D - P$ will be positive.

The 65 students in the class reported data on 211 aunts and uncles, as shown in Table 5.1.

TABLE 5.1　Raw Data on Sentiment, Proximity, Interaction

PROXIMITY (X)	INTERACTION (T)	SENTIMENT (Y) −	+
+	+	29	49
+	−	13	0
−	+	17	21
−	−	68	14
		$N = 211$	

The zero orders are given in Table 5.2.

TABLE 5.2　Zero-Order Correlations in Table 5.1

	LOWER LIMIT	SAMPLE VALUE	UPPER LIMIT
Sentiment and interaction	+.67	+.80	+.92
Proximity and interaction	+.76	+.86	+.95
Proximity and sentiment	+.26	+.48	+.70

[2] George Homans, *The Human Group*, Harcourt, New York, 1950.

All three are positive, and since the lower limits are all positive, all three are statistically significant.

Next, the partials and differentials (Table 5.3).

TABLE 5.3 Partials and Differentials in Table 5.1

RELATIONSHIP	CONTROLLING	PARTIAL	DIFFERENTIAL	$D - P$
Sentiment and interaction	Proximity	+.79	+.80	+.01
Proximity and interaction	Sentiment	+.85	+.86	+.01
Proximity and sentiment	Interaction	+.03	+.66	+.63

The data, as examples in textbooks often do, lend support to the model. The partial for XT, $+.85$, is positive and $D - P$ is a negligible $+.01$. The partial for TY, $+.79$, is positive, and $D - P$ is a negligible $+.01$. The partial for XY, $+.03$, is negligible and $D - P$ is a nonnegligible $+.63$.

Figures 5.5 and 5.7 contain one or two mutual relationships, but we also should look at two-assertion models where both assertions are nonmutual (asymmetric, directed, one-way, etc.). The possibilities are given in Figure 5.8, calling the middle variable T.

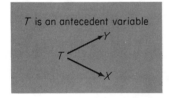

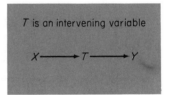

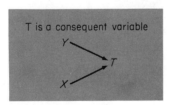

FIG. 5.8 Two-assertion models with asymmetrical relationships.

When T affects X and T affects Y, T is called an *antecedent variable* because it precedes X and Y in a causal sequence. When T is in the middle, it is called an *intervening variable*. From a statistical point of view, the predictions are the same for both and the same as our two previous two-assertion models. We predict three zero orders, one of which will vanish and two of which will be unaffected.

You will note that for type II models (1) models with one or two mutual relations, (2) models with an antecedent variable, and (3) models with an intervening variable all give the same statistical predictions. Consequently, there is no way we can detect a difference between them from the data in our eightfold table. Traditionally, however, the XY relationship in the case of an antecedent variable has been called spurious. Good, clean examples are hard to come by, but Kendall and Lazarsfeld offer a famous hypothetical one. They say that there is a spurious correlation between the number of fire engines at a fire and the damage done. The model asserts that the size of the fire is an antecedent variable and when it is controlled the correlation will vanish—big fires cause more damage and attract more fire engines. The concept of spurious correlation is a useful one and you will run into it repeatedly in sociology. However, you should remember this: It is not the correlation which is spurious (there probably is a demonstrable, palpable, significant correlation between fire engines and fire damage); it is the implicit causal model which is spurious, and we have no operational way to distinguish where XY is spurious and where it is not.

Hajda's data (Figure 5.9) are a good example of a model with an intervening variable. Table 5.4 shows that the Hajda data fit the predictions nicely.

FIG. 5.9

TABLE 5.4 Complete Analysis of the Data in Table 4.3

VARIABLES	ZERO ORDER	CONTROLLING THIRD VARIABLE PARTIAL	CONTROLLING THIRD VARIABLE DIFFERENTIAL	$D - P$
Age and reading	−.24	−.01	−.48	−.47
Age and education	−.62	−.62	−.62	.00
Education and reading	+.76	+.76	+.76	.00

Granted that the difference is intuitive rather than statistical, you will probably not feel that the correlation between age and reading is phony in the way the fire engine–fire damage relationship is, even though both partials vanish. With an intervening variable we feel that the antecedent and consequent variables do have a causal relationship, an indirect one through the intervening variable. This is a prime example of explanation, for an intervening variable explains how the other two are linked.

Now Rule 5.3! Take a good look at the bottom diagram in Figure 5.8. At first glance, it looks like the other two-assertion diagrams, but it has an important difference. There is no way to "get from" X to Y following the arrows, no way to get from Y to X following the arrows, and no way to get from T to both X and Y following the arrows. Consequently, there is no way to deduce any causal connection between X and Y from the model. To repeat in slightly different terms, any argument about the XY correlation from a causal model amounts to tracing a path from X to Y ("X affects Y" or "X affects T which affects Y") or Y to X ("Y affects X" or "Y affects T which affects X") or from the third variable to both ("T affects X and T also affects Y") following routes defined by the arrows. When T is a consequent variable, no such paths can be traced because—although the two lines are there—the directions of the arrows make such routes impossible.

We are now agreed that by definition a consequent variable neither raises nor lowers the correlation "behind" it. But we are also in agreement that a consequent variable will produce a nonnegligible value of $D - P$. (Remember that in three-variable models we always test $D - P$ for each side of the triangle, regardless of how the arrows run.) This second agreement also makes sense. Using the bottom diagram in Figure 5.8 as an example, we infer that T's tend to "have been" X's and Y's, while $NOT\ T$'s "tend to have been" $NOT\ X$'s and $NOT\ Y$'s. If so, pairs differing on T will have a surplus of consistent XY pairs, which is to say that $D - P$ will be positive.

These two agreements would collide were it not for Rule 5.3. If we were to test the XY relationship using the partial we would be in the bind of claiming that T has no effect on XY and simultaneously claiming that the XY relationship is reduced when T is controlled. Rule 5.3 saves us from this contradiction. We merely ignore the consequent variable when assessing the prior relationship. Since, in a certain sense, "T has not happened yet" when the XY relationship was forged, we leave it out. In other words, we predict the zero order rather than the partial. A specific example may clarify the reasoning.

Here is an example of an actual three-variable model with a consequent variable, with data from a 1954 national survey of adult American attitudes toward Communists and atheists.[3] Variable X is region (South vs. all other), T is age (40 and older vs. 39 and younger), and Y is tolerance of atheists (an index combining answers to questions such as "Should an atheist be allowed to give a speech in your town?").

The model assumes that age affects tolerance negatively (older people are less tolerant), region affects tolerance negatively (Southerners are less tolerant of atheists), and there is no causal connection between age and region. The model is shown in Figure 5.10. The data are given in Table 5.5.

[3] The study is reported in Samuel A. Stouffer, *Communism, Conformity, and Civil Liberties*, Doubleday, New York, 1955. Data reported here are reanalyzed from copies of Stouffer's raw data on file in the data bank of the Dartmouth College Department of Sociology.

TABLE 5.5   Raw Data on Age, Region, Tolerance of Atheists

REGION	AGE	LOW	HIGH
South	40 and older	659	259
	Under 40	331	289
Other	40 and older	1031	898
	Under 40	529	924

$N = 4920$
No answer on one or more = 13
Total = 4933

When predicting for TY and XY, nothing special happens because they do not have a consequent test variable. For each we predict a negative partial and a negligible value of $D - P$.

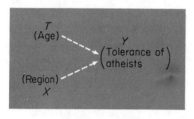

FIG. 5.10

Returning to our problem child, TX, Rule 5.1 predicts that $D - P$ should be positive ($- * - = +$), which is to say that the differential Q should be more positive than the partial Q. Is this plausible in terms of causal reasoning? Surely it is, if we are willing to put our propositions historically("tend to have been") rather than propheti- cally ("tend to become"). From the discussion of the differential in Chapter 4, our prediction means this: Tolerant people "tend to have been" younger non-Southerners, while less tolerant people "tend to have been" older Southerners. Thus, we apply Rule 5.1 *whether or not* there is a consequent variable.

Before considering the partial, $Q_{TX:\text{TIED } Y}$, let us reason together about the zero-order correlation for TX, arguing from the model rather than the rules. The model asserts that T and X have no direct relationship (from the blank between them) and no indirect relationship (from the logic of consequent variables) and variables with no direct or indirect relationship should have zero-order correlations of zero.[4]

Remembering that the three terms in the equation must add up, we are led to deduce a *negative* partial! What? Well, if the zero order is zero and the dif- ferential is positive, the partial must be negative to compensate if the equa- tion is to add up. But such a mathematically necessary result is ridiculous.

[4] "But," you say, "some fourth variable might be producing a correlation between age and region." The rule of the game in causal models is "Speak for yourself, John." Any vari- able that wants credit must appear in the model and the methodological assumption is that no other variable is related to any of the three. The assumption is often wrong, but the cure is to move to a four-variable model, not to invoke hobgoblins.

Even if it turned up, we would be embarrassed to say that two unrelated causes have a negative relationship produced by their effects. Putting the same idea another way, a consequent variable will tend to produce spurious partials just as an antecedent variable produces spurious zero orders.

The abstract principle is this: If we know the answer for two parts of the equation, the answer for the third follows mathematically. When there is no consequent variable, the differential and partial are causally plausible and the zero order is treated as a statistical consequence. When there is a consequent variable, the zero order and differential are causally plausible and the partial is treated as a statistical consequence.

To predict the XT coefficient we use Rule 5.3 and strip Y from the model. The result is a two-variable model with no line connecting the variables, i.e., the prediction that X and T have a negligible zero-order correlation. The data are given in Table 5.6.

TABLE 5.6 Analysis of Data in Table 5.5

	AGE AND TOLERANCE	REGION AND TOLERANCE	AGE AND REGION
Zero order			
Upper limit	−.30	−.30	+.12
Sample value	−.35	−.36	+.05
Lower limit	−.40	−.41	−.01
Partial	−.34	−.36	−.01
Differential	−.35	−.35	+.11
$D - P$	−.01	+.01	+.12

Another triumph for sociological theory! Age and tolerance have a partial of −.34 and $D - P$ is a negligible −.01. Region and tolerance have a partial of −.36 and $D - P$ is a negligible +.01. Age and region have a negligible zero-order coefficient, +.05, and $D - P$ is a nonnegligible +.12. Notice that, although it is negligible, the partial for age and region, −.01, is negative as implied by the previous discussion.

Because of the differences introduced when there is a consequent variable, we subdivide type II models into type IIC, where there is a consequent variable, and type II for all others.

We can now summarize types II and IIC.

A type II model gains credibility when the variable with the zero assertion has a negligible partial and a nonnegligible value of $D - P$ (its sign depending on the signs of the two other assertions) and the other variables have nonnegligible partials (whose signs match the lines in the model) and negligible values of $D - P$.

A type IIC model gains credibility when the variable with the zero assertion has a negligible zero order and a nonnegligible value of $D - P$

(its sign depending on the signs of the other two assertions) and the other variables have nonnegligible partials (whose signs match the lines in the model) and negligible values of $D - P$.

Type III: Three Causal Assertions

The remaining possibility is that the model claims a causal relationship for each of the three sides of the triangle. Again, one of the variables may be a consequent. We call such models IIIC. However, we will save this possibility for discussion after the more simple situations.

Three-variable models may be divided into groups even when there is no consequent variable. Figure 5.11 illustrates types IIIR and IIIS.

Consider first a model with three positive assertions, the triangle with all positive sides in Figure 5.11. Following Rules 5.1 and 5.2 we predict

1. All three partials will be positive.
2. Since all three doglegs are positive, D will exceed P for each relationship.
3. Since all the partials and all the differentials are positive, all three zero orders must be positive.

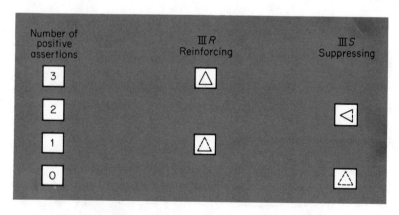

FIG. 5.11   Three assertion models—no consequent variable.

The model is of some interest. In the first place, it provides a plausible rationale for two-variable analyses that end up in the twilight zone, that ambiguous outcome region which defied clear description in Chapter 4. In each pair of variables, the partial should be reduced but not vanish when the third variable is controlled.

In the second place, it suggests an interesting causal system where each variable tends to raise the correlation between the other two, making the zero-order correlations higher than one would expect from the two-variable assertions. We dub the model a "reinforcing system" because each variable acts to reinforce the causal relationship for the other two.

Reinforcing systems may or may not have a "cycle," a path starting out from some variable and returning to it on a route following the arrows. Cyclic models are common in sociological theory. Such notions as "vicious circles" often boil down to reinforcing systems, and although it is not presented exactly this way, Arthur Stinchcombe's concept, "historicist causal imagery," is closely related to a reinforcing system with a cycle.[5]

By the dogleg multiplication rule (and the fact that when we reverse the labels "high" and "low" for a variable with two negative relationships, they both become positive), a model with one positive and two negative assertions has exactly the same structure.

Here is an example, again from Stouffer's 1954 study (see note 3 above). The three variables are

$T =$ educational attainment (high school graduate vs. less than high school)

$Y =$ tolerance toward Communists (high equals greater tolerance toward Communists on the basis of a scale similar to the tolerance toward atheists scale in the previous example)

$X =$ authoritarian attitudes toward child rearing (high equals a favorable answer to the question "If a child is unusual in any way, his parents should get him to be more like other children")

Granting that X is a pretty crude measure of the complex psychological dimension called authoritarianism, we will use that label for simplicity.

Our causal model, as illustrated in Figure 5.12, is that education tends to lower authoritarianism and raise tolerance, while the latter two have a

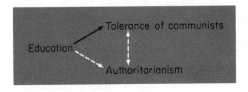

FIG. 5.12

[5] Arthur L. Stinchcombe, *Constructing Social Theories*, Harcourt, New York, 1968, pp. 101–125.

mutual negative relationship (authoritarians tend to be intolerant; intolerant people tend to be authoritarian). Note that although both relationships with education are asymmetrical, the arrows run away from education, not toward it, and the model contains no consequent variable. The raw data are shown in Table 5.7, and the calculations are shown in Table 5.8.

TABLE 5.7 Raw Data on Education, Tolerance, and Authoritarianism from Stouffer's Survey

EDUCATION	AUTHORITARIANISM	TOLERANCE OF COMMUNISTS −	+
High school	High	613	251
	Low	655	522
Less than	High	1669	247
high school	Low	722	219

$$N = 4898$$
No answer on one or more = 35
$$Total = 4933$$

TABLE 5.8 Analysis of Data in Table 5.7

	EDUCATION AND AUTHORITARIANISM	EDUCATION AND TOLERANCE	AUTHORITARIANISM AND TOLERANCE
Zero order			
Upper limit	−.42	+.56	−.37
Sample value	−.47	+.52	−.42
Lower limit	−.52	+.47	−.48
Partial	−.42	+.46	−.33
Differential	−.53	+.56	−.49
$D − P$	−.11	+.10	−.16

All three partials are nonnegligible and have the signs predicted by the model. In all three cases, $D − P$ is 10 units or more (though the differences are not whopping), and the sign of the difference is that predicted by the dogleg rule (Rule 5.1). In sum, the data provide some support for the causal model; we infer that education, tolerance, and authoritariansim tend to reinforce each other.

The other two models, type IIIS, in the right-hand column of Figure 5.11, operate in the *opposite* fashion. In each case, the third variable serves to squelch or inhibit the size of the relationship for the other two because the dogleg product and the partial have opposite signs. When the partial is positive, the dogleg product is negative and the differential will be less positive than the partial. When the dogleg is negative, the opposite happens. As a consequence, each variable acts as a suppressor for the other two, using the terminology of Chapter 4. Thus, the package may be called a "suppressing system" in contrast with the "reinforcing system" just discussed.

What statistical predictions does one make for a suppressing system?

First, one predicts three nonnegligible partials, with signs given by the signs in the model.

Second, one predicts that each $D - P$ will have an absolute difference of 10 Q units or more, with the sign of the difference opposite to that of the partial.

We have no clear-cut example of such a system to present here, but one much like it turns up when we get to consequent variables (Figure 5.16).

Mutually suppressing models are particularly interesting when they contain a cycle because they give an operational definition of a popular concept in sociological theory, the homeostatic or functional system.[6] While sociological "theorists" have written many books and articles about homeostatic systems, they are very shy about giving concrete examples, so we will have to use the weary example of the thermostat. Consider a three-variable system of room temperature, instructions to the furnace, and furnace output. In this famous equilibrium system, when room temperature goes up, instructions to the furnace go down (i.e., the thermostat tells the furnace to lower its output), and when room temperature goes down, the opposite happens. This gives us a negative arrow running from room temperature to instructions. Similarly we would draw a positive arrow from instructions to furnace output and a positive arrow from furnace output to room temperature. The three arrows constitute a mutually suppressing system with a cycle. You can see that the main consequence is that changes in any one variable will set off a boomerang which will act to reverse the changes. Thus the system as a whole is "homeostatic" or "tends to resist change."

We now turn to three-assertion systems that have a consequent variable, i.e., type IIIC.

What happens when a system which otherwise would be "reinforcing" contains a consequent variable? One would get a model such as the one shown in Figure 5.13.

As a specific example, consider occupation (white collar vs. blue collar and farm), education, and earnings in the 1960 census (Figure 5.14). It seems plausible to assume that

 or

FIG. 5.13   FIG 5.14

6 Stinchcombe, *op. cit.*, pp. 80–101.

1. Education affects occupation, but not vice versa.
2. Education affects earnings, but not vice versa.
3. Occupation affects earnings, but not vice versa.

Since earnings has two one-way arrows coming in, it is a consequent variable. What shall we predict?

As before, we make the same predictions as in the reinforcing model for the relationships *involving* the consequent variable—positive partials, positive zero orders, and a positive difference for $D - P$. We still assume that the third variable reinforces relationships involving the consequent variable.

For the relationship between education and occupation, we predict a positive value of $D - P$ and then follow Rule 5.3, giving us merely the relationship depicted in Figure 5.15, which is to say we predict a positive zero-order correlation between education and occupation.

But that is essentially what we would have predicted anyway. Thus, we are not led to a different prediction. We make the same predictions we would have for a reinforcing

FIG. 5.15

system. There is, however, an important difference in meaning. We are no longer predicting that the three variables have a mutually reinforcing effect; only two of them do.

Table 5.9 gives the actual data, for men only. Again, since they are taken from the U.S. census of 1960 and rounded to the nearest 10,000, we do not present confidence limits. The coefficients are presented in Table 5.10.

Five of the six predictions are supported by the data. The partials for education, income and for occupation, income are positive, as is the zero-order correlation for education, occupation. The $D - P$ predictions for

TABLE 5.9 Education, Occupation, and Earnings in 1959 among Employed Men

| | | EARNINGS | |
OCCUPATION	EDUCATION	UNDER $4000	$4000 OR MORE
White collar	High school	345	729
	Less than high school	238	199
Blue collar or	High school	419	382
farm	Less than high school	1330	587

Total = 4229

TABLE 5.10

	EDUCATION AND INCOME	OCCUPATION AND INCOME	EDUCATION AND OCCUPATION
Zero order	+.49	+.48	+.71
Partial	+.37	+.36	+.67
Differential	+.58	+.56	+.74
$D - P$	+.21	+.21	+.07

education, income and for occupation, income are also supported. Both differences are positive and nonnegligible.

The sixth prediction, a positive $D - P$ for education and occupation, is not supported. The difference, $+.07$, is correct in sign but does not reach the conventional magnitude of 10 units. The prediction—that higher earners "have been" better educated white collar workers while lower earners "have been" less educated blue collar workers—is not fully supported by the data.

It is only in methodology texts that data give monotonously clean results and the outcome for this model is fairly typical of what happens in practice where data seldom give perfect support or humiliating rejection. One must apply personal judgments, but our judgment is that when five predictions are supported and the sixth "comes close," the model is reasonable.

Finally, let us consider IIIC models with zero or two positive assertions. Again, we would predict the same results for relationships involving the consequent variable as in the suppressing system: nonnegligible partials with signs predicted from the model, $D - P$ differences of 10 units or more, and the sign of $D - P$ opposite to the sign of the partial. In the case of the other relationship, again, we predict the sign of the zero order as well as $D - P$.

The data on sex, occupation, and earnings presented in Table 4.11 in the previous chapter are a nice example. Intuition (and our previous findings) suggests that the appropriate model is as shown in Figure 5.16. And we predict

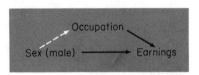

FIG. 5.16

1. For occupation and earnings, a positive partial, a $D - P$ difference of 10 or more units, and the sign of $D - P$ being negative.
2. For sex and earnings, ditto.
3. For sex and occupation, a negative zero order and a positive value of $D - P$.

Completing the analysis begun in Chapter 4, we get the coefficients given in Table 5.11.

TABLE 5.11 Coefficients for Occupation, Earnings, and Sex

	OCCUPATION AND EARNINGS	SEX AND EARNINGS	SEX AND OCCUPATION
Zero order	+.28	+.81	−.40
Partial	+.50	+.88	−.57
Differential	+.02	+.75	−.20
$D - P$	−.48	−.13	+.37

The data support the model. For occupation and earnings there is a positive partial $(+.50)$ and a $D - P$ difference of $-.48$, and the difference is opposite in sign when compared with the partial. For sex and earnings there is a positive partial ($+.88$) and a $D - P$ difference of $-.13$, and the difference is opposite in sign when compared with the partial. And there is a negative zero order for sex and occupation ($-.40$), along with a positive value of $D - P$, $+.37$.

Because there is a nonnegligible $D - P$ difference for sex and occupation and its sign is positive while the partial is negative, the data also fit the general model of a suppressing system. In Figure 5.16, we could have drawn any of the arrows anyway our fancy dictated and the data would support the model. Again we see that data which support a given model do not necessarily rule out all competing models. Intuition, of course, argues for the directions we assumed in Figure 5.16, but in this case the statistical pattern could not care less what intuition argues.

In summary, we have completed our catalogue of three-variable models by adding the three-assertion types, IIIC, IIIR, and IIIS, to types 0, I, II, and IIC, giving a total of seven basic models into which one may sort the 7^3 or 343 possible causal diagrams for three variables.

Summary of Types IIIC, IIIR, IIIS

In a type IIIC model there are three causal assertions and one of the variables receives two one-way arrows. The rule is to delete the consequent variable when predicting the correlation between the others, which amounts to predicting their zero-order correlation to be the same as the sign in the model. One examines all three $D - P$'s and the other two partials, following the usual procedure.

In a type IIIR model there are one or three positive assertions (zero or two negative assertions) and no consequent variables. In such models all three partials should have the same sign as the assertions in the model, and for all three, $D - P$ should be nonnegligible and have the same sign as the line to which it refers. Type IIIR models are called reinforcing systems because each variable operates to strengthen the size of the correlation between the other two.

In a type IIIS model there are zero or two positive assertions (one or three negative assertions) and no consequent variables. In such models all three partials should have the same sign as the assertions in the model, and for all three, $D - P$ should be nonnegligible and have a sign opposite to that of the line to which it refers. Type IIIS models are called suppressing systems because each variable operates to reduce the size of the correlation between the other two.

How to Proceed

The discussion has been lengthy and detailed to make clear the variety of causal models that may occur in three-variable systems, but testing such models is not all that difficult. The steps are these:

1. Draw your model, making sure that the signs of the relationships and the directions of the arrowheads are exactly what you want. In case of doubt, make the assertion symmetrical.

2. Inspect the model to see whether it has a consequent variable, one variable with two asymmetrical relationships coming into it.

3. If there is no consequent variable:

   a) Predict the sign of each partial from the sign of its leg of the triangle.

   b) Predict the $D - P$ difference and its sign by multiplying the signs on the appropriate doglegs.

4. If there is a consequent variable in your model:

   a) Predict the zero order for the relationship not involving the consequent variable from the sign of that leg in your model.

   b) Predict $D - P$ for each relationship, as usual.

   c) Predict the partial for the other two variables as in step 3.

5. Calculate the zero orders, partials, and differentials for all three variables.

   a) When working with a desk calculator it is a good idea to calculate the weights and check your results by seeing whether you can obtain the correct zero orders from the partial, differential, and weights.

   b) Remember the rule of thumb that $D - P$ must be 10 Q units or more to be considered other than negligible.

Working the other way—trying to find appropriate causal models for a particular set of data where you have made no prediction—is much harder. The best way is to begin with the three values of $D - P$, using Table 5.12 to locate the more promising model types. Within these groups you can usually sort things out from the signs of the coefficients and the match between the coefficients and the signs of $D - P$.

TABLE 5.12 $D - P$ Difference and Model Type

NUMBER OF RELATIONSHIPS WHERE $D - P$ is NONNEGLIGIBLE	MODEL TYPE
3	IIIC, IIIR, IIIS
2	None
1	IIC, II
0	0, I

Returning to the very beginning of this discussion, we remind you that the causal models treat *selected* outcomes and there is no guarantee that every set of data will meet the criteria of some model.

This leads to the important question: What should I do if it does not work —if my model does not work, or if the data do not meet the criteria for any model? There are no clear answers, but the following notions may be of use.

First, of the three statistics, $D - P$, the zero order, and the partial, the partial is the "most dubious" in that it provides only relative control of the third variable. (See Rule 4.3 in Chapter 4 and its explanation.) Thus, if $D - P$

and the zero orders fit your model, but the sizes of the partials are inappropriate, you might try the technique of "refinement" discussed in Chapter 4.

Second, if multiple measures of your variables exist (see Rules 1.1c and 1.1d), try your model on alternative measures of the same variables. If none of them fit, clearly something is wrong with your model, but if some do, then you should think hard about the meaning and operational definitions of your variables. Thus, for example, if your model for SES works when you use income as a measure of SES but not when you use education, maybe you should refine your definition of SES.

Third, perhaps your model is correct but incomplete. A fourth variable might be operating to suppress some relationship you predicted or to produce a relationship which is not predicted. Chapter 6 explains how to test four-variable models. The fourth variable may be an additional causal variable, in which case you should use the procedures in Chapter 6. However, it might be a specifier for your whole model. For instance, your model might work among men but not among women, or it might work for long-term residents but not newcomers. All you have to do is to divide your cases into categories of the potential specifier and repeat your three-variable analysis within each. However, you should remember that each of these samples will be smaller than the original sample and thus it will be harder for your zero order relations to attain significance.

IN A NUTSHELL

A. With three variables analyzed simultaneously no neat classification of all possible outcomes exists. However, causal models serve to clarify a number of interesting possibilities.

B. Causal models boil down to three rules:

1. Predicting partials from the signs in the models,

2. Predicting $D - P$ from doglegs in the models, and

3. Looking at one zero order and two partials when one variable is assumed to be consequent.

C. Even in three-variable systems there are many different causal models. They may be classified by the number of causal assertions, 0, 1, 2, 3. Within type II models, one distinguishes those with a consequent variable from all the others. Within type III models, one distinguishes reinforcing systems and suppressing systems as well as consequent variable models. From the viewpoint of sociological theory, three-assertion models containing a cycle of arrowheads are especially important because they provide operational definitions of "historical" and "functional" theories.

D. It is easy to determine whether the data fit a particular model, but sometimes very difficult to tell which model the data fit best.

Rules

RULE 5.1

For all pairs of variables, the sign of $D - P$ is the product obtained by multiplying the signs of the causal relations involving the third variable.

RULE 5.2

The partial for each pair of variables should have the sign of the causal assertion in the model, except when there is a pair of one-way arrows running into the test variable.

RULE 5.3

When there are two one-way arrows running into the test variable, delete the test variable when predicting the relationship between the other two.

Major Concepts

---

1. Antecedent variable
2. Consequent variable
3. Cyclic model
4. $D - P$
5. Dogleg

6. Intervening variable
7. Reinforcing system
8. Spurious correlation
9. Suppressing system

FURTHER READING

Causal models are the "hottest" thing in sociological methods at the time when this is being written. There is a rapidly developing literature, but unfortunately it is developed in terms of interval scale measures and the statistics of regression. Among the most important discussions are

H. M. BLALOCK, JR., *Causal Inferences in Nonexperimental Research*, University of North Carolina Press, Chapel Hill, 1964.

H. M. BLALOCK, JR., *Theory Construction*, Prentice-Hall, Englewood Cliffs, N. J., 1969.

OTIS D. DUNCAN, "Path Analysis: Sociological Examples," *American Journal of Sociology*, 1966, *72*, 1–16.

ARTHUR L. STINCHCOMBE, *Constructing Social Theories*, Harcourt, New York, 1968, pp. 57–148.

APPENDIX: FORMULAS FOR THREE-VARIABLE ANALYSIS

Layout and cell notation

$$Y$$

T	X	$-$	$+$
$+$	$+$	A	B
$+$	$-$	C	D
$-$	$+$	E	F
$-$	$-$	G	H

I (X and Y)

1. $Q(XY)$
$$= \frac{[(B+F)*(C+G)] - [(A+E)*(D+H)]}{[(B+F)*(C+G)] + [(A+E)*(D+H)]}$$

2. $Q(XY)$ TIED T
$$= \frac{[(B*C)+(F*G)] - [(A*D)+(E*H)]}{[(B*C)+(F*G)] + [(A*D)+(E*H)]}$$

3. WEIGHT TIED T
$$= \frac{(B*C)+(F*G)+(A*D)+(E*H)}{[(B+F)*(C+G)] + [(A+E)*(D+H)]}$$

4. $Q(XY)$ T
$$= \frac{(B*C)-(A*D)}{(B*C)+(A*D)}$$

5. WEIGHT T
$$= \frac{(B*C)+(A*D)}{[(B+F)*(C+G)] + [(A+E)*(D+H)]}$$

6. $Q(XY)$ *NOT* T
$$= \frac{(F*G)-(E*H)}{(F*G)+(E*H)}$$

7. WEIGHT, *NOT* T
$$= \frac{(F*G)+(E*H)}{[(B+F)*(C+G)] + [(A+E)*(D+H)]}$$

8. $Q(XY)$ DIFF T
$$= \frac{[(B*G)+(F*C)] - [(A*H)+(D*E)]}{(B*G)+(F*C)+(A*H)+(D*E)}$$

9. WEIGHT DIFF T
$$= \frac{(B*G)+(F*C)+(A*H)+(D*E)}{[(B+F)*(C+G)] + [(A+E)*(D+H)]}$$

II (X and T)

1. $Q(XT)$
$$= \frac{[(B+A)*(H+G)] - [(F+E)*(D+C)]}{[(B+A)*(H+G)] + [(F+E)*(D+C)]}$$

2. $Q(XT)$ TIED Y $= \dfrac{[(B*H)+(A*G)]-[(F*D)+(E+C)]}{(B*H)+(A*G)+(F*D)+(E*C)}$

3. WEIGHT TIED $Y = \dfrac{(B*H)+(A*G)+(F*D)+(E*C)}{[(B+A)*(H+G)]+[F+E)*(D+C)]}$

4. $Q(XT)$ Y $= \dfrac{(B*H)-(F*D)}{(B*H)+(F*D)}$

5. WEIGHT Y $= \dfrac{(B*H)+(F*D)}{[(B+A)*(H+G)]+[(F+E)*(D+C)]}$

6. $Q(XT)$ NOT Y $= \dfrac{(A*G)-(E*C)}{(A*G)+(E*C)}$

7. WEIGHT NOT Y $= \dfrac{(A*G)+(E*C)}{[(B+A)*(H+G)]+[(F+E)*(D+C)]}$

8. $Q(XT)$ DIFF Y $= \dfrac{[(B*G)+(A*H)]-[(F*C)+(D*E)]}{(B*G)+(A*H)+(F*C)+(D*E)}$

9. WEIGHT DIFF $Y = \dfrac{(B*G)+(A*H)+(F*C)+(D*E)}{[(B+A)*(H+G)]+[(F+E)*(D+C)]}$

III (*T* and *Y*)

1. $Q(TY)$ $= \dfrac{[(B+D)*(E+G)]-[(A+C)*(F+H)]}{[(B+D)*(E+G)]+[(A+C)*(F+H)]}$

2. $Q(TY)$ TIED X $= \dfrac{[(B*E)+(D*G)]-[A*F)+(C*H)]}{(B*F)+(D*G)+(A*F)+(C*H)}$

3. WEIGHT TIED $X = \dfrac{(B*E)+(D*G)+(A*F)+(C*H)}{[(B+D)*(E+G)]+[(A+C)*(F+H)]}$

4. $Q(TY)$ X $= \dfrac{(B*E)-(A*F)}{(B*E)+(A*F)}$

5. WEIGHT X $= \dfrac{(B*E)+(A*F)}{[(B+D)*(E+G)]+[(A+C)*(F+H)]}$

6. $Q(TY)$ NOT X $= \dfrac{(D*G)-(G*H)}{(D*G)+(G*H)}$

7. WEIGHT NOT X $= \dfrac{(D*G)+(G*H)}{[(B+D)*(E+G)]+[(A+C)*(F+H)]}$

8. $Q(TY)$ DIFF $X = \dfrac{[(B * G) + (D * E)] - [(A * H) + (F * C)]}{(B * G) + (D * E) + (A * H) + (F * C)}$

9. WEIGHT DIFF $X = \dfrac{(B * G) + (D * E) + (A * H) + (F * C)}{[(B + D) * (E + G)] + [(A + C) * (F + H)]}$

6

Four Variables

The addition to the T, X, Y trinity of a fourth variable, S, does not lead to any *fundamentally* new concepts. The big jump is from two to three and after that additional variables can be handled by extension of the concepts developed in Chapters 4 and 5.

This does not mean that four-variable analyses are easy. Additional variables multiply the volume of statistics even though each statistic is relatively familiar. Three variables generate 9 coefficients; but a similar job for four variables requires that one examine at least 24 different numbers!

You can see that four-variable analyses are not something to undertake to kill 15 or 20 minutes between engagements. However, they are well worth study for two reasons. First, if you can pull off a neat four-variable analysis, you have really accomplished an intellectual feat. There are few parts of sociology where we have well-worked-out four-variable systems and you might as well be a pioneer. Second, a thorough understanding of the principles for four-variable analyses will prepare you for Chapter 7, which gives some simpler rough-and-ready techniques for handling large sets of variables.

This chapter is organized as follows:

First, we will explain the working parts of four-variable systems in terms of causal models and an extension of "the equation."

Second, we will work through some sample four-variable models.

Third, we will use the principles developed in the first section to state some strategies for the frequent problem of finding two test variables that explain Q_{XY} better together than each does alone.

The Working Parts

In a causal model four-variable problems amount to adding one variable and as many as three lines to our triangles. Figure 6.1 illustrates.

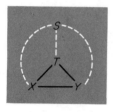

We call the new variable S and draw all of its causal assertions as negative to make visually clear the difference between the old XTY system and the new one. Note that adding a single variable has added three relationships rather than one, doubling the total, which is now six. This is one reason large causal systems are so complex (and fascinating); as they increase in size, the number of relationships increases much faster than the number of variables. A system with as "few" as 10 variables could have as many as 45 causal assertions. (See the formula for the total number of distinct pairs in Table 2.7.)

FIG. 6.1

A four-variable system not only has more pairs of variables, but the relationships between two variables become more complex.

With four dichotomies there are 2^4 or 16 cells in the raw data table. Again using a notation that focuses our eyes on the A, B, C, and D cells for the XY correlation, examine the 16-fold table in Table 6.1.

TABLE 6.1

			Y	
S	T	X	−	+
+	+	+	ATS	BTS
+	+	−	CTS	DTS
+	−	+	$A\bar{T}S$	$B\bar{T}S$
+	−	−	$C\bar{T}S$	$D\bar{T}S$
−	+	+	$AT\bar{S}$	$BT\bar{S}$
−	+	−	$CT\bar{S}$	$DT\bar{S}$
−	−	+	$A\bar{T}\bar{S}$	$B\bar{T}\bar{S}$
−	−	−	$C\bar{T}\bar{S}$	$D\bar{T}\bar{S}$

For example, the $C\bar{T}S$ in the fourth row, left-hand column stands for the frequency of cases that are (1) *NOT T*, (2) S, and (3) in the C cell of the XY relationship, i.e., *NOT X* and *NOT Y*.

Now let us consider the various statistics we can calculate with four-variable data from a 16-fold table. Obviously there are six zero orders (XT, XY, XS, TY, TS, SY). And each can be broken down into weighted parts just as the zero order in a three-variable analysis can. Inevitably there are many more parts in each than in the case of three variables. In general a zero-order Q can be expressed as a weighted average of the Q's calculated among pairs tied and differing on the variable(s) not included in the zero order. We now have two test variables, and for each, pairs can be tied or differing. Calling the Q in question XY and the other variables S and T, this leads to Table 6.2.

TABLE 6.2   Possible Pairs in a Four-Variable Equation

		T	
		Differing	Tied
S	Tied	II	I
	Differing	IV	III

In case I we calculate Q_{XY} only among pairs that are tied on both S and T. The coefficient is $Q_{XY:\text{TIED }S,T}$ and it obviously is some sort of partial. It can be called either a "partial partial" or a "second-order partial." It is a "partial partial" in the sense that when it is compared with the partial in three-variable analysis, it shows how the three-variable partial is affected when a second test variable is introduced and held constant, i.e., when the partial is partialed. You will remember that by the *order* of a coefficient we mean the number of letters which appear after the term Q_{XY}. The zero-order coefficient has zero letters after the colon and the second-order partial has two letters, S and T.

To calculate this coefficient we need two sums, the sum of the positive $(B * C)$ cross products for cells where the two test variables are tied and the sum of the negative $(A * D)$ cross products for cells where the two test variables are

TABLE 6.3   Cross-Product Cells for a Second-Order Partial

tied. In terms of Table 6.1 the former boils down to finding all $B * C$ cells where the other two letters are identical and for the latter, all $A * D$ cells where the other two letters are identical (see Table 6.3).

You can see that if we were to multiply all the frequencies connected by lines in the left half of Table 6.3, their cumulative sum would be the total cross product for consistent pairs and a similar cumulative sum for the right half would give the total cross product for inconsistent pairs. The second-order partial, $Q_{XY:\text{TIED }S,T}$, would be the difference in these two sums divided by their total.

In cell IV in the opposite corner of Table 6.2 we find the association between X and Y among pairs where both S and T differ. It extends the notion of a differential to two test variables and is written as $Q_{XY:\text{DIFF }S,T}$. It can be called a second-order differential (two letters appear after the colon) or a "differential differential," following the same reasoning which led us to the catchy phrase "partial partial."

To find the relevant cell multiplications for a second-order differential, we note that we need $B * C$ cells where *both* of the other letters differ and similarly $A * D$ cells where the other two letters do not match. Table 6.4 illustrates.

TABLE 6.4   Cross-Product Cells for a Second-Order Differential

			POSITIVE CROSS PRODUCTS		NEGATIVE CROSS PRODUCTS	
			Y		Y	
S	T	X	$-$	$+$	$-$	$+$

Again, we would carry out the calculation by multiplying all frequencies connected by a line in Table 6.4, summing those from the left side to get the total for $(B * C)$ and summing those on the right side to get the total for $(A * D)$. The coefficient, as usual, is the difference in these cumulative totals divided by their sum.

Cases II and III appear to be something new, but they are merely a new combination of old possibilities. Each combines the properties of a partial and a differential since each has one test variable tied and one differing. Case II is $Q_{XY:\text{DIFF }T,\text{TIED }S}$, and case III is $Q_{XY:\text{DIFF }S,\text{TIED }T}$. What shall their nicknames be? Obviously both are second-order coefficients, but are they partial differentials or differential partials? It depends on the comparison you wish to make. When they are compared with the second-order differential, they are *partial* differentials since they tell us what happens to the second-order differential when S or T is partialed. On the other hand, when compared with the second-order partials, they are *differential* partials since they tell us what happens to the second-order partial when S or T differs. The distinction is one that would appeal to the statistician son of grammarian parents, but we will generally call them partial differentials because that sounds a little better.

To calculate the correlation between X and Y among pairs differing on S while tied on T, we need cells in Table 6.1 where the notation for S differs while the notation for T matches (Table 6.5).

TABLE 6.5   Cross-Product Cells for $Q_{XY:\text{DIFF }S,\text{ TIED }T}$

As usual, multiplication and summing of the frequencies connected by the lines will provide the total consistent and inconsistent pairs for the coefficient. With this strong hint, you should be able to lay out a table like Table 6.5 for the other partial differential, $Q_{XY:\text{DIFF }T,\text{ TIED }S}$.

We have now labeled all four cells in Table 6.2, as shown in Table 6.6. With appropriate weights (as usual the number of pairs involved expressed

TABLE 6.6   Second-Order Coefficients

		T	
		Differing	Tied
S	Tied	Partial differential or Differential partial	Partial partial or Second-order partial
	Differing	Differential differential or Second-order differential	Partial differential or Differential partial

as a proportion of the total pairs differing on X and Y) one can write a formula expressing Q_{XY} in terms of these four coefficients. Without presenting any algebra, the expanded equation looks like this:

$$Q_{XY} = (Q_{XY:\text{TIED } S,T} * W\text{I}) + (Q_{XY:\text{DIFF } T, \text{TIED } S} * W\text{II})$$
$$+ Q_{XY:\text{DIFF } S, \text{TIED } T} * W\text{III}) + (Q_{XY:\text{DIFF } S,T} * W\text{IV})$$

One can apply the equation to any other pair of variables in the system by switching the letters around, and in principle it can be extended to systems with any number of variables. With, for example, 37 variables, one could define a thirty-fifth-order coefficient for 2 of them among pairs tied on a particular 30 and differing on a particular 5. No example will be presented.

The equation combines a two-variable analysis (the zero order) and a four-variable analysis (the second-order coefficients to the right of the equal signs). If we shift back to a fourfold table like Table 6.2 or 6.6, we can see how three-variable results fit into this system. Table 6.7 illustrates.

TABLE 6.7 Zero-Order, Three-Variable, and Four-Variable Coefficients for XY

		T		
		Differing	Tied	Weighted sum
S	Tied	$Q_{XY:\text{DIFF } T, \text{TIED } S}$	$Q_{XY:\text{TIED } S, T}$	$Q_{XY:\text{TIED } S}$
	Differing	$Q_{XY:\text{DIFF } S, \text{DIFF } T}$	$Q_{XY:\text{DIFF } S, \text{TIED } T}$	$Q_{XY:\text{DIFF } S}$
	Weighted sum	$Q_{XY:\text{DIFF } T}$	$Q_{XY:\text{TIED } T}$	Q_{XY}

What Table 6.7 means is that any first-order coefficient in the right-hand column or bottom row of Table 6.7 can be expressed as the weighted average of two second-order coefficients inside the table. Thus if we multiplied the second-order partial by weight I and added to it $Q_{XY:\text{DIFF } T, \text{TIED } S}$ times WII (i.e., working across the top row of the table), we could obtain the value of $Q_{XY:\text{TIED } S}$ and the sum of WI and WII would equal the weight for the partial in the three-variable analysis using S as the test variable. We can similarly obtain the other second-order partials and differentials by weighted averages of the appropriate coefficients inside the table. Formulas for these calculations appear in an appendix to this chapter.

Table 6.7 shows how the whole works fits together like a set of nested boxes. For example,

1. A first-order partial is the weighted sum of the second-order partial and the appropriate partial differential.

2. A first-order differential is the weighted sum of the second-order differential and the "other" partial differential.

3. The zero order may be seen alternatively as:

a) The weighted average of the four second-order coefficients.

b) The weighted average of either pair of first-order coefficients.

c) The weighted average of the *four-variable* coefficients in a particular row (column) and the *three*-variable coefficient for the other row (column).

The table will be of considerable use in deducing the properties of four-variable systems. For now we merely note that it can be used in two different ways: Given four-variable results (or assumptions about them), we can make a number of inferences about three-variable results as well as about the zero-order coefficient. Conversely, given three-variable results (or assumptions about them), we can make certain inferences about four-variable results.

We can complete the warm-up by noting the correspondences between the coefficients in Table 6.7 and the parts of a causal system diagram. Two are easy, and one is harder. For now, we ignore consequent variables.

First, the sign of a given line corresponds to the second-order partial. If we were testing the model in Figure 6.1, we would require a negative second-order partial between S and Y controlling for T and X; a positive second-order partial between X and T, controlling for S and Y; and so on.

Second, the two-assertion doglegs correspond to partial differentials— they are assertions about the differential for one test variable, with the other test variable held constant. The two dotted lines running from S to X and Y in Figure 6.1 have a positive product, and thus we would predict that $Q_{XY:\text{DIFF } S,\text{TIED } T}$ would be greater than the second-order partial. For each variable there are now two doglegs, one for each test variable, holding the other constant. With six pairs of variables, this gives us $6 * 2 = 12$ dogleg predictions to test along with six partials. Note that such dogleg effects are merely friendly old $D - P$ with a test variable controlled.

The last coefficient, the second-order differential $Q_{XY:\text{DIFF } S,T}$, is a conglomerate. It should be thought of as the sum of effects of various causal structures rather than a causal structure per se. It is sensitive to (1) the independent effect of S on XY, (2) the independent effect of T on XY, and (3) the joint effect of S and T together on XY. Putting it another way, pairs differing on *both* S and T should have an XY correlation different from the second-order partial if differences in S produce an XY correlation *and/or* differences in T produce an XY correlation *and/or* differences in S and T jointly produce an XY correlation.

Because the effect of S and the effect of T on the XY correlation is through their doglegs, we will predict that positive doglegs in the model make the second-order differential positive and negative doglegs (strictly speaking, negative products for doglegs) make it negative. Clear enough, but what about point (3), the joint effect of S and T? To nail it down, it is necessary to turn back to tables like Table 6.6.

Four-variable coefficient tables have two rows and two columns, with four coefficients inside the cells. Table 6.8 gives some examples with fictitious data.

TABLE 6.8   Fictitious Four-Variable Results for Q_{XY}

a

		T			
		Differs	Tied	Effect	
S	Tied	+.42	+.31	+.11	
	Differs	+.64	+.53	+.11	.00
	Effect	+.22	+.22		
			.00		

b

		T			
		Differs	Tied	Effect	
S	Tied	+.42	+.31	+.11	
	Differs	+.85	+.53	+.32	+.21
	Effect	+.43	+.22		
			+.21		

c

		T			
		Differs	Tied	Effect	
S	Tied	+.42	+.31	+.11	
	Differs	+.20	+.53	−.33	−.44
	Effect	−.22	+.22		
			−.44		

Beginning with Table 6.8a, the upper right-hand corner has a value of +.31 for the second-order partial, the correlation between X and Y controlling for both S and T. If our model had a positive line connecting X and Y, this would be good news. To the left of the value +.31 there is a value of +.42, the partial differential for XY when T differs and S is tied. To the right, under the word "Effect," is the value +.11, which is (+.42) − (+.31), the difference between the two coefficients. Since the effect exceeds 10 units, the data suggest a positive dogleg product for T. When T differs (but not S), the correlation between X and Y is raised 11 units. We call this "the effect of T on XY" and say that the effect of T on XY is 11 units.

Shifting to the right-hand *column* of the same table, we arrive at a similar conclusion about the effect of variable S. The effect of S on XY in Table 6.8a is +.22, or 22 units.

The second-order differential has nothing whatsoever to do with the conclusions drawn so far, but when we shift our attention to the bottom row or left-hand column, the conglomerate coefficient looms out of the mists.

In Table 6.8a the second-order differential has a value of +.64, which is the correlation between X and Y among pairs differing on both S and T. The positive sign is plausible because both the S and T effects are positive. It is also larger than either of the partial differentials, again plausible if the second-order differential is a sum of positive effects.

Now, that joint effect. Reading across the bottom row in Table 6.8a and subtracting +.53 from +.64, we get another effect for T, the effect of varying T when S is also varying. Since this new effect, $+.11$, is the same as the old T effect, we infer that the effect of T is the same whether S is tied or differs. Carrying out the same gyrations in the columns, we draw a similar conclusion, an S effect of $+.22$ in both columns.

Table 6.8a boils down to this: There is a positive T effect on the XY correlation of the same magnitude in each row and a positive S effect of the same magnitude in each column.

In Table 6.8b, however, we increase the value of the second-order differential from $+.64$ to $+.85$, an increase of 21 units, leaving the other three coefficients unchanged. What happens to the effects? Well, nothing and something. Nothing happens to the effects in the top row or right-hand column because the second-order differential has nothing to do with them. The other two effects increase 21 units, the 21 units we added to the second-order differential. The bottom row effect is now $+.32$ instead of $+.11$ and the left-hand column effect is now $+.43$ instead of $+.22$. The interpretation would be revised this way: There is an effect of T and an effect of S and each is higher when the other varies—T has a stronger effect on XY when S varies compared to its effect when S is tied—S has a stronger effect on XY when T varies compared to its effect when T is tied.

And this difference in the effects is what we mean by the joint effect of S and T, an increase in their effect on XY when both test variables differ, in comparison to the effects when only one or the other differs. (In the abstract the notion of the size of a relationship varying with the state of some other variable should be familiar from the discussion of specification in Chapter 4. In a specification, the coefficient varies with the category of the test variable, while here the coefficient varies with the degree of control of the test variable.)

What can go up can also go down, and Table 6.8c shows a hypothetical situation where the joint effect of S and T is to lower the XY correlation, not raise it. The effect of S and T on XY is less positive when both differ.

We may assess the joint effect by comparing the two row effects (.11 vs. .11, .32 vs. .11, $-.33$ vs. .11) or by comparing the two column effects (.22 vs. .22, .43 vs. .22, $-.22$ vs. .22), but of mathematical necessity we will obtain the same answer whether we look at rows or columns.

To summarize: The joint effect of S and T on the XY correlation appears as the difference between row (column) differences in tables like Table 6.6. As usual the difference is considered negligible unless it is 10 or more units in magnitude.

We now know *how* to test predictions about the second-order differential, but we do not yet know *what* to predict. However, we did gain some simplicity. Of the three components, the T effect, the S effect, and the joint ST effect, we may ignore the first two because they are built into the base line for the joint effect. For example, the prediction of a negligible joint effect is equivalent to predicting that the second-order differential is the sum of the S and T effects.

When does a model lead us to predict a joint effect? The key concept is "secondary dogleg" or dogleg of a dogleg. (You were warned that four-variable models have no new principles but merely use the old ones in a more complex way.) Consider the four-variable model illustrated in Figure 6.2.

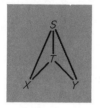

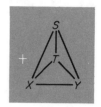

FIG. 6.2   FIG. 6.3

Focusing on the XY relationship and the test variable T, we see that the T effect should be positive because XT and TY have a positive dogleg product. We call XT and TY a primary dogleg. In a four-variable model, each dogleg relationship has a dogleg of its own. XT has the dogleg (XS, TS) and TY has the dogleg (TS, YS). The dogleg for a relationship in a primary dogleg is a secondary dogleg. (A moment's reflection will lead you to the horrifying insight that a five-variable model will have tertiary doglegs, doglegs of doglegs of doglegs! This is why we stop at four-variable models in this book.)

When we examine the partial differential $Q_{XY:\text{DIFF } T, \text{TIED } S}$, we are controlling for the secondary doglegs, but in the second-order differential they are running around loose, unleashed as it were. What will they do? In Figure 6.2 the familiar three-variable principles tell us that the magnitude of the positive TX and TY correlations will be increased when S differs because both secondary doglegs have positive products. The result will be to strengthen both relationships in the T dogleg and make the XY correlation even stronger. (Implicit in the sign rule is the principle that the stronger the relationship, the stronger its impact on a correlation.) Making the T effect stronger when S differs is joint effect by definition. And there we are. We predict a joint effect when we expect that the secondary doglegs raise or lower the correlations in the primary doglegs in such a way as to make the primary dogleg effects more positive or less positive.

Unfortunately, there is no simple multiplication rule for such predictions. One must grind out separate forecasts for all combinations of signs in the primary and secondary doglegs. At the end of this section we present a table, Table 6.11, that does this job for you; but before lifting the veil we will discuss some four-variable models and their joint effect predictions to give you a feel for the reasoning and also to acquaint you with some of the more interesting four-variable models.

We assume in this section that all relationships are mutual. The problem of asymmetrical relationships and one-way arrows will be handled in the next section of this chapter.

First, consider a model (Figure 6.3) where all six relationships are predicted to be positive.

In such a system all six relationships will have positive partials, all primary doglegs will have positive effects, and all joint effects will be positive. An all-positive four-variable model is akin to the reinforcing systems discussed in Chapter 5. Each relationship tends to increase all the other relationships and each pair of variables raises the correlations beyond the effects produced by single variables.

Four-variable reinforcing systems need not have only positive assertions. We will not present the mathematical proof, but it can be shown (Figure 6.4) that any four-variable model with six nonnegligible assertions will be a reinforcing system if each of the four triangles (XTY, TYS, XTS, SXY) has exactly one or three positive lines (if none of the four has exactly zero or two positive lines).

XTY has one positive line, TYS has one positive line, XTS has three positive lines, and SXY has one positive line. Thus Figure 6.4 is a reinforcing system. Each dogleg and each joint effect will have the same sign as the relationship to which it refers.

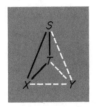

FIG. 6.4

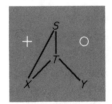

FIG. 6.5

In reinforcing systems, the secondary doglegs strengthen both relationships in the primary doglegs, but joint effects also occur when only one line in a primary dogleg is reinforced.

Figure 6.5 illustrates such a system. In this and similar four-variable diagrams we adopt the following four conventions: (1) The relationship being predicted is at the bottom, (2) the primary dogleg variable is in the middle, (3) the secondary dogleg variable is at the top, and (4) the sign products for the secondary doglegs appear next to them. A complete analysis requires two such diagrams with the test variables alternating top and bottom positions. See Figure 6.7 as an example.

We predict that when S differs, TX will become more positive, but TY will not change one way or another. Nevertheless, the T effect should increase because we anticipate an increased impact on XY when either dogleg relationship increases in magnitude, providing that the other is not zero or is not lessened.

It is not necessary that the variable have a nonnegligible primary dogleg in order to have a joint effect. We next rearrange Figure 6.5 so that our interest is in the primary dogleg for S rather than the primary dogleg for T (Figure 6.6).

For SX, the secondary dogleg will accentuate a positive relationship, but for SY it will *produce* one. We predict that the S effect is negligible (its primary dogleg product is zero), but when T also varies, differences in T will have a positive effect on the XY correlation.

Pushing things to an extreme, consider a "string" model, as depicted in Figure 6.7.

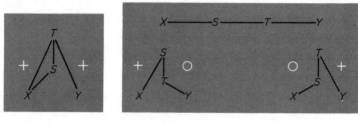

FIG. 6.6   FIG. 6.7

The prediction is that both partial differentials will be negligible. However, since S "creates" a positive TX relationship and T "creates" a positive SY relationship, we predict a positive joint effect. The table of coefficients is shown in Table 6.9.

TABLE 6.9 Hypothetical Data for XY Relationship in Figure 6.7

		\multicolumn{2}{c}{S}		
		Differs	Tied	Effect
	Tied	.00	.00	.00
T	Differs	+.65	.00	+.65	+.65
	Effect	+.65	.00	
		\multicolumn{2}{c}{+.65}	

In a string model the correlation between the end variables is a function of the joint effect only, the single variable effects being nil.

So far we have seen that joint effects are anticipated when the secondary doglegs reinforce or "create" primary dogleg relationships. But secondary doglegs can also be suppressors, as shown in Figure 6.8.

In Figure 6.8(a) the STX triangle is a suppressing system and as a consequence the secondary dogleg will tend to lower or reverse the positive TX

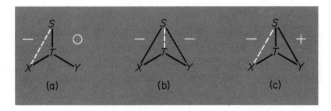

FIG. 6.8

correlation. The other primary relationship, TY, is unaffected. Our prediction would be that the joint effect is negative.

Cases (b) and (c) (in Figure 6.8) introduce ambiguity. In (b) S will tend to lower both TX and TY, but we do not know how much. (Remember that one cannot deduce the zero-order correlations in a suppressing system.) If S merely lowers them a little, a negative joint effect would be predicted, but if it reverses both of them, it *could* produce two strong negative relationships for TX and TY, resulting in a more positive dogleg than the one we started with. Because of this ambiguity, we make no prediction when both second-order doglegs are suppressor systems. In (c), one secondary dogleg acts to raise a positive relationship and the other to lower a positive relationship. How they will "average out" is unknown. Here again no prediction can be made.

Having seen how secondary doglegs can reinforce, "create," and suppress relationships in primary doglegs with diverse consequences for the correlation, we move on to another possibility. Figure 6.9 gives yet another model, a diamond.

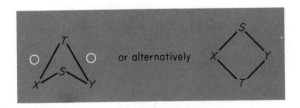

FIG. 6.9

The important line in Figure 6.9 is the missing one. T and S are unrelated. All four secondary dogleg products are necessarily zero because ST appears in all four of them. The result? When S and T are predicted to be unrelated, we always predict that the joint effect is zero.

A variant of this is the four-variable cycle shown in Figure 6.10.

From the principles discussed so far we obtain a simple set of predictions for a four-variable cycle: Predict negligible partial-differential effects and

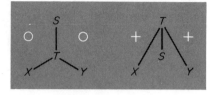

FIG. 6.10   FIG. 6.11

nonnegligible joint effects and second-order partials for variables connected by a line; predict negligible partials and joint effects but nonnegligible partial differentials for variables not connected by a line. (Quiz time: If you see how this rule emerges, you have a good grasp of the discussion so far.)

One last model, Figure 6.11. The point here is that predictions for the two sets of secondary doglegs are not necessarily identical. On the left side we get secondary dogleg products of zero, while on the right-hand diagram we get positive products. Could this happen? Certainly, as shown in Table 6.10.

TABLE 6.10 Hypothetical Results Consistent with Figure 6.11

		S		
		Differs	Tied	Effect
T	Tied	.00	.00	.00
	Differs	+.40	+.40	.00
	Effect	+.40	+.40	
		.00		

The table says that when only S differs the correlation remains negligible, but when T differs also there is a correlation of $+.40$. T increases the S effect. But we also see that the T effect is 40 units whether or not S differs. S has no impact on the T effect. From all of this, it follows that the joint effect will be negligible.

In general then, we only predict a joint effect when S's secondary doglegs move the correlation in the same way that T's secondary doglegs do. If either secondary effect is predicted to be negligible, the joint effect is predicted to be negligible.

The author has never seen a model with conflicting predictions—one secondary dogleg raising the correlation, the other lowering it—but he has no proof that they are impossible. If you find one, the advice is to make no prediction at all.

In the next section of this chapter you will see how all of this actually works in concrete examples. For now, we summarize by presenting the following rules:

Rules for predicting the XY correlation in a four-variable model with no consequent variables

RULE 6.1

Predict the second-order partial from the line for XY.

RULE 6.2

Predict the difference:

$(Q_{XY}:$ DIFF T, TIED $S) -$ second-order partial	from the sign product for the T dogleg
$(Q_{XY}:$ DIFF S, TIED $T) -$ second-order partial	from the sign product for the S dogleg

RULE 6.3

Predict the joint effect, as follows:

  a) Predict the impact of S from the primary and secondary doglegs using Table 6.11.

  b) Predict the effect of T using Table 6.11, substituting SX for the rows and SY for the columns.

  c) If:

   both cell entries are >, predict a positive joint effect.
   both cell entries are <, predict a negative joint effect.
   one or both cell entries are =, predict a negligible joint effect.
   the cell entries are > and <, make no prediction.
   either cell entry is ?, make no prediction.

TABLE 6.11   Prediction Table for Joint Effects

	Secondary Dogleg Product	Sign for TY —			Sign for TY 0			Sign for TY +		
		−	0	+	−	0	+	−	0	+
Sign for TX +	+	<	<	?	<	=	>	?	>	>
	0	<	=	>	<	=	>	<	=	>
	−	?	>	?	?	=	?	?	<	?
Sign for TX 0	+	<	<	?	<	=	>	?	>	>
	0	=	=	=	=	=	=	=	=	=
	−	>	>	?	>	=	<	?	<	<
Sign for TX −	+	?	>	?	?	=	?	?	>	?
	0	>	=	<	>	=	<	>	=	<
	−	>	>	?	>	=	<	?	<	<

> = Difference is positive
= = Difference is negligible
< = Difference is negative
? = No prediction

Examples of Four-Variable Models

The actual work of deriving predictions for a four-variable model is easy and takes no more than 5 minutes, once you get the hang of it. All you do is to apply Rule 6.1 to the six relationships, Rule 6.2 to the 12 different doglegs, and Rule 6.3 to the six different four-variable diagrams and then check the predictions against the calculated values in the data (computational formulas are given at the end of this chapter). To illustrate the process we will walk slowly through two different case histories.

Proximity, interaction, sentiment, and norms

In Chapter 5 (Figure 5.7) we analyzed some data relevant to a famous three-variable model, George Homans' trinity of proximity, interaction, and sentiment. In a related and well-known study,[1] Daniel Wilner and his associates argue that a fourth variable, social norms, should be added. Wilner was looking at the effect of segregated and integrated public housing on racial attitudes. His main argument is that integrated housing will make whites more favorable to Negroes through the intervening variables of interaction (whites who live near Negroes will tend to interact with them and interaction leads to liking, liking to interaction) and also norms (integrated housing developments will tend to develop social norms favoring positive interracial sentiments and people tend to adopt the sentiments favored by local norms). In addition, we assume that norms and interaction have a mutual positive relationship.

This gives us the four-variable model shown in Figure 6.12.

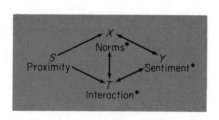

We have drawn the XY relationship as mutual even though the verbal hypothesis is not put exactly that way; but otherwise the drawing is a straightforward translation of the verbal arguments. Because none of the variables receives two one-way arrows, we can ignore consequent variables and the problems of order and deletion.

FIG. 6.12 Asterisk indicates a relationship toward (with) negroes, among whites.

[1] Daniel M. Wilner, Rosabelle P. Walkley, and Stuart W. Cook, *Human Relations in Interracial Housing: A Study of the Contact Hypothesis*, University of Minnesota Press, Minneapolis, 1955.

Wilner collected data on the four variables in interviews with roughly 600 women living in public housing projects with varying degrees of spatial segregation. For present purposes, we can describe his measures as follows:

S (Proximity): $+$ = living close to a Negro family, $-$ = living less close to a Negro family

T (Interaction): $+$ = more frequent contacts with Negroes in the project, $-$ = less frequent contacts

X (Norms): $+$ = belief that respondent's friends are favorable to Negroes, $-$ = belief that friends are less favorable to Negroes

Y (Sentiment): $+$ = more favorable attitudes toward Negroes in general, $-$ = less favorable attitudes toward Negroes in general

Table 6.12 gives the raw data,[2] recalculated from a percentage table in Wilner's book, another example of the reason for Rule 3.1.

TABLE 6.12 Raw Data for Variables in Wilner Study

S	T	X	Y −	Y +	S	T	X	Y −	Y +
+	+	+	33	76	−	+	+	20	43
+	+	−	31	25	−	+	−	37	36
+	−	+	19	14	−	−	+	36	27
+	−	−	27	15	−	−	−	118	41
									$N = 598$

In Table 6.13 we have ground out all the possible Q's that can be extracted from a four-variable table. The three-variable and zero-order results are also presented, à la Table 6.7, though we do not use them in our predictions. At the right of each subtable all possible four-variable effects are presented.

The question is whether the differences in the right side of Table 6.13 are those predicted from the model. Figure 6.13 presents all the subdiagrams needed to make the predictions.

Away we go! Of the six second-order partials, Figure 6.13 shows us that all but one, SY, have positive lines. Thus we predict five positive partials and one negligible. Checking Table 6.13 we see that the predictions are all supported. Except for SY, which has a negligible partial of $+.064$, all the partials are positive and exceed 10 units in magnitude.

[2] *Ibid.*, p. 106.

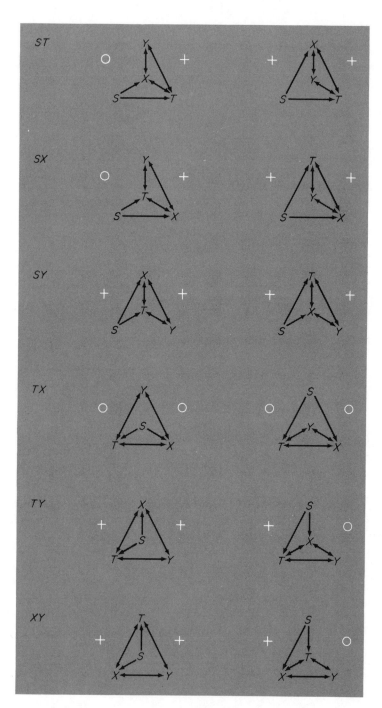

FIG. 6.13   Diagrams used to derive predictions for model in Fig. 6.12.

TABLE 6.13 Four-Variable Results for Data in Table 6.12

Q_{ST}

		Y				
		Differs	Tied	3 Variable	Second-order partial	+.517
	Tied	+.499	+.517	+.508	X effect	+.056
X	Differs	+.638	+.573	+.610	Y effect	−.018
	3 Variable	+.580	+.546	+.564 = Zero order	Joint effect	+.083

Q_{SX}

		Y				
		Differs	Tied	3 Variable	Second-order partial	+.376
	Tied	+.349	+.376	+.363	T effect	+.092
T	Differs	+.566	+.468	+.524	Y effect	−.027
	3 Variable	+.480	+.425	+.455 = Zero order	Joint effect	+.125

Q_{SY}

		X				
		Differs	Tied	3 Variable	Second-order partial	+.064
	Tied	+.155	+.064	+.111	T effect	+.181
T	Differs	+.452	+.245	+.366	X effect	+.091
	3 Variable	+.335	+.162	+.258 = Zero order	Joint effect	+.116

Q_{TX}

		Y				
		Differs	Tied	3 Variable	Second-order partial	+.310
	Tied	+.450	+.310	+.387	S effect	+.154
S	Differs	+.601	+.464	+.542	Y effect	+.140
	3 Variable	+.534	+.394	+.473 = Zero order	Joint effect	−.003

Q_{TY}

		X				
		Differs	Tied	3 Variable	Second-order partial	+.452
	Tied	+.528	+.452	+.491	Effect of S	−.024
S	Differs	+.591	+.428	+.523	Effect of X	+.076
	3 Variable	+.563	+.440	+.508 = Zero order	Joint effect	+.087

Q_{XY}

		T				
		Differs	Tied	3 Variable	Second-order partial	+.389
	Tied	+.470	+.389	+.431	Effect of S	−.020
S	Differs	+.560	+.369	+.485	Effect of T	+.081
	3 Variable	+.520	+.380	+.459 = Zero order	Joint effect	+.110

Turning to the dogleg effects, Figure 6.13 shows them to be all positive (both lines positive) or zero (one line positive, one line zero). Our batting average is not so good here. The four doglegs predicted to be negligible turn out that way (−.018 for the effect of Y on ST, −.027 for the effect of Y on SX, −.024 for the effect of S on TY, −.020 for the effect of S on XY) but of the eight doglegs predicted to have positive effects only three exceed 10 units (+.181 for the effect of T on SY, +.154 for the effect of S on TX, +.140 for the effect of Y on TX). The remainder are correct in sign, but fail to reach 10 units (+.056 for the effect of X on ST, +.092 for the effect of T on SX, +.091 for the effect of X on SY, +.076 for the effect of X on TX, +.081 for the effect of T on XY).

So far we have made 18 predictions, of which 13 turn out to be correct and 5 incorrect. This leaves the six joint effects, which we will take at a slower clip to illustrate the procedure.

First is *ST*. Our impression is that it will be positive. On the left side we see a positive line reinforced; on the right side we see one positive line reinforced and another "created." We can check this in Table 6.11.

We will adopt the following conventions for using Table 6.11. When the diagram is arranged in standard form, à la Figure 6.13 (relationship on the bottom, primary dogleg variable above it, joint effect variable on top), the left-hand primary dogleg relationship (the line from the primary dogleg variable to the left-hand bottom variable) refers to the rows of the table, and the right-hand primary dogleg relationship refers to the columns.

We begin with the left diagram for *ST* in Figure 6.13. The primary dogleg relationship on the left side (of the left diagram), *SX*, is positive. This tells us that we will be in the top three rows of the table. The product for the secondary dogleg is zero (*XY* is positive, *SY* is zero), which places us in the second row from the top of the table. Turning to *XT* we find it positive, which means we will be in the right-hand three columns of the table. Its secondary dogleg product is positive (*XY* and *TY* are positive) so we are in the extreme right-hand column. At the intersection of the second row and extreme right-hand column, the cell entry is >, which means a positive prediction. Now we repeat the process for the right-hand diagram for *ST*. The zero assertion for *SY* places us in the middle three rows and its positive secondary dogleg product (*SX* and *XY* are positive) puts us in the fourth row from the top. Moving to *TY*, its positive sign and positive secondary dogleg product (*XY* and *XT* are positive) puts us in the right-hand three columns and then in the extreme right-hand column. At the intersection of the fourth row from the top of Table 6.11 and the extreme right-hand column we see another >. Since both cell entries are >, Rule 6.3 tells us to predict the joint effect to be positive. However, Table 6.13 tells us that, while positive in sign, it falls short of 10 units, being +.083. Thus our prediction for the joint effect of *X* and *Y* on *ST* is not supported.

You now see the general procedure for using Table 6.11. First, lay out the subdiagrams as in Figure 6.13. Second, choose the top, middle, or lower third of the table from the sign of the left line in the primary dogleg in the left-hand diagram. Third, choose the specific row from the secondary dogleg product for that relationship. Fourth, choose the left, middle, or right section of the table from the sign of the right-hand line in the primary dogleg (still in the left-hand diagram). Fifth, choose the specific column from the secondary dogleg product for that relationship. Sixth, read off the cell entry. Seventh, repeat the same procedure for the other diagram and compare the cell entries.

The second joint effect is *SX*, which is easy enough to predict since the diagrams are identical with those for *ST*. We again predict a positive joint effect, and this time we get one, +.125.

Third is SY. Since both diagrams are the same as Figure 6.2 we anticipate a positive joint effect. Doing it the hard way, we end up in the top row, extreme right-hand column of the table for both diagrams and the cell entry is indeed $>$. The prediction is supported by a joint effect of $+.116$ in Table 6.13.

Fourth is TX. We note immediately that the test variables, S and Y, are unrelated, and from the principles stated above we anticipate a negligible joint effect. Using Table 6.11, we end up in the second row from the top, second column from the right, where the entry is $=$. The figures in Table 6.13 support the prediction because the coefficient is a negligible $-.003$.

Fifth is TY. Operating from Table 6.11 or from the observation that the diagrams are the same as those for ST and SX, we obtain a positive prediction. The prediction is not borne out, as the actual effect in Table 6.13 is $+.087$, not of the required 10 units of magnitude.

Sixth is XY, which, being identical in form with TY, gives the same prediction, positive. This prediction is supported, as the effect in Table 6.13 is $+.110$.

Of the six predictions regarding joint effects, four were supported and two failed. Our final score for the 24 predictions is 17 correct and 7 incorrect. This would be a good batting average in professional baseball, but a sheer success count is probably not the best way to assess the results in a four-variable model. A more revealing technique is to cross-tabulate predictions against the actual differences and coefficients. The degree of correlation in Table 6.11 is (by definition) a measure of the extent to which the predictions line up with the results. Table 6.14 is such a correlation table for our model. (Note that we use the intervals from Table 2.8 for the vertical scale.)

TABLE 6.14 Results and Predictions for Wilner Data

		PREDICTION		
		Negative	Negligible	Positive
	+.70 or higher			
	+.50–.69			1
	+.30–.49			4
Actual	+.10–.29			6
difference	+.00–.09		1	7
or	−.00–.09		5	
coefficient	−.10–.29			
	−.30–.49			
	−.50–.69			
	−.70 or less			

The table shows a healthy relationship. Indeed if we were to calculate the value of gamma (see Chapter 3), it would be $+1.00$. The relatively more positive differences and coefficients are indeed the ones predicted to be positive, while the negligible differences tend to be the ones predicted to be negligible.

A sheer mechanical test like Table 6.14 is not sufficient though. One should always consider the substance of a model as well as its 24 individual predictions. The "main idea" in this model is that proximity leads to positive attitudes through the intervening variables of norms and interaction. Table 6.13 supports this theme. There is a zero-order correlation between proximity and sentiments ($Q = +.26$, and other calculations show it to be significant). When either norms or interaction are controlled, the correlation is reduced (the three-variable partials are $+.111$ and $+.162$), and when both are controlled, the correlation becomes negligible ($+.064$). Granted that the model fails in a number of predictions, we must also grant that it comes through for the substantively more important ones.

Sex, education, occupation, and earnings

The proximity–interaction–norms–sentiment model was a good way to begin because all of the relationships are positive and there are no consequent variables. For our second example, however, we will work with a more tricky set of variables, combining Figures 5.14 and 5.15 into a four-variable model for sex, education, occupation, and earnings. The variables have been defined before, but as a refresher we note that the positive ends of the dichotomies are male, high school graduate, white collar occupation, and 1959 earnings of $4000 or more.

The model consists of the following assertions:

1. Sex and education are unrelated.
2. Sex affects occupation negatively.
3. Sex affects earnings positively.
4. Education affects occupation positively.
5. Education affects income positively.
6. Occupation affects income positively.

Stooping to the vernacular: Men and women do not differ much in education, men are more likely to have blue collar and farm jobs, men earn more, high school graduates get better jobs, high school graduates earn more, and white collar workers earn more.

The first step is to diagram the model. Since all the assertions except the first are asymmetrical, we have to pay careful attention to the directions of the arrows. When there are a number of one-way arrows in a model, it is worth the trouble to arrange it in the best possible order, which boils down to an arrangement in which all the one-way arrows run in the same direction. Our model is given in Figure 6.14, and the data are given in Table 6.15.

Figure 6.15 and Table 6.16 give us the necessary numbers and diagrams. Because this model is a little more fancy, we will take it relationship by relationship, numbering our predictions as we go along.

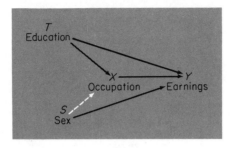

FIG. 6.14

The first relationship, *ST*, has no line in Figure 6.15. Our impulse is to predict its second-order partial to be negligible. A closer look at the figure, though, shows two one-way arrows running into *X* and two one-way arrows running into *Y*. In other words, both test variables are consequents. If, as Chapter 5 explained, we have no use for a single consequent variable when predicting a relationship, we have less use for a pair of them.

From the discussion in Chapter 5 you should be able to guess what to do. Right! You delete *X* and *Y* and predict a negligible zero order for *S* and *T*.

In four-variable systems the structure is not always so obvious, the main reason being that variables can be connected by a direct line and also an indirect two-step path. The theme is the same as ever; we want to delete (ignore) a test variable where pairs that differ on it would have a higher (or lower) correlation for the relationship in question but where it would be illogical to claim that the test variable affects the relationship causally. To cover the broader class of cases, we must state Rule 5.3 in a more general form.

R U L E   6.4

Definition: A test variable *T* is a consequent for variables *X* and *Y* if there is a path from *X* to *T* and a path from *Y* to *T* following the arrows, but *none* of the following paths exist: (1) *X* to *T* to *Y*, (2) *Y* to *T* to *X*, or (3) *T* to *X* and also *T* to *Y*.

Rule: If one test variable is consequent, test the relationship in a three-variable analysis, controlling the nonconsequent test variable. If both test variables are consequent, predict the zero-order correlation.

As an example, delete the *SY* and *TY* relationships from the top diagrams in Figure 6.15. While *Y* would not be a consequent variable for *ST* using the rule in Chapter 5 (there are no one-way arrows now from *S* to *Y* and *T* to *Y*), one can "go" from *S* to *X* to *Y* and *T* to *X* to *Y*, but there is no way to "get" from *S* to *Y* to *T*, *T* to *Y* to *S*, or *Y* to *S* and *Y* to *T* following the one-way streets defined by the arrows. Thus *Y* is a consequent variable by Rule 6.4.

Since in our example both *X* and *Y* are consequents, Rule 6.4 tells us to predict the zero-order correlation for *ST*.

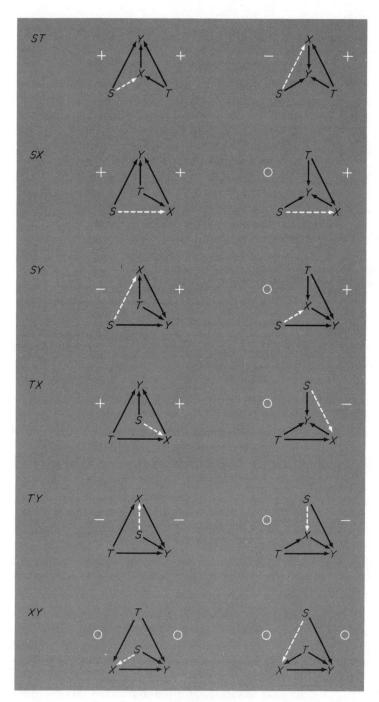

FIG. 6.15 Diagrams used to derive predictions for model in Fig. 6.14.

TABLE 6.15 Raw Data for Sex, Education, Occupation, and Income (figures are from 1960 U.S. census tables, rounded to the nearest thousand)

S	T	X	Y		S	T	X	Y	
			Income					Income	
Sex	Education	Occupation	−	+	Sex	Education	Occupation	−	+
+	+	+	3451	7294	−	+	+	6982	1150
+	+	−	4188	3817	−	+	−	2005	76
+	−	+	2397	1986	−	−	+	2538	168
+	−	−	13303	5871	−	−	−	6063	107

$N = 61396$

TABLE 6.16 Four-Variable Results for Data in Table 6.15

Q_{ST}

		Y				
		Differs	Tied	3 Variable	Second-order partial	−.126
	Tied	+.184	−.126	+.019	X effect	−.395
X	Differs	−.047	−.521	−.305	Y effect	+.310
	3 Variable	+.042	−.373	−.182	Joint effect	+.164

Q_{SX}

		Y				
		Differs	Tied	3 Variable	Second-order partial	−.510
	Tied	−.283	−.510	−.406	T effect	−.102
T	Differs	−.155	−.612	−.404	Y effect	+.227
	3 Variable	−.206	−.572	−.405	Joint effect	+.230

Q_{SY}

		X				
		Differs	Tied	3 Variable	Second-order partial	+.884
	Tied	+.800	+.884	+.849	T effect	−.017
T	Differs	+.713	+.867	+.772	X effect	−.084
	3 Variable	+.748	+.877	+.810	Joint effect	−.070

Q_{TX}

		Y				
		Differs	Tied	3 Variable	Second-order partial	+.705
	Tied	+.748	+.705	+.726	S effect	+.059
S	Differs	+.748	+.764	+.757	Y effect	+.043
	3 Variable	+.748	+.733	+.740	Joint effect	−.059

Q_{TY}

		X				
		Differs	Tied	3 Variable	Second-order partial	+.372
	Tied	+.585	+.372	+.495	S effect	−.112
S	Differs	+.202	+.260	+.225	X effect	+.213
	3 Variable	+.414	+.326	+.378	Joint effect	−.271

Q_{XY}

		T				
		Differs	Tied	3 Variable	Second-order partial	+.365
	Tied	+.576	+.365	+.495	S effect	−.475
S	Differs	+.112	−.110	+.024	T effect	+.211
	3 Variable	+.369	+.146	+.282	Joint effect	+.011

1. The zero-order correlation for sex and education is predicted to be negligible. Inspection of the three-variable results in Table 6.16 reveals a zero-order coefficient of $-.182$. The prediction is not supported.

Moving on to the dogleg effects for X and Y, a new problem arises, or rather, a new version of the same old problem. In a four-variable model the two primary dogleg relationships can have a consequent variable, although this is a logical impossibility in a three-variable model. Looking at the X dogleg for ST, this is what we find. Y is a consequent variable for SX and TX. What do we do? You guessed it, we delete Y and test the X dogleg from the three-variable model S,T,X. The dogleg product being negative (SX is negative, TX is positive), we predict:

2. $D - P$ will be negative in the three-variable analysis of ST with X as a test variable. Table 6.16 supports the prediction. $D = -.305$, $P = +.019$, and $D - P = -.324$.

The other dogleg effect, Y, does not have a consequent variable (it is logically impossible for Y to be a consequent for X and X to be a consequent for Y) and so we make the regular four-variable prediction. Since SY and TY are both positive

3. The effect of Y should be positive, and it is, being $+.310$.

The last prediction for ST is the joint effect. Because it involves all four variables it cannot have a consequent "beyond" it just as $D - P$ cannot have a consequent in three-variable analyses. Table 6.11 gives us two question marks so no prediction can be made, the structure being like Figure 6.8(c).

The second relationship is SX. The diagram reveals that Y is a consequent, but not T, so we predict the first-order partial as Rule 6.4 tells us to:

4. $Q_{SX:\text{TIED } T}$ should be negative, and is, with a value of $-.406$.

For the T dogleg, Y is a consequent variable (you can always spot a variable consequent to both dogleg relationships because it will have three incoming one-way arrows), so, as in prediction 2,

5. $D - P$ for Q_{SX} with test variable T should be negligible. The prediction is supported. $D = -.404$, $P = -.406$, and $D - P = -.002$.

For the Y dogleg we make the usual four-variable prediction.

6. The effect of Y should be positive, and it is ($+.227$).

The joint effect for SX is predicted to be positive, following the usual rationale.

7. The joint effect for SX, +.230, is positive as predicted.

For SY, the third relationship, there is no consequent variable. We proceed with the usual four-variable partial prediction:

8. The second-order partial for SY is predicted to be positive. The calculated value, +.884, supports the prediction.

But we are not yet back on completely familiar territory. When we come to the dogleg prediction for T, we observe the following: X is a consequent variable for ST, but X is not a consequent variable for TY. The dilemma is insoluble. If we control X, we may get that spurious partial effect of a consequent variable; if we ignore X, we cannot partial out its predicted effect on TY. We ease out of such situations by making no prediction at all. We are now ready to state a general rule for dogleg predictions in four-variable models:

RULE 6.5

When predicting dogleg effects in four-variable models:

If the other test variable receives three incoming one-way arrows, delete it and predict $D - P$ in a three-variable tabulation.

If the other test variable is a consequent for one primary dogleg relationship but not the other, make no prediction.

In all other cases, predict the four-variable effect.

The X dogleg for SY is a conventional situation and is predicted to be negative.

9. The X effect for SY is predicted to be negative, but the prediction is not supported, the difference, −.084, being less than 10 units.

10. The joint effect of T and X on SY is predicted to be negative but is of insufficient magnitude, being −.070.

The fourth relationship, TX, raises no problems that have not been considered previously. Noting that Y is a consequent variable for both TX and the primary dogleg relationships, we predict away.

11. The correlation between T and X, controlling for S, should be positive, and is (+.726).

12. $D - P$ for TX, controlling for S, should be negligible, and is (.757 − .726 = −.031).

13. The effect of Y in the four-variable data should be positive. This prediction fails as the effect is only +.043.

Table 6.11 tells us to make no prediction for the joint effect as the left-hand structure is ambiguous.

The fifth relationship is TY. Its only "abnormality" is that X is a consequent for the dogleg relationship ST but not for SY, so the second part of Rule 6.5 applies. We steam along with more predictions.

14. The second-order partial, $+.372$, is positive, as predicted.
15. The effect of X, $+.213$, is positive, as predicted.

Again, Rule 6.3 tells us to make no prediction for the joint effect.
The last relationship, XY, is as common as dirt. No exceptions or special rules at all. We predict

16. The second-order partial, $+.365$, is positive, as predicted.
17. The effect of S, $-.475$, is negative, as predicted.
18. The effect of T, $+.211$, is positive, as predicted.
19. The joint effect, $+.011$, is negligible, as predicted.

Table 6.17 shows how the whole thing looks.

TABLE 6.17   Results and Predictions for Model in Figure 6.14

| | | PREDICTION | | |
		Negative	Negligible	Positive
	+.70 or higher			2
	+.50–.69			
	+.30–.49			3
	+.10–.29			5
Actual difference	+.00–.09		1	1
or coefficient	−.00–.09		2	
	−.10–.29	1	1	
	−.30–.49	3		
	−.50–.69			
	−.70 or lower			

Again a healthy positive relationship with a gamma of $+1.00$. Our second model does about as well as the first.

Reviewing the results in terms of substance, there is no "key" proposition as there was in the public housing data. Where a model has a clear order, though, one may summarize it by working from antecedent to consequent variables. Our model can be boiled down to the following:

Education leads to better jobs (prediction 11) and it leads to higher earnings both directly (prediction 14) and indirectly through better jobs (prediction 15). Men earn more (prediction 8) but they tend to get lower status blue collar jobs (prediction 4). According to the model, this should tend to bring down the sex difference in earnings, but this prediction (prediction 9) is not fully supported by the data. Regardless of sex and education, white collar workers have higher earnings (prediction 16).

In this sense, the model looks a little less successful since one of the seven key inferences is not supported.

Having trotted along while two models were tested, you should be able to test your own four-variable models using diagrams and the rules.

At this point you may feel that testing a four-variable model is "a lot of trouble." In a sense you are right, and we began the chapter by warning you that four-variable models are not something to while away a 10- or 15-minute gap in your round of activities. In another sense, though, you are wrong— or at least you fail to see the point of sociological theory. The fact that a plethora of predictions emerges from six simple assertions and a few rules is the intellectual beauty of theoretical work as opposed to sheer number crunching. A theory that can produce a large number of specific predictions on the basis of a logical system is the best kind of theory there is. The bane of modern sociology is theories that do not predict anything (this is what most of you study in your courses called "Sociological Theory") and long lists of statistical findings that have no intellectual coherence, and our little models avoid these swamps. This is not to say that either of our models provides a particular poignant insight into the human condition or reveals insights never before suspected—but that is not the purpose of theory. The purpose of theory is logical articulation of propositions and operational rules for testing then empirically. Theorywise, poignancy is lagniappe; deductions pay the bill.

Introducing a Second Test Variable

When one is attempting to explain some zero-order correlation, XY, it is very common to find that in each of a number of three-variable analyses the test variable reduces the first-order partial but does not eliminate it. In other words, the results for XY may fall in the "twilight zone" for a number of test variables, $R, S, T. \ldots$

At this point one usually wonders whether controlling two test variables might explain XY even though no one of them is powerful enough to do the trick alone. Sometimes you can and sometimes you cannot. A review of four-variable structures sheds light on how it works.

Let us assume the following hypothetical results:

$$Q_{XY} = +.40$$

$$Q_{XY:\text{TIED } T} = +.20$$

$$Q_{XY:\text{TIED } S} = +.20$$

Our problem is this: Given these data, what conditions must obtain for the second-order partial, $Q_{XY:\text{TIED } S,T}$ to disappear?

We can fill in parts of a table like Table 6.18 and work from there.

TABLE 6.18   Hypothetical Four-Variable Results

		T Differing	*T* Tied	*T* Weighted sum
S	Tied		.00	+.20
S	Differing			>+.40
	Weighted sum	>+.40	+.20	+.40

The answer is obvious. Because the results have to add up, we see that both partial differentials must be positive and greater in magnitude than the first-order partials, as shown in Table 6.19.

TABLE 6.19   Implications of Table 6.9

		T Differing	*T* Tied	*T* Weighted sum
S	Tied	>+.20	.00	+.20
S	Differing	?	>+.20	>+.40
	Weighted sum	>+.40	+.20	+.40

Notice that the differential differential is not defined. It could even be negative, provided that the partial differentials are extremely high.

Must one obtain such felicitous results when a second test variable is introduced into the analysis? Alas, no. Consider the outcome shown in Table 6.20, given the same assumptions.

TABLE 6.20   Alternative Hypothetical Results

		T Differing	*T* Tied	*T* Weighted sum
S	Tied	+.20	+.20	+.20
S	Differing	>+.40	+.20	>+.40
	Weighted sum	>+.40	+.20	+.40

In Table 6.20 the four-variable results are not a whit better than the three-variable results even though the initial assumptions are unchanged.

We may draw this conclusion: Four-variable explanations may or may not be better than two-variable explanations, and when they are, both partial differentials must have the same sign as the zero order which is explained.

Can we say anything about the factors which differentiate the blissful outcome of Table 6.19 from the discouraging revelations of Table 6.20?

The answer is "yes and no." It is "no" in the sense that one can never deduce the exact results of higher-order tabulations from the results of lower-order tabulations, a fact of life we accepted in three-variable analysis. It is "yes" in the sense that we can spot the crucial principles and learn some useful tips from them.

Where the test variables S and T fit the sign rule, their zero-order relations can have only one of three patterns: (1) TXS and TXY are both suppressing systems, (2) S and T have a negligible relationship, and (3) TXS and TXY are both reinforcing systems.

When TSX and TSY are both suppressing systems, we expect that both partial differentials will be strong. From the rules for three-variable analysis, we anticipate that when S is controlled, TX and TY will become stronger, and when T is controlled, SX and SY will become stronger. This should enhance both dogleg effects in four-variable analysis and improve the explanation (i.e., drive the second-order partial down below either first-order partial.)[3]

When ST is negligible, the suggestion is that the joint effect will be negligible, because zero ST relationships are the hallmark of a negligible joint effect. This is good news, although not as good news as a double suppression.

When TSX and TSY are both reinforcing systems, the suspicion arises that there will be a definite joint effect (see Figure 6.3 and its discussion). This is not necessarily disastrous because one may have negligible second-order partials and healthy joint effects, provided that the dogleg effects are quite robust. However, it is not particularly gratifying news, especially when ST is very strong and one of the four dogleg correlations is rather weak. The latter situation suggests that in four-variable tabulations, one of the dogleg relationships would vanish, rather than the XY correlation.

Putting these ruminations together, we obtain Rule 6.6:

RULE 6.6

When a number of test variables affect, but do not explain XY in three-variable tabulations and one seeks pairs providing a better explanation (i.e., a smaller second-order partial), examine the zero-order coefficients for the triangles STX and STY :

When both are suppressing systems, the pair is promising and the stronger the magnitude of ST, the greater the promise.

When S and T are unrelated, the pair is promising.

When both triangles are reinforcing, the pair is less promising, and the greater the magnitude of ST, the less the promise.

---

[3] The assiduous reader will note that this advice contradicts our previous reasoning about Figure 6.8(b). The difference boils down to this. Before, we eschewed such structures because of the remote possibility that the suppression would be so strong that one set of doglegs would "reverse sign" in four-variable tabulations. While this could happen, it is very rare in practice. Since our aim here is not to make predictions but to screen a set of data for further tabulations, we take the chance, knowing that the four-variable tabulations will settle the matter one way or another.

A Note on Larger Models

Although the author has not attempted to do so, it would seem that our approach could be extended to models with five or more variables.

One could deduce all the possible coefficients quite easily. In any higher-order coefficient a given variable has two possibilities—it is tied or it varies. With N variables there are $N - 2$ test variables and consequently $2^{(N-2)}$ coefficients. Thus, with six variables there would be 2^4 or $2 * 2 * 2 * 2 = 16$ fourth-order coefficients. . . for each of 15 pairs of variables.

Furthermore, it would not be too difficult to find structural analogues to the coefficients. Those where all the test variables are tied are partials and correspond to the lines in the model; those where all but one test variable are tied correspond to the doglegs in the model; and (presumably) the remaining coefficients can be seen as various joint effects.

What is debatable is whether such an attempt is worthwhile. Beginning research students (particularly the better ones) frequently try to test five- or six-variable models, believing that this indicates professional sophistication. Generally, the result is a mass of statistics and a limited insight into the phenomenon being studied.

In scientific work, economy and simplicity are given high priority, and beginners fail to realize that a large model is a sign of failure, not success. The best model of all is a two-variable one ($X \longrightarrow Y$): It says that X influences Y and nothing else in the world makes a damn bit of difference. To show that in sociology would be a remarkable feat. It is only when one is forced to admit that T influences X and Y that one is driven to a three-variable model, and one falls back on a four-variable model only when the additional effects of S cannot be ignored.

Thus, some advice: Seek the smallest model that does justice to your data, not the largest. Unless you have compelling substantive theoretical reasons to do so, treat data with five or more variables by the procedures of Chapter 7, not as large models.

IN A NUTSHELL

A. Analysis with two test variables involves elaboration of "the equation" into four terms whose weighted average equals Q_{XY}.

1. The second-order partial Q_{XY}:TIED S, T
2. The partial differential for T or Q_{XY}:DIFF T, TIED S
3. The partial differential for S or Q_{XY}:DIFF S, TIED T
4. The second-order differential or Q_{XY}:DIFF S, T

B. These coefficients may be used to test causal models by adopting the following conventions:

1. The second-order partial should have the sign of the causal assertion for *XY* unless there is a consequent variable.
2. The partial differential effects should have the signs of the relevant dogleg products unless the fourth variable is consequent.
3. The joint effect—the difference between the row (column) differences in a table of second-order coefficients—should have the sign given by Rule 6.3.
4. Consequent variables are deleted for relationships and doglegs.

C. Applying these concepts to the problem of explanation, we conclude that:

1. Two test variables may or may not provide a better explanation of *XY* than either taken alone in three-variable tabulations.
2. Successful four-variable explanations usually have relatively small joint effects, or joint effects opposite in sign to *XY*.
3. Inspection of the zero-order relations for the *STX* and *STY* triangles, following Rule 6.6, can help one to spot promising and less promising pairs of test variables.

Rules (in condensed form)

R U L E 6.1

When there is no consequent variable, predict the second-order partial from the line for *XY*.

R U L E 6.2

When there is no consequent variable, predict the difference between the partial differentials and the second-order partial from the relevant dogleg sign products.

R U L E 6.3

Predict the joint effect from Table 6.11.

R U L E 6.4

When predicting *XY*, delete *S* or *T* or both if they are consequent variables, using the zero-order or first-order partials as appropriate.

R U L E 6.5

When predicting dogleg effects, delete the other test variable if the secondary doglegs both lead to a consequent; make no prediction if one secondary dogleg leads to a consequent.

RULE 6.6

When seeking promising pairs of variables for two-variable explanations, examine the zero-order correlations for *STX* and *STY*. Prefer pairs where both are suppressing systems and eschew pairs where both are reinforcing systems, the latter especially when *ST* is a strong correlation.

Major Concepts

1. Partial differential (differential partial)
2. Primary dogleg
3. Second-order differential
4. Second-order partial
5. Secondary dogleg

APPENDIX: FORMULAS FOR FOUR-VARIABLE ANALYSIS

Note: The formula is for the zero-order correlation Q_{XY} with test variables S and T. You may, of course, use it for other tabulations by relettering the variables as is appropriate.

Raw data table and cell notation

S	T	X	Y −	+	S	T	X	Y −	+
+	+	+	A	B	−	+	+	I	J
+	+	−	C	D	−	+	−	K	L
+	−	+	E	F	−	−	+	M	N
+	−	−	G	H	−	−	−	O	P

Formulas

$$Q_{XY} = \frac{[(B+F+J+N)(C+G+K+O)] - [(A+E+I+M)(D+H+L+P)]}{[(B+F+J+N)(C+G+K+O)] + [(A+E+I+M)(D+H+L+P)]}$$

$$Q_{XY:\text{TIED }S,T} = \frac{[(B*C)+(F*G)+(J*K)+(N*O)] - [(A*D)+(E*H)+(I*L)+(M*P)]}{[(B*C)+(F*G)+(J*K)+(N*O)] + [(A*D)+(E*H)+(I*L)+(M*P)]}$$

$$Q_{XY:\text{DIFF } S, \text{TIED } T} =$$

$$\frac{[(B*K)+(J*C)+(F*O)+(N*G)]-[(A*L)+(I*D)+(E*P)+(M*H)]}{[(B*K)+(J*C)+(F*O)+(N*G)]+[(A*L)+(I*D)+(E*P)+(M*H)]}$$

$$Q_{XY:\text{DIFF } T, \text{TIED } S} =$$

$$\frac{[(B*G)+(F*C)+(J*O)+(N*K)]-[(A*H)+(D*E)+(I*P)+(M*L)]}{[(B*G)+(F*C)+(J*O)+(N*K)]+[(A*H)+(D*E)+(I*P)+(M*L)]}$$

$$Q_{XY:\text{DIFF } S,T} =$$

$$\frac{[(B*O)+(F*K)+(N*C)+(J*G)]-[(A*P)+(E*L)+(M*D)+(I*H)]}{[(B*O)+(F*K)+(N*C)+(J*G)]+[(A*P)+(E*L)+(M*D)+(I*H)]}$$

Weights

To find the weight for each of the second-order coefficients, divide its *denominator* by the denominator for Q_{XY}. It is a good idea to check your work by calculating each weight and adding them to see whether they sum to 1.000.

First-order coefficients

First-order coefficients may be obtained from the second-order coefficients and their weights, using the following notation for the weights:

			T	
			Differing	Tied
S	Tied		II	I
	Differing		IV	III

$$Q_{XY:\text{TIED } S} = \left(Q_{XY:\text{DIFF } T, \text{TIED } S} * \frac{\text{II}}{\text{I}+\text{II}} \right) + \left(Q_{XY:\text{TIED } S,T} * \frac{\text{I}}{\text{I}+\text{II}} \right)$$

$$Q_{XY:\text{DIFF } S} = \left(Q_{XY:\text{DIFF } S,T} * \frac{\text{IV}}{\text{III}+\text{IV}} \right) + \left(Q_{XY:\text{DIFF } S, \text{TIED } T} * \frac{\text{III}}{\text{III}+\text{IV}} \right)$$

$$Q_{XY:\text{TIED } T} = \left(Q_{XY:\text{TIED } S,T} * \frac{\text{I}}{\text{I}+\text{III}} \right) + \left(Q_{XY:\text{DIFF } S, \text{TIED } T} * \frac{\text{III}}{\text{I}+\text{III}} \right)$$

$$Q_{XY:\text{DIFF } T} = \left(Q_{XY:\text{DIFF } T, \text{TIED } S} * \frac{\text{II}}{\text{II}+\text{IV}} \right) + \left(Q_{XY:\text{DIFF } S,T} * \frac{\text{IV}}{\text{II}+\text{IV}} \right)$$

7

(Too) Many Variables

In some sciences data are rare and costly. A team of physicists may spend a year of time and tens of thousands of (other people's) dollars to obtain observations on one or two variables. An archeologist may travel halfway around the world to obtain one elderly tooth. An experimental social psychologist may mount something close to a Broadway production in a small group experiment that generates data we have seen to be equivalent to a zero-order correlation.

Sociologists have worse luck—they are victims of "data glut." Good sociological data may be costly, and there are many important aspects of social life where little or no valid data are available; but when a sociologist collects data, he usually collects a lot.

For example, it is "normal" for a public opinion survey to produce data which fill all 80 columns of five or six different IBM cards per respondent. In other words, 400 or more variables!

There are two reasons for data glut in sociology. First, the additional cost of extra measures is relatively slight in personal interviews and questionnaires. So much of the cost (in time and money) goes into drawing the sample, obtaining cooperation from the respondents, organizing a staff to carry out the project, and the like, that "a couple more questions" do not seem to add any appreciable burden to the project or to the subjects who provide the data.

Second, sociological theory and research have not yet developed to the point where the research worker is confident that he can predict his results ahead of time. Thus, there is a tendency for the designer to develop lengthy attitude batteries (because he does not trust the validity of his individual items) and endless test variables (because "Who knows? Maybe brother-in-law's political preference is correlated with the respondent's job satisfaction").

The upshot is that when you actually begin your first research project you will find yourself confronted with much more information than you can handle by strict application of the procedures treated in the previous chapters. The problem is not mathematical: We saw in Chapter 6 that the skeleton for multivariate analysis may be extended to any number of variables. The problem is mostly psychological. Psychologists tell us of "the magic number seven, plus or minus two" by which they mean that it is extremely difficult for us to grasp much more than half a dozen concepts or facts at the same time. Remembering from Chapter 1 that the aim of research is to generate conclusions, not just churn numbers, the research worker is usually faced with a formidable intellectual task in handling large numbers of variables.

From this point of view, survey analysis is misnamed because the crucial task is not analysis, breaking things down into smaller parts, but synthesis, organizing them into intellectually coherent packages. The high art of sociological research is to cut through all the numbers to find a simple set of conclusions that make sense without distorting the findings.

Remember this: Stacks and stacks of "output" are the sign of an amateur, not a professional.

In this chapter we will present a set of rules and procedures which will help you in handling voluminous sets of data. If you follow them, you can usually extract meaningful results, even though you will not wring the data dry.

We warn you that these are rules of thumb, and it cannot be shown mathematically that they are the most efficient procedures. However, so many beginners flounder around in their first attempts at analysis that we urge you to follow these rules—if only to keep from going around in circles. Later on, after you become sophisticated, you should feel free to ignore these rules and rely on your intuition.

State Your Problem

Never loath to embrace the obvious, we begin with this advice: *State your problem.*

If you hang around sociology laboratories you will frequently see research workers who seem to be idly cross-tabulating and running correlations in defiance of our advice above. There is no great harm in this *in the beginning stages* of analysis where it is a good idea to idly cross-tabulate this-that-and-the-other to get the "feel" of how your variables work and hang together. But, sooner or later, you must take charge because analyses do not emerge spontaneously from the data.

So far our advice borders on a truism, but it becomes less so when we complete the sentence.

State your problem in one of these three ways:

1. Is my hypothesis (model) plausible?
2. What explains Q_{XY}?
3. What are the major correlates of Y?

In other words, the great bulk of research problems fall into one of these three categories,[1] and if you cannot state your problem in these terms, you do not yet have a researchable problem.

In problem (1) the research worker states a particular two-variable hypothesis ("Social science students are more liberal on domestic political issues than engineering students") or a more complex three- or four-variable causal model and then proceeds to collect and tabulate data to see whether the hypothesis is plausible or not. In problem (2) the research worker observes a correlation $(Q_{\text{field of study and liberalism}} = +.38)$ and attempts to explain it through introducing appropriate test variables. In problem (3) the research worker picks a single variable, Y, and attempts to find a number of other variables which are all correlated with it ("What are the social characteristics associated with undergraduate major?").

As the hypothetical example makes clear, the problems are not wildly different and as the research proceeds the problem may shift. One might begin by asking what are the social characteristics associated with field of undergraduate study (problem 3), find that liberal attitudes are very strong predictors, then attempt to explain why social science students are more liberal (problem 2), and end up with a four-variable model involving parental variables, student values, and career choice (problem 1). However, at each stage in the game you should be able to state exactly what problem you are working on at the moment because the issues and techniques vary considerably.

It is ironic that the difficulty of the problem is inverse to its complexity. Problem 1, which may involve a very fancy initial model, is the easiest in the sense of knowing what to do about it, while problem 3, which only involves

---

[1] The professional will note that certain technical research problems such as developing a good measure of some variable, comparing alternative sample designs, estimating a particular parameter, and the like do not fall neatly into this list. However, anyone working on such problems needs training beyond the level of this book.

coming up with the name of some variable, is the toughest to handle from a purely technical point of view. Which is just another way of saying: The more hard thinking you do before you begin your analysis, the easier it will be to know what to do.

To sum up, it is perfectly permissible to begin your research with a vague interest in some phenomenon ("career choice" or "values" or "socialization"), particularly if you are working with someone else's data, but sooner or later it has to be turned into a specific research problem. This means stating particular variables and a definite research problem of type 1, 2, or 3. Obviously if you are collecting your own data you are under greater pressure to state your problem precisely, but even when you are fishing in someone else's pond, you have not really begun your work until you have stated a definite research problem.

Testing a Hypothesis or Model

The most straightforward research is testing a hypothesis or causal model. · This does not mean that you are destined to have great luck. One of the reasons experienced research workers break into howls of laughter when they hear someone say "Sociology is merely a documentation of the obvious" is that the obvious seldom comes out that way when put to the test of data. Nevertheless, problem 1 has the advantage that it is possible to outline a clear set of steps to follow.

Note: Our rules and steps assume that your data have already been collected and are ready for tabulation. If you are starting from scratch, exactly the same principles apply, with the modification, "Design your study so that you can...."

Steps in testing a hypothesis or causal model

I. State your hypothesis. If it involves three or more variables, draw a causal diagram paying careful attention to the direction of the arrows. (If you are in doubt about direction, assume symmetry.)

II. Consider the measures of your variables.

    A. Run the marginals for the measures you are considering, entering the category frequencies in a code book to use as a check on your later results.

    B. Combine items into indices if necessary to obtain reasonable marginal distributions.

    C. If several items seem equally appropriate as indicators of the same variable, pick the one you think is "best," but keep a record of the others.

D. Pick the cutting point for each variable and indicate it in your code book.

III. Run the appropriate zero-order or multivariate tabulations, checking the marginals for all items against the code book to make sure you ran the right data.

We are now at a fork in the road, depending on whether your hypothesis "works" or "fails."

IVa. If it fails:

A. If the failure lies in a partial that should vanish but is only reduced a little, refine the partial if possible, following the suggestions of Chapter 4.

B. Check for mechanical errors. Can you reconstruct the correct marginals from the frequencies in your cross-tabulation? Did you keep the signs of the correlations straight? Do the terms in "the equation" add up to the correct zero orders?

C. Check for a possible suppressor variable or set of suppressor variables that may be distorting your results. Use the sign rule as a guide.

D. Substitute alternative measures for various items. If your hypothesis works using the other measure, ask what reformulation or limitation of your hypothesis is suggested.

E. If all else fails, search blindly for specifiers. Your hypothesis might be "right" within one category of T but "wrong" in the other. Note, however, that the best you can hope for is a watering down of the original hypothesis, which now applies only to a particular category of T.

F. Consider prayerfully the distinct possibility that you are just plain wrong.

IVb. If it "succeeds":

A. Test sensitivity to your measurement decisions. In other words, check to see whether your predictions are still supported when you measure the same variables in other ways.

1. Try other cutting points and cell analysis (see Chapter 3) for your variables, particularly the nominal ones.

2. Try other alternative measures for your variables. If your predictions work for some but not others, ask yourself how you should change or limit the meaning of your hypothesis.

B. Introduce test variables that might threaten your results.

1. Use the sign rule to locate variables in your data that might produce spurious support for your hypothesis.

2. Even when the sign rule does not apply, it is good practice to introduce as test variables measures of the standard sociological variables: education, occupation, sex, age, region, city size, ethnicity, etc., just because they have a "good track record."

3. Consider what variables, not measured in your data, are likely to have a sign rule pattern that threatens your hypothesis.

C. If possible, repeat (replicate) your results on other data. At the least, check sociological journals and books for other research findings that support or challenge your findings.

Explaining a Correlation

The second classic research problem is to explain a correlation between X and Y through multivariate analysis. The same steps apply to the less frequent case where one wants to explain why there is no correlation or only a small correlation between X and Y, though the "content" of the sign rule is reversed.

Steps in explaining a correlation

I. Pick an appropriate correlation to be explained. Before grinding away on statistical analysis, you should consider whether you really want to explain Q_{XY}. Ask yourself two questions:

A. Is the correlation substantively interesting? If, for example, you observe a positive correlation between income and the length of a man's yacht, there is no feeling of puzzlement or itch to dig further into the matter. Matters of intellectual taste are involved here and many scientific careers have been made by treating as problematical findings everyone else considers to be obvious. Nevertheless, you should ask yourself whether the correlation is worth explaining.

B. Is the size of the correlation appropriate? If the correlation is too high, you will not be able to explain it; if it is too low, it is hardly worth the trouble. Beginners frequently make the mistake of trying to explain the largest correlation in their data, but the sign rule reminds us that correlations are explained by larger correlations, not smaller ones. At the other extreme, you may be able to reduce a zero-order correlation of $+.12$ to $+.02$ and thus "explain" it according to the rules of the game, but a correlation of $+.12$ is (usually) not a prey worthy of your skills as a huntsman. Content aside, the best correlations to explain are the middling ones, high enough to be worth the trouble but low enough so that there are reasonable test variable relations.

C. Make sure that your correlation is statistically significant before you attempt to explain it through multivariate analysis. "Sampling error" is the first explanation to consider for any relationship, and one should seek others only when it can be rejected as a plausible hypothesis.

II. Look for half a dozen or so promising test variables.

A. Think hard about X and Y, and what sort of variables might be correlated with both. Use your common sense, use preliminary results from your own data, or draw on your readings in social science. The trick is to come up with test variables that are related to *both* X and Y, and the most common failure of the beginning researcher is to end up with a list of test variables that have strong correlations with X *or* Y but not both.

B. Avoid test variables that are obviously causally consequent to both X and Y.

C. Run the zero-order correlations of your potential test variables with both X and Y, checking the marginals for all items against your code book.

D. If you have a considerable number of test variables, you may screen them by multiplying their zero-order coefficients. For example, if Q_{TX} is $+.48$ and Q_{TY} is $-.34$, their product is $-.1632$. The product should have the same sign as Q_{XY}, the correlation to be explained. This rough index gives higher priority to larger correlations and also to those pairs where the correlations are even in size. (If $TX = +.80$ and $TY = +.20$, the product is $+.160$. If $TX = +.50$ and $TY = +.50$, the product is $+.250$. The average of the pair is the same in both examples, but the latter is more promising because the correlations are even in magnitude.)

III. Run half a dozen or so of the more promising test variables in three variable tabulations, checking the marginals against your code book.

A. If, for one of the test variables, the partial $Q_{XY:\text{TIED }T}$ is negligible and $D - P$ is 10 units or more, you have explained Q_{XY}. Then go back to step IVb in the previous section on hypothesis testing.

B. If your best test variable ends up in the twilight zone, try refining it according to the instructions in Chapter 4. If the refined partial becomes negligible, you have explained Q_{XY}. Then go back to step IVb in the previous section on hypothesis testing.

C. If none of your test variables affects the correlation appreciably, you are probably stuck. You might find some helpful tips in step IVa of the previous section on hypothesis testing.

D. If two or more of your test variables end up in the twilight zone, go to step IV below.

IV. Consider the possibility that two test variables, S and T, taken together might explain Q_{XY}. As explained in Chapter 6, pairs of test variables sometimes provide better explanations when operating in tandem, but sometimes they do not. (Mathematically, it is even possible for the second-order partial to be stronger than either first-order partial, though such an outcome would be rare when the test variables are chosen using the sign rules.) There is no way to know for sure until you run four-variable tabulations, but when you have a flock of test variables that show promise in three-variable tabulations, you may use Rule 6.6 to screen the more promising pairs. Do this by examining the zero-order coefficients for the various STX and STY triangles.[2] Give priority to pairs where these triangles are suppressing and within that group to *strong ST* relationships. Give lesser priority to triangles that are reinforcing and among them still less priority to strong ST relationships. In other words, you want strong ST relationships when the systems are suppressing and weak ST relationships when the systems are reinforcing. This done, run the higher-priority pairs in four-variable tabulations. If you find a pair where the second-order partial becomes negligible *and* where both dogleg effects are nonnegligible, you may say that S and T explain XY. Then go back to step IVb in the previous section on hypothesis testing. Remember that you can "refine" two test variables as easily as one. Merely cross-tabulate the categories of S against the categories of T, layout fourfold XY tables within each resulting subgroup, sum the positive cross products over all the subgroups, sum the negative cross products over all the subgroups, and compute the partial Q from the two sums.

V. If the results with two test variables produce a smaller partial for Q_{XY} than that obtained in three-variable tabulations but the relationship does not drop below the absolute value of .10, you may continue to add test variables as long as your patience holds out. The following points should be noted:

---

[2] This requires that you know the zero-order correlations among all the promising test variables. In point of fact, where computation facilities permit, it is a good idea to have a matrix of zero-order correlations for all the variables in your analysis. This is cumbersome when there are more than, say, 25 variables, but the theme here is that you should not have many more than 25 variables. Dragnet operations are not a good idea in survey analysis. Indeed, the major liability of modern computers is the ease with which they lead to massive —and confusing—assaults on massed phalanxes of variables.

A. First, to calculate a higher-order partial, cross-tabulate all the test variables against each other, lay out a fourfold XY table within each resulting subgroup, and sum cross products in the now familiar fashion.

B. Second, generally speaking, each new test variable will take a smaller "bite" out of Q_{XY}, and if you are not on the edge of an explanation with two or three variables, you may well have to go to 15 or 20 test variables to reduce the correlation sufficiently. To avoid endless nibbling, it is a good idea to have a decision rule for a nonnegligible impact on a higher-order partial, just as we used "D minus P" to evaluate the impact of a single test variable. Following the discussion in Chapter 6, the appropriate rule seems to be this: Add an additional explainer only if its dogleg effect (partial differential vs. nth-order partial) is 10 units or more. To calculate a higher-order partial differential for variable S, (1) cross-tabulate the test variables other than S; (2) within *each* of the resulting subgroups, lay out a pair of fourfold tables like these:

		Y					Y	
S	X	$-$	$+$		S	X	$-$	$+$
$+$	$+$				$-$	$+$		
$-$	$-$				$+$	$-$		

(3) calculate all the positive cross products and sum them (there will be twice as many as there are subgroups on the other test variables), do the same for the negative cross products and calculate the coefficient from the difference and total for these sums.

C. Third, do not be unduly eager to add explainers. Given a large number of measures, considerable patience, and easy access to computation equipment, there is nothing to prevent you from introducing 10 or 20 test variables simultaneously. However, the intellectual gain from such massive assaults is minimal. To say that the relationship between X and Y is explained by 15 test variables amounts to saying that the relationship defies any simple interpretation. Putting the same point another way: Add explainers to your analysis when they "tell you something," not merely because they drive the partial down a little.

The Major Correlates

Perhaps the most common research problem of all begins with questions such as "What are the differences between delinquents and nondelinquents?

What sort of people vote for right-wing political candidates? What conditions are necessary for democratic trade unions?" In each there is a key variable, *Y*—delinquency, political preference, degree of democracy—and the question amounts to this: "What are the major correlates of *Y*?"

The question can be broken into two problems, *whether* a particular variable is correlated with *Y*, and *how* it is correlated with *Y*. To find out whether, you (hold your breath!) cross-tabulate it against *Y* and calculate the zero-order correlation. Easy enough. But to discover how a particular variable is correlated with *Y*, you must turn to multivariate analysis because the relationship may not be simple and direct. Other variables may reinforce, suppress, or even explain the correlation.[3]

Because we have been talking about multivariate analysis for three and one half chapters, there is nothing very new here. What is different is this: Because we are on a sort of fishing expedition (by definition we are not testing a specific hypothesis or model), we are likely to have a boatload of variables. A complete analysis of each (its highest order partial, the scads of partial differentials, and the highest order differential) would produce a bucket of coefficients and a thimble of sociological understanding. Therefore, we seek shortcuts so that we can undertake a reasonably systematic search with a minimum number of tabulations. The following steps are suggested.

Steps in analyzing correlates of *Y*

I. Measure *Y* carefully. Because your key variable, *Y*, will appear in every tabulation, the results cannot be any better than your measure of that variable. Granted that any variable worth tabulating is worth careful measurement, you should be especially concerned with *Y*. Check its marginals, weigh alternative measures, brood about its validity—in short, make sure that *Y* is worth all the time and effort you will spend working with it. Too many studies are devoted to exquisite statistical analyses of dubious key variables.

II. Choose a set of predictors. Until you have actually run correlations between your predictors and *Y* there is no way to tell which variables have promise, and if you are a patient person, you can run dozens of predictors. Nevertheless, three pieces of advice may be given.

---

[3] A note for the statistically sophisticated reader: With interval data and regression statistics, one may pursue a different tack, finding a set of predictors that maximizes the multiple correlation with *Y*. Throughout this book we have managed to find rough analogues of most regression techniques, but here we fail. There seems to be no satisfactory multiple correlation for *Q* and gamma, although many investigators are working on the problem. For advanced students, "dummy variables" may be a useful compromise but they are beyond the scope of this volume.

A. First, it is generally wise to pick predictors that are all consequent variables or none consequent, rather than a mixture. Sometimes your problem is "What does Y lead to?" and sometimes your problem is "What leads to Y?" and where causal direction is intuitively clear, your results will be more tidy if you stick to one or the other.

B. Second, you should avoid other measures of Y as best you can. If you have a number of predictors that are really measures of Y (e.g., intelligence test items, where Y is an intelligence test), any one of them will show a strong correlation with Y. However, you do not learn much when you find that one of the major predictors of preference for the Democratic party is the item, "On the whole, do you approve of the Democratic party?"

C. Third, and this is rather tricky, select sets of predictors that are substantively homogeneous or substantively heterogeneous. In general, substantive heterogeneity is better. You will learn more from your fishing expedition if you try a variety of choices from the sociological bait bucket—attitude measures, SES variables, demographic variables, measures of reference groups, peer group characteristics, etc. Indeed, sometimes the main result is finding which sort of variables have the strongest correlations with Y. Sometimes, however, one goes to the opposite extreme, for example, finding how a number of SES measures operate jointly or independently in affecting Y or teasing out the ways a set of attitude items are associated with Y. What is bad, however, is an awkward mixture, say, seven attitude items plus religious denomination or ten political variables plus two items on personal adjustment. Putting it another way, choose your items to give a broad sweep across the variables sociologists use, or go to the opposite extreme, a fine-grain analysis within a particular domain of content.

III. Run the zero-order correlations for all pairs of variables, giving the Q coefficients for all pairs of predictors and each predictor and Y. This may involve a bit of work, particularly if you do not have access to a computer (6 variables give 15 pairs, 9 variables give 36, 12 give 66). However, a matrix of intercorrelations is the secret for making your analysis systematic rather than hunt-and-peck.

To illustrate, let us consider 7 variables from Samuel A. Stouffer's 1954 survey of the U.S. adult population, discussed above in Chapter 5. The dependent variable, Y, is "tolerance of communists," an attitude scale combining 15 items that tap a person's willingness to grant civil liberties to "communists" and persons accused of being "communists." We use Stouffer's cutting point giving 25% "more tolerant" and 75% "less tolerant" even though it falls outside our 70–30 rule.

Stouffer's own analysis involves a variety of attitudinal (authoritarianism, interest, optimism, etc.) and "background" items. Remembering step IIC, we here select 6 background items. Their definitions and marginal percentages are as follows:

(A) Sex (+ = Male, 47%; − = Female, 53%)
(B) Age (+ = 40 or older, 57%; − = 21–39, 42%)
(C) Region (+ = South, 32%; − = Other, 68%)
(D) City size (+ = 100,000 or over and suburbs of same, 38%; − = Other, 62%)
(E) Education (+ = High school graduate or more, 41%; − = Less than high school graduate, 58%)
(F) Frequency of church attendance (+ = Within last month, 63%; − = Other, 37%)

Here is the matrix of correlations.

TABLE 7.1   Intercorrelations of Stouffer Items

	Sex A	Age B	Region C	City D	Education E	Church F	Tolerance Y
Sex A		+.08	−.04	−.02	−.11	−.26	+.15
Age B			+.05	−.06	−.48	+.04	−.23
Region C				−.38	−.35	+.16	−.46
City D					+.17	−.04	+.29
Education E						+.15	+.52
Church F							−.18
Tolerance Y							

IV. Make a sign matrix for the correlations. To do this, lay out a square matrix with as many rows and columns as variables. Enter a plus sign for every positive correlation of +.10 or higher and a minus sign for every negative correlation of −.10 or lower. Leave blank the cells for negligible correlations. Unlike Table 7.1, fill in both halves of the matrix. Table 7.2 presents the sign matrix for the data in Table 7.1.

TABLE 7.2   Sign Matrix for Data in Table 7.1

	A	B	C	D	E	F	Y
A					−	−	+
B					−		−
C				−	−	+	−
D			−		+		+
E	−	−	−	+		+	+
F	−		+		+		−
Y	+	−	−	+	+	−	

V. "Reflect" the sign matrix. *Reflection* is the process of reversing the high and low labels for categories to minimize the number of negative signs in the matrix. Why eliminate the negatives? Simply because it is easier to keep track of the variables if the signs are the same. In Table 7.1, for example, we see that sex has a positive correlation with tolerance, age has a negative correlation, region has a negative correlation, and so forth. It would be a lot clearer to reverse the meaning of age (making young positive and older negative) and region (making North positive and South negative) so that we can say that men, young people, and northerners are more tolerant, rather than saying that men tend to be more tolerant, older people less tolerant, and southerners less tolerant.

How do you do it? The principle is simple. If you switch the assignment of positive and negative to the categories of one variable in a correlation you automatically reverse the sign of the correlation. If you find a variable with more negative than positive correlations and reverse its labels, you will reduce the number of negative signs in the matrix. Reflection means to keep doing this until there are no more variables with more negative than positive signs. Sometimes you can eliminate all the minus signs. Usually you can reduce them to a handful.

In Table 7.2 we can count the number of positive and negative signs in each row, as summarized in Table 7.3. Table 7.3 shows that variables A, B, and C have an excess of negative signs and that B and C have the largest excess. We arbitrarily choose B as the first variable to reflect and make a new matrix reversing the sign of each correlation involving B, that is, the correlations in the second row and second column from the left. We also put a bar over the letter B, like this, $\bar{B}$, to denote a reflected variable. The new sign matrix appears in Table 7.4.

TABLE 7.3 Summary of Signs for Variables in Table 7.2

VARIABLE	TOTAL POSITIVE	TOTAL NEGATIVE	DIFFERENCE
A	1	2	+1
B	0	2	+2
C	1	3	+2
D	2	1	−1
E	3	3	0
F	2	2	0
Y	3	3	0

TABLE 7.4 Sign Matrix After Reflection of Variable B

	A	$\bar{B}$	C	D	E	F	Y	POSITIVE	NEGATIVE	DIFFERENCE
A					−	−	+	1	2	+1
$\bar{B}$				+			+	2	0	−2
C				−	−	+	−	1	3	+2
D			−		+		+	2	1	−1
E	−	+	−	+		+	+	4	2	−2
F	−	+		+	+		−	2	2	0
Y	+	+	−	+	+	−		4	2	−2

The figures at the right side of Table 7.4 reveal that variables A and C still have an excess of minus signs, C's being the largest. Therefore, we make a new matrix (not shown), the same as Table 7.4, except that C is reversed. Inspection of the new matrix shows A to have a surplus of 1 and F a surplus of 2. Therefore, we make still another matrix reversing F. This turns out to be the final matrix because there are no more variables with more minus than plus signs. In general, one continues until there is no variable with more minuses than pluses. If variables remain with an equal number of pluses and minuses, they should be flipped only if one of their minuses is with Y. Table 7.5 shows the final table for our Stouffer data. Note that the values of the nonnegligible correlations are entered.

TABLE 7.5   Final Matrix for Data in Table 7.1

	A	$\bar{B}$	$\bar{C}$	D	E	$\bar{F}$	Y
A					−.11	+.26	+.15
$\bar{B}$					+.48		+.23
$\bar{C}$				+.38	+.35	+.16	+.46
D			+.38		+.17		+.29
E	−.11	+.48	+.35	+.17		−.15	+.52
$\bar{F}$	+.26		+.16		−.15		+.18
Y	+.15	+.23	+.46	+.29	+.52	+.18	

VI. Select promising test variables for each variable by multiplying the values of the relevant correlations. The idea here is to use the final reflected matrix to spot those test variables that should be considered for each predictor variable and to ignore those whose impact is probably nil. The result is a tabulation plan for each separate predictor, the number of test variables depending on the values in the matrix. This may mean that we run only the zero-order correlation for a given variable or that we will control all the other predictors. It all depends on what the application of the sign rule suggests. To illustrate, we continue our analysis of correlates of tolerance.

We start with A (sex) and search Table 7.5 for other variables that have nonnegligible correlations with both A and Y. There are two of them, E (education) and $\bar{F}$ (church attendance). Table 7.6 shows how to summarize the data, using the multiplication index explained in step IID for explaining a correlation.

TABLE 7.6 AG $(Q = +.15)$

Variable	CORRELATION WITH		Product
	A	G	
E	−.11	+.52	−.0572
$\bar{F}$	+.26	+.18	+.0468

There is no magic number for evaluating the product, but here we note that all four correlations are close to the value of Q_{AG} so we decide to control for both. We further note that E might be a suppressor (its product is opposite in sign to the AG correlation). Table 7.7 gives the results of the four-variable tabulation.

TABLE 7.7 Four-Variable Results for Q_{AG}

		E Differs	Tied	
$\bar{F}$	Tied	+.11	+.16	Effect of E: .11 − .16 = −.05
	Differs	+.14	+.20	Effect of $\bar{F}$: .20 − .16 = +.04

Following the usual rules for four-variable analyses, we conclude that the effects of education (E) and church attendance ($\bar{F}$) are in the anticipated direction, but neither meets the ten-unit standard. Thus we conclude that sex is correlated with tolerance and that the relevant test variables, education and church attendance, do not affect the correlation.

Similar analyses of the other five predictors are summarized in Table 7.8.

TABLE 7.8 Condensed Summary of Multivariate Analyses

ITEM	ZERO ORDER	TEST VARIABLE	TX	TY	PRODUCT	EFFECT TERM*	PARTIAL	DIFFERENCE**
Age B	+.23	E	+.48	+.52	+.2496	+.33	+.10	+.23**
Region C	+.46	E	+.35	+.52	+.1820	+.54	+.39	+.15**
		D	+.38	+.29	+.1102	+.48	+.39	+.09
		$\bar{F}$	+.16	+.18	+.0288	not tested		
City D	+.29	$\bar{C}$	+.38	+.46	+.1748	+.36	+.22	+.14**
		E	+.17	+.52	+.0884	+.22	+.22	.00
Educ. E	+.52	$\bar{C}$	+.35	+.46	+.1610	+.56	+.47	+.09
		$\bar{B}$	+.48	+.23	+.1104	+.50	+.47	+.03
		D	+.17	+.29	+.0493	not tested		
		$\bar{F}$	−.15	+.18	−.0270	not tested		
		A	−.11	+.15	−.0165	not tested		
Church F	+.18	E	−.15	+.52	−.0780	+.16	+.18	−.02
		$\bar{C}$	+.16	+.46	+.0736	+.20	+.18	+.02
		A	+.26	+.15	+.0390	+.22	+.18	+.04

* In three-variable tabulations value is that of the differential; in higher order tabulations value is that of relevant partial differential. Calculation of partial differentials is explained in the previous section of this chapter.

** Indicates difference of 10 units or more.

Now, an English translation.

Education is the only variable related to both age and tolerance.

When it is controlled, it has a distinct impact on the correlation, D minus P being 23 units and the first-order partial dropping to a borderline value of $+.10$. In "real research" one would proceed to refine education and probably achieve an unambiguous explanation.

Three variables, education, city size, and church attendance, are correlated with both region and tolerance. However, the church attendance correlations are so low that we decided not to use them as controls (you might have made the opposite decision; it is a matter of judgment). When we control for education and city size, it is seen that education does has an effect (15 units) but city size does not quite meet the ten-unit standard. Since the second-order partial is $+.39$, we say that education affects but does not explain the correlation between region and tolerance.

City size is the next variable. Region and education appear as relevant test variables, and the four-variable tabulations show that region does affect, but not explain, the correlation while education has no clear impact.

The next variable, education, has all five predictors as potential test variables. All the other measures have a nonnegligible correlation with education and with tolerance. However, our judgment is that only two, age and region, seem worth testing. The four-variable data show that neither has a ten-unit impact magnitude.

The last variable is church attendance. Here age, education, and region are potential test variables, education possibly being a suppressor. However, the five-variable tabulations show that none of the three has an acceptable impact on the correlation between church attendance and tolerance.

VII. Summarize your results in a chart. It is often helpful to summarize such complex data with a chart in which predictor variables are arranged in order of size of zero-order correlation (unless there is a strong suppressor effect; if the partial is stronger than the zero order, one should use it rather than the zero order to place the variable in the ranking), and test variables are classified by their impact. Table 7.9 illustrates.

We may use Table 7.9 to state the major findings of our "project."

A. Education is the strongest correlate of tolerance in this set ($Q = +.52$ with 95% confidence limits of $+.47$ and $+.56$). Better educated persons are more likely to be tolerant. Although region and age are correlated with both education and tolerance, neither has a clear-cut impact on the correlation.

B. Region is the second strongest correlate ($Q = +.46$, with 95% confidence limits of $+.39$ and $+.52$). Northerners are more likely

TABLE 7.9 Summary of Analysis of Correlates of Tolerance of Communists

Variable + Category	Zero Order Q*	Partial	TEST VARIABLES USED			
			Explains	Reinforces	Suppresses	No Effect
Education High school graduate	+.52	+.47				Region Age
Region Non-South	+.46	+.39		Education		City size
City size Larger	+.29	+.22		Region		Education
Age Younger	+.23	(**)	Education			
Church attendance Infrequent	+.18	+.18				Age Region Education
Sex Male	+.15	+.16				Education Church att.

* All zero-order correlations are statistically significant, using 95% confidence limits.
** We assume that refinement of educational levels would bring the partial down below the three-variable value of +.10.

to be high on tolerance. Educational differences contribute to this correlation, northerners being better educated and more highly educated people being more tolerant. City size, a variable associated with both region and tolerance, has no definite impact. When both education and city size are controlled, the partial Q for region and tolerance is +.39.

C. City size has a low correlation with tolerance ($Q = +.29$, with 95% confidence limits of +.23 and +.35). People in larger cities are more likely to be high on tolerance. Two variables, education and region, associated with both city size and tolerance, were introduced as controls. When both are controlled, the partial correlation drops to +.22 and it is seen that region, but not education, has an impact on the correlation. Big-city residents are more tolerant, in part because they tend to be northerners and northerners tend to be more tolerant.

D. Age has a low correlation with tolerance ($Q = +.23$, with 95% confidence limits of +.17 and +.29). Younger adults are more likely to be high on tolerance. The correlation is explained by education. It is the higher educational attainment of young adults that accounts for their greater tolerance. (See note at the bottom of Table 7.9).

E. Church attendance has a low correlation with tolerance ($Q = +.18$, with 95% confidence limits of +.12 and +.25). Infrequent church attenders are more likely to be high on tolerance. Although age, region, and education are associated with both church attendance and tolerance, none of the three has a clear impact on the correlation.

F. Sex has the lowest correlation in this set ($Q = +.15$, with 95% confidence limits of +.09 and +.22). Men are more likely to be tolerant. Education and church attendance, although correlated with both sex and tolerance, do not contribute to the relationship. In practice, such reporting would be unduly laconic. Stouffer himself devotes about half of his book to a detailed exegesis of these findings. However, you can see that our strategy provides a systematic framework, forcing the investigator to examine all relationships in his set of variables, but allowing him to shortcut a complete analysis of all possible statistics on the basis of the sign rule and his personal judgment.

Our little report not only lacks a full explanation of sampling, measurement, and procedures. It is also deficient in "interpretation," the sociological overtones, conjectures, references to other studies, and similar nontechnical ideas that make the difference between a research report and a set of numbers. Our six steps will provide a reasonable skeleton, but the investigator must also provide sociological flesh. Harkening back to the beginning of Chapter 1, remember that it is the task of the investigator to make the jump from findings to conclusions.

IN A NUTSHELL

A. Steps in testing a hypothesis or causal model:

1. State your hypothesis or model.
2. Consider the measures of your variables.
3. Run the appropriate tabulations.
4. Assess the results:

a) *If the hypothesis fails, consider: refining your variables, possible mechanical errors, suppressor variables, alternative measures, specifiers—and the possibility that you are wrong.*

b) *If the data support the predictions, test the effects of measurement decisions, introduce or consider test variables that threaten your results, and attempt to replicate your findings.*

B. Steps in explaining a correlation:

1. Pick an appropriate correlation to be explained, considering substance, size, and significance.
2. Look for appropriate explainer variables, considering causal direction and the product of the zero orders.
3. Run the most promising test variables in three-variable tabulations, refining the measure if appropriate.
4. If no single test variable explains *XY*, consider promising pairs of test variables.

5. If the correlation is not explained by two test variables, you may continue to add test variables, although you are not encouraged to use large sets of explainers.

C. Steps in analyzing correlates of Y:

1. Measure Y carefully.
2. Choose a set of predictors:
   a) *All consequent or none consequent to Y.*
   b) *Avoiding measures of Y.*
   c) *That give a broad sweep or a fine-grain analysis.*
3. Run the zero-order correlations for all pairs of variables.
4. Make a sign matrix for the nonnegligible correlations.
5. Reflect the sign matrix to minimize negative signs.
6. Select promising test variables for each predictor by multiplying values of the relevant correlations. Run multivariate analyses, using the difference between partial differentials and partials to assess impact of test variables.
7. Summarize your findings in a chart, with predictors arranged in terms of size of correlation with Y.

Conclusion

In addition to the specific procedures explained in this chapter, our advice represents a philosophy or style of research summarized in the following aphorisms.

Bite less, chew more

Tabulation and analysis are a strange combination of tedium and fascination. It is easy to become hypnotized by the sheer operation of making tables and calculations. You do not "owe" your data a complete analysis that makes use of every variable. You merely wish to wrench from the data a meaningful answer to some research question.

Always keep in mind what you are trying to find out and avoid the tendency to "make one more run" as an excuse to avoid the challenge of writing up and integrating the data you already ran.

Remember that a clean, systematic analysis of three or four variables is more valuable (and more difficult) than a lengthy treatise with dozens of variables and dozens of loose ends.

Explain people, not just correlations

Research, as you may have guessed, is a highly technical procedure and it is commendable to seek technical elegance in your work. However, you should not forget that your aim is to find out something interesting about the people or groups you are studying. It is a marvelous thing to see a partial shrivel up and vanish, but it is not worth going to the trouble to show that T explains XY when XY is a relationship that nobody gives a damn about or T's effect is a truism substantively. It is splendid to document a list of correlates, but each correlate on the list should be of some interest to somebody.

To test whether you have become a mere technician rather than a sociologist, ask yourself at each point in your analysis whether you could explain the gist of what you are doing (in English) to a freshman sociology class—and whether you would feel silly if you did.

Check, mates!

Check your marginals against your code book. Calculate the confidence limits for your zero orders. Check your calculations by using the complete equation with weights. Make sure that you have the signs of your correlations straight. In general, assume that all smashing findings are mechanical errors until your checks demonstrate the opposite.

Seek simplicity and distrust it

Appendix:
Alternative Decompositions
of a Relationship: What
Lazarsfeld Really Said

The central idea of this text has been "the equation," a formula for decomposing Q or gamma into two conditional (partial) coefficients and a differential, the four being glued together by weights, the pair proportions.

In Chapter 4 we attributed the decomposition formula to the British statistician G. Udny Yule and its application for outcome regions to U.S. sociologists Patricia Kendall and Paul F. Lazarsfeld. The time has come to admit to a fib, or rather a web of half truths. The whole truth is that there are actually three different decomposition formulas, one proposed by Yule, one proposed by Kendall and Lazarsfeld, and one appearing for the first time in this volume. They are similar in spirit, which justifies the fib, but have some very important differences, which necessitates this appendix.

The story goes like this: Following the academic rule of prior publication, the discoverer of the decomposition is Yule. In "an early edition"[1] of his

---

[1] The author does not know the exact date, which is not given in an unpublished manuscript by Lazarsfeld reviewing the history of the idea. The first edition of Yule's text appeared in 1911 and it had run to 10 editions by 1935.

classic statistics text he presented a formula which, when scrambled around a little, reveals a decomposition of *delta*, the difference between observed and expected cell frequencies. Yule, however, never developed the many research implications of the formula, treating it as an interesting algebraic property.

In 1939 Paul Lazarsfeld independently discovered the idea and went beyond the algebra to develop the crucial concepts of explanation, no effect (though he uses a different term for it), and specification. Lazarsfeld did not publish his results until 1950 in a joint essay with Patricia Kendall.[2] Even there the exact formula is not given, but, instead, the general idea is discussed. The algebra was presented in a rather technical essay in 1961.[3] Despite its fugitive character, Lazarsfeld's work has become famous through the many sociologists who studied with him over the years at Columbia University.

Lazarsfeld's own equation differs from Yule's in that he decomposes the cross-product difference (the numerator of *Q*) rather than delta and his weights are a little different. You will remember, however, that delta and the cross-product difference are closely related. Therefore the Yule and Lazarsfeld equations are mathematically quite similar.

Before presenting the actual equation, two technical notes:

1. The Lazarsfeld equation "works" only when the data have been transformed into proportions or probabilities, i.e., when each cell frequency is divided by *N*. The lowercase letter *p* is used to designate proportions.

2. Lazarsfeld uses brackets to denote the cross-product difference and designates his variables by the numbers 1, 2, and 3. In presenting his formula we will compromise by using brackets and our familiar letters *X*, *Y*, and *T*.

Here is his equation:

$$[XY] = \frac{[XY:T]}{p_T} + \frac{[XY:NOT\,T]}{p_{NOT\,T}} + \frac{[TX] * [TY]}{p_T * p_{NOT\,T}}$$

In words: the cross-product difference equals (1) the cross-product difference among *T*'s divided by the proportion *T*, plus (2) the cross-product difference among *NOT T*'s divided by the proportion *NOT T*, plus (3) the zero-order cross-product difference for *TX* multiplied by the zero-order

---

[2] P. L. Kendall and P. F. Lazarsfeld, "Problems of Survey Analysis," in R. K. Merton and P. F. Lazarsfeld, eds., *Continuities in Social Research*, The Free Press, New York, 1950, pp. 147–167.

[3] Paul F. Lazarsfeld, "The Algebra of Dichotomous Systems," in Herbert Solomon, ed., *Studies in Item Analysis and Prediction*, Stanford University Press, Stanford, Calif., 1961, pp. 111–157.

cross-product difference for TY, this product being divided by the product of the T marginals—for data expressed as proportions.

Since dividing by p produces a sort of average,[4] we can also describe the equation this way: The cross-product difference for XY equals the product of the average cross-product differences for TX and TY plus the sum of the average conditional cross products.

The various archetypal outcomes are handled as follows:

1. In explanation, the partial terms are zero and the XY relationship is identical to the value of the extreme right-hand term.
2. In what we call "no effect"[5] the extreme right-hand term is zero and the XY relationship is the sum of the two conditional terms.
3. Specification, of course, is a substantial difference between the two conditional terms.
4. Suppression is not defined in the 1950 paper, but was apparently developed later to cover situations where the sum of the partial terms exceeds the value of the zero order.

For comparison, if we were to decompose the cross-product differences rather than Q's (in proportions or raw frequencies, it makes no difference), our formula would look like this:

$$[XY] = [XY:T] + [XY:NOT\,T] + [XY:\,\text{DIFF}\,T]$$

The first two (conditional) terms are similar in the two equations. Lazarsfeld's partial terms amount to our partials divided by their marginal proportions; ours amount to his multiplied by their marginal proportions. Note that because the marginal proportions are always less than 1.00, Lazarsfeld's partials will always be larger in magnitude (except when the value is zero; then both will be zero).

It is the extreme right-hand term where the two systems diverge radically. Ours, the differential, is a second-order coefficient. Lazarsfeld's uses the two zero-order relationships for the test variable. He calls his term a "marginal" for the same reason noted in Chapter 4—the TX and TY correlations provide the marginals for the two conditional tables.

Because our partial terms are always smaller than Lazarsfeld's, our differential must always be larger than his marginal term (because both equations add up to the same value, XY). Thus, we can write the following rough equation:

[4] The "sort of" is required because the cross product is a property of pairs, not cases. Strictly speaking, to obtain an average cross product we should divide by the total number of pairs, but this would change the structure of the decomposition considerably.

[5] Lazarsfeld calls this situation "partial-type elaboration" for reasons that make perfect sense in the context of his essay but will not be explained here.

$[XY: \text{DIFF } T]$ = (sum of Lazarsfeld partials) $-$ (sum of our partials)

$$+ \frac{[TX] * [TY]}{p_T * p_{NOT\,T}}$$

What are the practical differences between the two systems? First, it is crucial to stress that both are correct, just as it is correct to assert that $2 + 2 = 4$ and equally correct to assert that $1 + 3 = 4$. What is important is the research decisions one would make using one or the other as a frame of reference.

Second, the key difference can be expressed as a dilemma: In Lazarsfeld's system the sign rule holds exactly and the degree of correlation is a rule of thumb; in our system the sign rule is a rule of thumb and the degree of correlation is stated exactly.

Consider first the sign rule. When using the Lazarsfeld system, the sign of the marginal term is given by multiplying the signs of the zero-order relationships for T. If the TX correlation is positive and the TY correlation is positive, the sign of the marginal term must be positive and (if XY is positive) the sum of the partials will be less than the zero order; i.e., the partials must be reduced. Or again, if TX or TY or both are zero, the marginal term must have a value of zero and the partials sum to the zero order. If we accept the framework, we can say that TX and TY literally add, subtract, or contribute nothing to the XY correlation. Our text in Chapter 4 involved a number of circumlocutions necessary to paste over the fact that our version of the sign rule is only a rule of thumb. That does not mean it is a bad rule of thumb. It is a good one, but it has no mathematical necessity in our system.

Consider second the degree of correlation. In Chapter 2 we argued that in order to state the degree of correlation, a coefficient must be normed. That is, it must have a denominator that guarantees a range from $+1.00$ to -1.00. Without this, it is impossible to compare cross-product differences within or between equations, except on a rule-of-thumb basis. For this reason we concluded that the cross-product difference standing alone is unsatisfactory as a measure of degree. The absence of a satisfactory degree of correlation makes analysis using the Lazarsfeld system rather ambiguous when one asks such questions as "How much impact does T have on XY? Which test variable has the greatest effect on XY? How small should a relationship be to be considered negligible?"

So far we have not really demonstrated that the difference produces a dilemma. Rather we showed an advantage for one system and another advantage for the other. Nevertheless, there is at least one point where the two systems clash head on. It goes this way.

The Lazarsfeld system defines partials in such a way that they must be raised or lowered when TX and TY are nonzero. Our system is such that partial Q's may be identical to the zero order even when TX and TY are correlated.

Empirical examples may be found in Tables 5.3, 5.4, and 5.5 and the matter is of some theoretical importance in causal models. Consider, for example, the two models shown in Figure A.1.

Fig. A.1

We would anticipate positive zero-order correlations among all three variables in either model even though the XY correlation in (b) should turn out to be spurious. Applying the Lazarsfeld framework, the marginal term should be positive in all three-variable analyses for each model, leading us to the conclusion that in each model, each variable affects the other two. However, in our system, we distinguish between the two models by requiring "no effect" for XT and TY in model (b). Thus our system for handling causal models *requires* the use of our decomposition and the nonliteral version of the sign rule.

Having told you all about our decomposition and little or nothing about Lazarsfeld's, it would be sheer cant to say "take your choice." We explained and developed our approach because we believe its advantages outweigh its disadvantages. Nevertheless, you should realize that the Lazarsfeld system is the classic approach and if you accept ours, you will hardly be accused of mindless acquiescence to majority opinion.

Index